Liquor Marketing and Liquor Advertising

LIQUOR MARKETING

and

LIQUOR ADVERTISING

A Guide for
Executives and Their Staffs
in Management, Sales
and Advertising

BY HENRY BRETZFIELD
Account Executive
Lawrence Fertig & Co., Inc.

Abelard-Schuman, New York

Library of Congress
Catalog Card Number: 55-6404

FIRST PRINTING

Printed and bound in the
United States of America

Published simultaneously in Canada
by Nelson, Foster & Scott, Ltd.

TO

the moderate drinker

Contents

Foreword xvii

Preface xix

1 Liquors, Liquor Marketing and Liquor Advertising . . . 1

Definition of "liquors," "liquor marketing" and "liquor advertising." Plan and scope of book.

2 An Outline of American Liquor History 3

Pre-Prohibition history. Liquors in colonial days. Three-cornered rum trade. Molasses Act. Sugar Act. Rum-smuggling. Decline of rum trade. Whiskey supersedes rum in historical importance. Farmer-distillers. Excise tax of 1791. "Whiskey Rebellion." Early distilling methods. First scientific distilling. The liquor industry expands with the nation. Early bottling, labeling, marketing, advertising. Emergence of brand names. Bottling in Bond Act. "Whiskey Ring." "Whiskey Trust." Straights vs. Blends. Prohibition movement from colonial days to the 18th Amendment. The Prohibition era. Bootlegging, organized crime, poison liquors. Rise in per capita consumption. Cost of Prohibition. Failure of Prohibition. Repeal societies. 21st Amendment. The post-Repeal period. Liquor legislation. NIRA, FACA, FAA ACT, ATU, ATTD. Bureau of Customs. Distilled Spirits Institute. Industry self-regulation. The "Big Four." Post-repeal marketing and advertising. National brand names. World War II. Conversion to war production. Shortages and rationing. Maintenance of brand names. The post-war period. Return to buyers' market. Changes in drinking preferences. High taxes. The consumer trades up. Continuation of dry agitation.

3 Aspects of the Liquor Industry 19

Size and importance: annual production, bottling, consumption; exports and imports; taxes; import duties; permit and license fees; payrolls; suppliers; consumer purchases; producers, importers, middlemen. Federal, state and local law: 21st Amendment. Revenue and control legislation: taxes, customs duties, government supervision of production, warehousing, bottling. Provisions of Federal Alcohol Administration Act. Federal Trade Commission. Adulterated and misbranded liquors. Fair trade. State and local law. State prohibition, revenue and control legislation. Wet and dry states and counties. Local option. License fees, excise taxes, sales taxes. Monopoly states legislation. Important industry problems: drys, bootleggers, alcoholism, bootlegging, teen-age drinking, drunken driving, retailing evils. Tax problems. Public relations problems. Problems created by aging requirements, by multiplicity of state laws, by illegal re-use of containers. National trade associations. Industry by-products: distillers feeds.

4 Products, Production, Warehousing and Bottling . . . 34

Definitions of commonly used terms. The distilling process. Raw materials. Distillation. Congeners. Aging. Charred and uncharred barrels. Rectification. Warehousing. Internal Revenue bonded warehouses. Customs bonded warehouses. Bottling houses. Bottling, labeling. Strip stamps. Whiskey. Whiskey production. Sour-mash bourbons. Production of grain-designated whiskies; straights; bonds; blends of straights; spirit blends; blended Scotch type whiskies; Scotch, Irish and Canadian whiskies. Gin. Distilled gin. Compound gin. Production methods. Neutral spirits, juniper berries, botanicals. Dry gin. Distilled (London) dry gin. English and Dutch gins. Cordials. Production methods. Dry cordials. Varieties of cordials. Flavored gins. Flavored brandies. Brandy. Production methods. Grape, apple and other fruit brandies. Lees, pomace and residue brandies. Cognac. Cognac region. Production methods. Stars and letters on labels. Armagnac. Calvados. Quetsch. Spanish brandies. Rum. Puerto Rican, Cuban, Jamaican and other West Indies rums. American rum. Production methods, light and heavy-bodied rums. Jamaica London Dock Rums. Demerara rums. Vodka. Sudden rise to success. Absence of taste and aroma. Production methods. Bottled mixed drinks. Bitters. Other distilled spirits: aquavit, tequila.

5 Package, Carton and Case 64

Importance of package in liquor marketing. Bottles. Earthenware containers. Closures. Red and green strip stamps. Labels. Federal labeling law. Mandatory and prohibited practices. Ribbons, foil, seals, etc. Carton. Year-round and holiday cartons. Types of cartons. Case. Use as shipping container, advertising vehicle, point-of-sale piece. Bottles and wine gallons per case. Marking of cases.

6 Marketing Channels 77

Marketing channels differ between open and monopoly states. List of open states. Wholesalers: types, functions. Retailers, off-premise and on-premise. Open states which prohibit on-premise retailing. Producers' and importers' local sales offices. List of monopoly states. State commissions. Retailers, off-premise and on-premise. State stores. Wholesale and retail functions of state stores. Privately owned package stores and bars. Monopoly states which prohibit on-premise retailing. Producers' and importers' local sales offices.

7 Markets 85

Liquor market restricted to adults who drink and buy lawfully in wet areas. Industry self-imposed restrictions. Market classified in terms of regular and occasional drinkers, urban and rural drinkers, sex, age, income, race, nationality. Wet and dry states and counties. Wet states in order of size of wet population. Markets lost to bootleg liquors. Government seizures of illicit stills. Largest bootleg markets. Bootleg and legal sales compared.

8 Prices, Pricing and Profits 93

Pricing for maximum profit. Relationship between retail price, sales volume and net profit. Factors which determine sales volume. Factors which determine pricing. Charges against gross profit. Sales, marketing, advertising and sales promotion expenses. Price control. F.O.B. price determines retail price class. Fair trade legislation. McGuire Act. State Fair Trade laws. Mandatory and voluntary Fair Trade. States without Fair Trade. Mandatory mark-up systems. Fair Trade laws unnecessary in monopoly states. Price cutting and price wars. "Dealing," legal and illegal. Price structures. Open state price structures. Components. Building price structures. Monopoly state price structures. Monopoly mark-up systems. Des Moines Warranty. Package store prices. Prices of bottle sizes compared. Bar prices. Determination of selling price per drink. Drink sizes. Retail pricing at varying mark-ups. Pricing of mixed drinks. Price classes. Price classes representing major sales volume. Major price classes for whiskey, gin, cordials, brandy, rum, vodka, prepared cocktails. Prices and price classes of leading brands.

9 Sales and Sales Patterns 112

Major producers and importers. The "Big Four": Seagram, National, Schenley, Walker. Annual dollar sales volume and advertising expenditures. Leading brands. Other producers, importers and vendors and leading brands. Sales of distilled spirits. Sales in open vs. monopoly states. Sales in individual states. Sales of domestic vs. imported spirits. Monthly, quarterly and semi-annual sales. Sales by sizes, by retail outlets. Comparative sales of whiskey, gin, cordials, brandy, rum and vodka in open and monopoly states; in individual states; domestic vs. imported; monthly, quarterly, semi-annually. Sales of each class of spirits in terms of national market; open vs. monopoly states; individual states; domestic vs. imported; monthly, quarterly, semi-annual sales; types; brands.

10 The Consumer 147

The consumer as an individual. Consumer buying. Purposes for which distilled spirits are purchased. Factors influencing consumer purchase and consumption. Consumer use of distilled spirits. Straight drinks. Mixed drinks. "On the rocks." Club soda, ginger ale and other mixers. Vermouth, fruit, fruit juices, sweeteners, bitters, and other ingredients. Glassware. Standard bar measures. Popular recipes for drinks made with whiskey, gin, cordials, brandy, rum, vodka.

11 Marketing and Advertising Law 160

Marketing law. Federal marketing law. Exclusive retail outlets, tied house, commercial bribery and consignment selling prohibited. Samples permitted. Wholesaling of non-liquor merchandise permitted. Minimum wholesale sale. Maximum retail sale. Shipments through mails prohibited. Other prohibited practices. State and local marketing law. No private wholesalers in monopolies, no on-premise retailing in some states, etc. State and local laws concerning retailing: hours of sale, sales on Sundays and holidays, container sizes, sales to minors, retail premises, manner of serving customers, etc. Advertising law. Federal advertising law. Mandatory statements: responsible advertiser, class and type, alcoholic contents, etc. Prohibited practices: false and misleading statements, statements disparaging competitive products, etc. Advertising exceptions to tied house prohibitory practices: point-of-sale material, dealer names in advertising, mat services, consumer and retailer advertising specialties. State and local advertising law. States requiring submission of copy for approval. State laws concerning copy and media. Advertising resolutions of the Distilled Spirits Institute. Other industry resolutions. Media restrictions on liquor advertising. Media refusing liquor advertising.

12 Marketing and Advertising Procedure 177

Marketing procedure. Developing the marketing and merchandising plan. Goals, obstacles, strategy. Research. Published data and other sources of research. Developing a brand name; requisites. Developing the package, carton and case. Pricing. Setting sales quotas. Distribution and sales checks. Evaluating middlemen. Determining the appropriation. Executing the marketing and merchandising plan. Helping middlemen sell. Marketing and merchandising in open states. Consumer advertising. Allowances. Sales meetings. Direct mail. Selling kits. Contests, prizes, bonuses. Truck panels. Mat services. Trade advertising and publicity, etc. Marketing and merchandising in monopoly states. Selling to commissions and to privately owned stores and bars. Consumer advertising, sales meetings, etc. Advertising procedure. Scope of liquor advertising. Developing the advertising and sales promotion plan. Advertising agencies. Research. The advertising appropriation. National, state and local advertising budgets. Planning the media schedule. Magazines, newspapers, outdoor, transportation and other media. The sales promotion appropriation. Advertising copy: developing a brand personality; long-term and short-term goals; special brand attributes; symbols and slogans; permitted and prohibited appeals; testimonials and other devices; adapting copy to specific media. Executing the advertising and promotion campaign. Legal approvals. Varying copy to meet individual state requirements. Mechanical production in accordance with media schedule. Merchandising the advertising and sales promotion campaign. Merchandising by producers, importers, wholesalers, media. Publicity. Consumer and trade publicity.

Appendices

A. The 21st Amendment 201

B. Federal Alcohol Administration Act 202

C. Standards of Identity for Distilled Spirits 215
(Article II, Regulations No. 5, FAA Act)

D. Advertising of Distilled Spirits 224
(Article VI, Regulations No. 5, FAA Act)

E. Inducements Furnished to Retailers 228
(Regulations No. 6, FAA Act)

F. Chronology 232

G. Glossary 234

Bibliography 247

Index 249

Illustrations, Maps, Charts, Tables

ILLUSTRATIONS

(Section between pages 104 and 105)

A pre-Prohibition whiskey advertisement
A current whiskey advertisement
Hiram Walker Distillery at Peoria, Ill.
Weighing barrels to compute gallonage
Examples of front and back labels
Decanter and carton
A self-service package store
A well-designed bar and cocktail lounge
A Virginia State Store
Making a purchase at an Ohio State Store
Filling an order for mixed drinks
An advertisement for the world's largest selling brand of distilled spirits

MAPS

Open, monopoly and dry states 79
Off-premise and on-premise states 81

CHARTS

Primary marketing channels 78
Drinkers and non-drinkers 86
% breakdown of retail price ('A' blend) 98
Sales of distilled spirits by months 119
Sales of distilled spirits by sizes 121

TABLES

Calculation of tax gallons and excise taxes—domestic spirits 37
Calculation of tax gallons, excise taxes and customs duties—imported spirits 37
Production specifications—principal domestic whiskies 42 and 43
Standards of fill 65
Number of bottles and gallons to the case 75
States in order of size of wet population 91

Calculation of net profit (varying sales volume, same retail price) 93
Calculation of net profit (varying sales volume, varying retail prices) 94
Calculation of straight whiskey cost per case 100
Calculation of manufacturer's cost 101
Calculation of F.O.B. price 101
Calculation of wholesaler's cost 102
Calculation of retailer's cost 102
Calculation of retail price 102
Price structures—'A' blend, 'A' straight, premium bond 103
Components of retail price 103
Retail prices in various states 104
Relationship of prices to sizes 105
Relationship of net contents per size to prices per size 105
Cost per case and cost per one-ounce drink 106
Mark-ups on cost per one-ounce drink 106
Comparison of gross profits—package stores and bars 106
Classification of distilled spirits by price classes 107
Classification of whiskey types by price classes 107
Classification of leading brands by price classes 109-111
Sales and sales relationship 113
Monthly, quarterly, and semi-annual sales of distilled spirits 117
States in order of distilled spirits sales volume 118
Sales of distilled spirits by sizes 120
Percentage of sales of each class of spirits to total sales 120
Percentage of open and monopoly sales of each class of spirits 120
Sales rank of classes of spirits in each state 122
Ten leading states for each class of spirits 123
Percentage of domestic and imported sales of each class of spirits 123
Domestic and imported spirits in order of sales volume 124
Percentage to total spirits sales of each class of domestic and imported spirits 124
Monthly, quarterly, and semi-annual sales of each class of spirits 125
Sales of domestic and imported whiskies 125
Monthly, quarterly, and semi-annual whiskey sales 126
Major whiskey types in order of sales volume 126

Percentage of sales of domestic whiskey types to total domestic whiskey sales 126
Percentage of sales of imported whiskey types to total imported whiskey sales 127
Percentage of sales of leading whiskey types to total whiskey and total spirits sales 127
Top selling whiskies in approximate order of sales 133
Percentage of open and monopoly sales of leading whiskey types 133
Ten leading states for each major whiskey type 134
States with largest sales volume for each major whiskey type 135
Monthly, quarterly, and semi-annual sales of major whiskey types 135
Comparison of gin sales to sales of each major whiskey type 136
Sales of domestic and imported gin 136
Monthly, quarterly, and semi-annual gin sales 137
Sales of domestic and imported cordials 138
Monthly, quarterly, and semi-annual cordial sales 139
Sales comparison—cordials, cordial specialties, flavored brandies and flavored gins 139
Comparison of prices of cordial varieties 140
Sales of domestic and imported brandies 141
Monthly, quarterly, and semi-annual brandy sales 141
Sales of domestic and imported rum 143
Monthly, quarterly, and semi-annual rum sales 143
Sales comparison—rum varieties 144
Monthly, quarterly, and semi-annual vodka sales 146
Distilled spirits mixed with other ingredients 151
Glassware and sizes 153
Standard bar measures 153
States which require submission of advertising for approval 172

Foreword

This is a book for which there has been a great need daily ever since Repeal, and for which the need is as acute today as at any time in the past 21 years.

The distilled spirits industry in the United States is a mass-distribution package-goods industry, in many respects like the other great package-goods industries of food, drugs and tobacco. Similarities to these industries would seem to make its functioning simple to an outsider. But once inside the industry, dissimilarities appear which make it extremely baffling to anyone who tackles its marketing and advertising problems.

Whereas food, drugs and tobacco may be sold freely in any of the 48 states and territories of the United States, distilled spirits are illegal objects of sale in two states. In other states liquors are so taxed, so hedged in by restrictions, laws, and regulations, that it becomes a near-miracle for the industry to exist at all on a national scale.

This volume puts together within its covers practically all of the basic data about the distilled spirits industry which any marketer or advertising man will need as fundamental guiding information about the industry.

It is not a "how to" book and I am very happy about this, because I do not believe anyone can give advice in a book as to how a particular product shall be marketed. Each product is different. Each company is different. Each set of marketing conditions is different. The natural instincts and abilities of the men guiding the advertising or marketing program in question must of necessity be the controlling factors in success or failure.

To this extent, then, no one can write a "how to" book. At the same time, everyone needs, either in his mind or at his hand, a large amount of basic information concerning the distilled spirits industry if he is to operate successfully in it. Up to now, while this information has been available, it could not be obtained without a tremendous amount of laborious digging from many varied and often obscure sources.

The virtue of this volume is that it puts all of this basic information together in thorough fashion. In my opinion no one operating within the liquor industry can fail to learn something from it.

Henry Bretzfield has had 20 years of continuous experience in the advertising and marketing of distilled spirits. His experience embraces virtually every phase of distilled spirits advertising and merchandising – copy, media, research, statistics, marketing and merchandising plans, and account management. He has earned the confidence and respect of all those who have come in contact with him for the wide scope of his knowledge of the distilled spirits industry and his comprehension of the basic facts concerning it. I know of no man whom I would consider more competent to put together a volume of this type with accuracy and authority.

PHILIP LUKIN,
Vice-President,
Lawrence Fertig & Co., Inc.

November 1, 1954

Preface

The purpose of this volume is to present and discuss the basic factual information which one must have in order to operate intelligently and successfully from day to day in liquor marketing and advertising.

This information is specifically intended for executives and their staffs in the management, sales, advertising, sales promotion and research divisions of distillers, rectifiers, importers, brokers, wholesalers and major retailers; government liquor administrative units; industry associations; advertising agencies; advertising media. It is also intended for the student, and for newcomers to liquor marketing and advertising: the young man or woman who is embarking on a business career and who has chosen the liquor industry; the seasoned businessman who is switching from another industry; the advertising agency that has won its first liquor account.

Newcomers to the industry will find here a short-cut to the knowledge which they must eventually acquire. Those who are veterans in liquor marketing and advertising will have at their disposal a refresher course, plus the convenience of a reference work which, for the first time, organizes, classifies, and compresses between two covers information which heretofore has been available only through many scattered sources.

A word to the student and to the neophyte:

The liquor industry enjoys the unique distinction, if not the honor, of being the object of two amendments to our Federal Constitution. The 18th Amendment declared alcoholic beverages illegal; the 21st Amendment restored their legality. In the years which have elapsed since the 21st Amendment became effective (1933), the industry has become one of America's economic giants. During this time, there has been a fervor of legislative activity. A mass of laws has grown up with the fertility, luxuriance and maze of a tropical jungle. As in the case of the two Constitutional amendments, much of this legislation is rooted in the fact that alcoholic beverages, if used to excess, are intoxicating and therefore potentially a serious sociological problem. The principle behind this legislation is manifestly sound.

The nature of the product is such that legal controls are desirable. Most of these controls are good controls. Whether others among them are necessary, or could stand revision and improvement, is another question.

Of course, not all legislation dealing with liquors stems from the sociological problem. Other industries are governed by laws which concern, for example, standards of product identity, trade practices and taxation. The liquor industry is governed by similar laws.

In view of the number and intricacy of liquor laws and regulations, not to mention rules set down by the industry for itself, and by those with whom it does business (e.g., advertising media), it is hardly surprising that liquor marketing and advertising are unique. As liquor products differ from other products, liquor markets differ from other markets. And as liquor markets differ, so do marketing, merchandising, advertising, and sales promotion practices differ. To put it another way—while the liquor industry responds to the same economic laws as do other industries, and is not in this sense "different," its response is conditioned by legislation and other forces to the point where its set-up and operation is in fact a good deal "different." As you go along from chapter to chapter, you will obtain a clear picture of these differences, an understanding and knowledge of which is essential to your successful progress.

* * *

In the preparation of this volume, I have been fortunate in receiving assistance from executives at the advertising agency with which I am associated, Lawrence Fertig & Co., Inc., from executives with our client, National Distillers Products Corporation, and from other industry executives. I would like particularly to thank those whose names appear below.

At Lawrence Fertig & Co., Inc.: Philip Lukin, Vice-President, for his valuable criticism of the manuscript as a whole; Kenneth Miller, Service Manager, for supervising the preparation of photographs, maps and charts; Robert K. Malkmus, Assistant Account Executive, for help with research.

At National Distillers Products Corporation: Reginald W. Maurer, Vice-President, for his aid on the subject of prices and pricing; Jeffrey W. Clapp, Vice-President, for his suggestions on parts of the manuscript concerning Monopoly States; Alynn Shilling, Director of Advertising, for permission to use requested National Distillers material; Stuart Cowan and Peter Cusack, executives in the Monopoly States

Division, the former for information relating to Monopoly States, the latter for background detail; I. D. Hall, Legal Department, for data on liquor legislation.

My thanks also go to Lew Schwartz, President and Publisher, Liquor Publications, Inc., for his guidance throughout, and to Daniel Hecht, Editor, Liquor Publications, Inc., for many of the photographs which appear herein.

Finally, my thanks go to Howard T. Jones, Executive Secretary, Distilled Spirits Institute, for a wealth of material on the industry.

HENRY BRETZFIELD

New York City

January, 1955

Liquor Marketing and Liquor Advertising

CHAPTER ONE

Liquors, Liquor Marketing and Liquor Advertising

Throughout this book the terms "liquors," "liquor marketing" and "liquor advertising" are used to express precise concepts. Let us examine these concepts, together with the scope of our discussion of each.

1. Liquors

The term "liquors" as I have used it refers to alcoholic beverages as follows:

DISTILLED SPIRITS. We will discuss only alcoholic beverages which are produced by distillation. Whiskey, gin, cordials, brandy, rum and vodka are examples of distilled alcoholic beverages. The liquor industry generally refers to distilled alcoholic beverages as "distilled spirits," and in so doing distinguishes them from wines, beers, and other alcoholic beverages which are fermented but not thereafter distilled.

We will exclude from these pages any discussion of non-distilled alcoholic beverages—not because they are produced differently, but because they involve marketing and advertising problems which vary sufficiently from those of distilled spirits to require separate treatment.

PACKAGE GOODS. We will discuss the marketing and advertising of distilled spirits which are bottled or otherwise packaged for use by the consumer.

NATIONAL BRANDS. We will discuss distilled spirits as marketed and advertised by brand name on a national (or regional) basis.

Liquor products will be examined in detail. Included will be an explanation of the production, warehousing and bottling of liquors; a description of each important class and type on the market today; information about bottles, labels, closures, cartons, cases.

2. Liquor Marketing

The term "liquor marketing" as used in this book refers to the marketing of distilled spirits by producers and importers, in liaison with advertising agencies, and as conducted through middlemen to the consumer.

A complete blueprint of liquor marketing will be developed. We will follow liquors from domestic bottling houses and customs warehouses to the highball, cocktail and shot glass. We will note methods of pricing and resultant price structures. We will observe the operations of producers, importers and middlemen. We will examine markets —as represented by license states and monopoly states, by sales and sales patterns, by the consumer. We will become acquainted with marketing law. We will learn the basic steps in marketing procedure.

3. Liquor Advertising

The term "liquor advertising" as used here refers to the advertising of distilled spirits by producers and importers, in liaison with advertising agencies, and as placed in consumer and trade media, both national and local. The term "media" refers to any means of communication which is ordinarily used to convey a selling message: magazines, newspapers, car cards, posters, trade papers, direct mail, match books, point-of-sale material.

As in the case of liquor marketing, a complete blueprint will be developed with respect to liquor advertising. We will become acquainted with advertising law; we will observe advertising procedure from the determination of the appropriation to finished advertisements as they reach the consumer.

* * *

As background to a detailed study of liquors, liquor marketing and liquor advertising, it is important that we become familiar with the liquor industry. We will want to have a general idea of its history in this country, and of its more significant characteristics today. American liquor history and current aspects of the industry are discussed in the next two chapters.

CHAPTER TWO

An Outline of American Liquor History

From the time of the earliest settlers to the present, the history of liquors in this country has been a history of struggle—a struggle not only for commercial success, but for existence itself. American distilling enterprise has been attacked by British kings and by a native army. It has been embroiled in industrial civil strife. It has been struck down by a centuries-old enemy and risen afterwards to a stature unmatched in the past. It has enlisted in a great war and helped see it through to victory.

The struggle has had its less spectacular, but nonetheless important aspects. There has been the long uphill effort to achieve both a better product and better techniques for marketing and selling it. There has been the patient fight to stamp out trade evils and to solve sociological problems. There has been steady plodding to create an effective body of law.

As we shall see, the long struggle in which the liquor industry has been engaged has resulted in notable success. As we shall also see, powerful enemies still exist, and continue on the offensive with persistent vigor.

The distilling industry has appeared frequently in the pages of our history, and has been a factor in shaping the course of events. At first rum played the major historical role among distilled spirits. Eventually this role was taken over by whiskey, which has continued in it ever since.

1. Pre-Prohibition History

Prior to the eighteenth century, we hear little of importance concerning liquors in this country. When the first settlers arrived, they brought spirits along with them; later they imported them from overseas. Some native distilling was accomplished in the 1600's. It is reported, for example, that William Kieft, the Director-General of the colony of New Netherlands, distilled spirits from grain (1640), thereby becoming the first man in America to do so. It is also reported that Kieft opened the first tavern in Manhattan, thus providing an outlet for his product. However, there was no really noteworthy distilling achievement until the following century.

In that century, in accordance with the Mercantile System, Britain insisted on mutual trade with the colonies to the exclusion, insofar as possible, of trade with other countries. The colonies were to ship their raw materials to Britain (in British ships) and were to purchase British manufactures. Britain would thus have less need to trade with other countries, at the same time that colonial trade with these other countries would be reduced to a minimum. This worked a particular hardship on the northern colonies, who had no raw materials of importance to ship to Britain, and had to pay for British manufactures in cold cash. One way to acquire this money was to produce rum and sell it. A startling method was developed. American ships brought molasses from the West Indies to New England distillers, who produced rum from it. Some of this rum found a domestic market and became immensely popular. In addition, however, substantial quantities were shipped to Africa and there traded for slaves. These slaves were brought to the West Indies and to the southern colonies. In the West Indies they were sold for molasses and put to work on sugar plantations for the production of additional supplies of molasses. The product was transported to New England, and the cycle repeated. This trading operation became tremendously profitable. At its height (about 1750), nearly a thousand ships regularly plied the triangular course: the West Indies, New England, Africa. Great fortunes were amassed by distillers and shipowners.

Meanwhile the mother country had been casting an uneasy eye on this development. The colonies were buying their molasses not only from the British islands in the West Indies, but from French and Spanish possessions there as well. In 1733, Britain, under King George II, decided to take action. Parliament passed the Molasses Act, which levied prohibitive taxes on French and Spanish molasses, permitting only the costly British molasses to be imported tax-free. The law contained no provisions for effective enforcement, however, and the colonies ignored it. The rum trade continued to increase.

In 1764, during the reign of George III, the Sugar Act provided enforcement measures which the Molasses Act lacked. The tax was reduced from sixpence to threepence per gallon, but the law provided that colonial vessels could be searched and seized. British warships soon were maintaining a constant patrol of New England waters.

Compliance with the law would have dealt a death-blow to the rum industry, which was the very foundation of the economy in some of the colonies. The law was defied, and rum smuggling thereupon contributed a tense chapter to colonial history.

The rum industry had a profound economic and social effect on eighteenth-century America, and contributed powerfully to the friction between colony and mother country which finally blazed forth in the Revolutionary War.

After the Revolution, commerce in rum continued, but when the African slave trade was abolished in 1808, it gradually declined.

Meanwhile, in the latter part of the eighteenth century, whiskey had been making a start toward replacing rum as America's most important liquor. The production of whiskey on a commercial scale was started because of a transportation problem which faced farmers who had settled at a distance from the Atlantic seaboard. There were no good roads leading back to coastal towns and cities, and it became tremendously difficult to get grain crops to market. The distillation of whiskey from grain provided a satisfactory solution. Whiskey would not spoil, was easily apportioned, easily packaged, and took up considerably less space than the grain used in producing it. Moreover, it brought a good price. Stills began to crop up on most farms in Pennsylvania and neighboring areas, and whiskey began to flow steadily into seaboard markets. (Washington himself is said to have produced whiskey on his farm at Mt. Vernon.)

Eventually this farm whiskey became a primary commercial product. As it grew in importance, it became a recognized medium of exchange (the same had been true of rum), especially when Continental currency became nearly worthless.

Just as rum had run into tax difficulties with England, whiskey was to run into tax difficulties with the federal government. During Washington's administration, Alexander Hamilton, as Secretary of the Treasury, embarked upon a comprehensive financial program. As part of the program, a distilled spirits excise tax was levied (1791) of 54¢ per gallon of still capacity, and 7¢ per gallon on production.

Many important figures of the time, notably Jefferson, were opposed to the tax, but their opposition was pale in comparison with that of the farmer-distillers themselves. Convinced that the tax was excessive and that their financial existence was threatened, these men defied the tax collectors. Stormy meetings were held and angry speeches delivered. Tension kept mounting until at last a mob marched on the garrison in Pittsburgh. Under General Henry Lee, Governor of Virginia, the federal government rushed fifteen thousand troops to the scene. This display of might awed the rebels, and the demonstration ended, fortunately without bloodshed.

This "Whiskey Rebellion," as it is called, took place in 1794, cost a half-million dollars to put down, and became a political issue between the administration and its opponents. When the Jeffersonians came into office, the tax was repealed (1800). From that day until 1862 (except as a war measure from 1812 to 1817), the government levied no taxes on distilled spirits.

The excise tax which led to the "Whiskey Rebellion" also produced another, if less dramatic, result. Many farmer-distillers migrated from the region in and around Pennsylvania to some less-developed areas which, through greater distance from the seat of federal government, or through difficulty of access, were generally out of the reach of revenue officers. Most of these migrating farmer-distillers settled in Kentucky, where they joined others who were already making whiskey there. From this small and haphazard start, Kentucky developed eventually into the largest whiskey-producing state in the country, and to this day out-produces all other states. In Pennsylvania, and also in Maryland, rye whiskey was produced from rye crops grown in those states. In Kentucky, however, corn was the crop and from this was distilled bourbon whiskey, which derives its name from Kentucky's Bourbon County, where farmer-distillers were concentrated.

By 1810, two years after the abolition of the slave trade, whiskey production was already far ahead of rum production.

As time passed, family stills gave way to commercial distilleries, which were fewer in number but which had, of course, a greater production capacity.

How was whiskey produced in these early days? Musing on distilling methods of the time, the *New York Sun* in 1897 described them as follows: "Distilling was not accomplished by any regularly defined rule, but rather after the manner of the old mammy's formula for bread-making by taking 'a passel' of meal, a 'passel' of malt, and about 'so much' water, 'biled down until it was done.' By this process there were frequently days when good whiskey was made, but just as often the run, like the old woman's bread, failed to produce the hoped-for result, the failure being invariably attributed to a change in the moon."

Apparently the first man to use scientific methods effectively in the production of American whiskey was James Crow, a Scottish physician and chemist, who is credited with founding the principles of Kentucky distilling as it is understood today. Crow arrived in Kentucky about 1830, and thereupon entered the distilling business. He standardized formulae and procedure, together with scientific apparatus, and maintained strict sanitation. As a result he was able to produce whiskey of uniform and recognizable quality. In this accomplishment lay the seeds of brand identification and development, and the marketing and advertising of brands on a national scale as we now know it. It is interesting to note, in this connection, that Old Crow, the whiskey which bears James Crow's name, has maintained its reputation down through the years and exists on the market today as a leading volume brand.

While Crow and contemporary distillers kept busy year in and year out, and as other distillers followed them, the nation kept steadily expanding westward. Transportation facilities improved and increased. First the steamboat, then the railroads sought new horizons, and with them went growing shipments of distilled spirits. Brands which had been known only locally began to win recognition regionally and even nationally. Some in fact found their way to overseas markets.

In time, taste preferences formed a pattern. Rye whiskey established itself as a favorite along the Eastern seaboard, while bourbon entrenched itself as a favorite in the vastly larger but less populous area west of the Alleghenies.

What about whiskey marketing in these by-gone days? At first, very few whiskies were sold on the basis of reputation and brand name. In fact, brand names as such did not emerge strongly until after the Civil War, and it was not until the present century that any great number became nationally known. Generally speaking, distillers in "the good old days" would appoint selling agents in various parts of the country. These agents sold the distiller's product to hotels and saloons, and to wholesalers. But what the distiller shipped and what his agents sold was not so many cases containing so many bottles. Instead, whiskey was shipped and sold by the barrel. Frequently, after it reached its destination, it was blended before bottling.

Sometimes the sales agent bottled it, sometimes the wholesaler or retailer. And as far as the consumer was concerned, if he wanted to take his whiskey home with him rather than drink it at the bar, he could present his own bottle to the retailer, who filled it from the tap. This became common practice.

When a middleman bottled whiskey, he usually put his name, plus a brand name of his own choosing, on the label. However, a few distillers' brands began to acquire a widening reputation. When this happened, middlemen saw the advantage of using labels bearing the distiller's brand name. Very often these middlemen designed their own labels. Thus, the traveler in those days might see different types of bottles, with differently designed labels, in different cities, all for the same brand.

As a service to his customers, and also because he realized the advantage to himself, a distiller of one of these early "name brands" would sometimes produce quantities of a stock label for those who bottled his product. However, the idea boomeranged. Brands in great demand soon found themselves counterfeited. With persistent frequency, their labels turned up on bottles containing unknown, inferior whiskies.

Litigation became the order of the day. In order to combat counterfeiting and other abuses, some distillers began to do their own bottling and labeling. In time others followed suit. Then, in 1897, another important step was taken in the direction of honest competition and consumer protection. This was passage of the Bottling in Bond Act, which prescribed exact standards for a certain type of straight whiskey, and provided for bottling of this whiskey at the distillery under the supervision of the federal government. Under this law a Kentucky bourbon, Old Hermitage, became America's first bonded whiskey.

How were liquors advertised prior to Prohibition? We need not spend much time on pre-Prohibition liquor advertising. It was certainly not conducted as expertly or as extensively as at present. Some brands advertised regularly, and relied to a great extent on a therapeutic approach. Magnificent if incredible superlatives claimed cures for gout, pleurisy, housemaid's knee and more serious ills.

During this pre-Prohibition period, which witnessed the growth of distilling, distilling skill, product quality and product standards, and also the emergence of brand names and the embryonic development of marketing and advertising techniques, the industry found itself involved with other difficulties and problems. To illustrate:

During Grant's administration, some unscrupulous distillers took part in the general corruption of the time. A "Whiskey Ring" in St. Louis conspired to defraud the government of millions of dollars in excise taxes.

As another example: within the industry about the turn of the century a small-scale civil war raged between producers of straight whiskey (Kentucky bourbon) and producers of blends. The Whiskey Trust (to be distinguished from the Whiskey Ring) claimed that only straight whiskies were entitled to be called whiskey, and that blends were not worthy of the designation. An Internal Revenue order provided that whiskies other than straight whiskies were to be labeled as imitations. Blend producers fought back bitterly and finally won the day. In 1909, during Taft's administration, the Internal Revenue order was rescinded and blends were permitted to be classified as whiskies. Just before Prohibition, blends (although not labeled as such) accounted for about 70% of the sale of all whiskies.

However, none of the problems of individual distillers or of the industry as a whole were of real importance while one problem in particular remained unsolved. A segment of the population was pledged to the complete overthrow of the industry. These anti-industry campaigners (drys) demanded that distilleries be shut down, that liquors be removed from the market, and that it be made a crime to manufacture or sell them. The problem grew in intensity. Pre-Prohibition distillers tried desperately to cope with it, but eventually it became too much for them.

Almost from the start of American history, there had been agitation for either curtailment or outright prohibition of the sale of liquors. The Pilgrims were talking about it as early as 1630. Sporadic legislation dots the pages of colonial history. For example, about 1650, Rhode Island decided to fine intoxicated persons the sum of five shillings, while Connecticut put a half-hour time limit on drinking by any individual. Some years later, Maryland passed a law which made the punishment for intoxication a six-hour stay in the stocks. At the start of the eighteenth century, New Hampshire forbade drinking in inns on Saturday nights and Sundays.

These were but straws in the wind. In 1733 came the first comparatively large-scale prohibition action when the colony of Georgia, under the authority of the British Parliament, outlawed the importation of liquors.

It was not until 1789, however, that the first organized "temperance society" was formed. This society, which was established in Connecticut, was followed by others, which mushroomed during the first few decades of the nineteenth century. In the 1830's, there were more than 5000 organized temperance groups with an estimated enrollment of one million members.

The labors of these early drys bore fruit. A state-wide prohibition law was passed at last (Maine, 1846). Throughout the nation thousands upon thousands of men, prodded by the drys, joined the teetotalers in pledging themselves to abstinence.

After the Civil War, the number of saloons increased. Unfortunately, many of them flaunted moderation and good taste by ignoring closing laws, by selling to minors and to intoxicated persons, and by failing to maintain order and decency.

In 1869, the National Prohibition Party was formed, proved ineffectual, and was followed five years later by the founding of the Woman's Christian Temperance Union (WCTU). In the 1880's four more states legislated prohibition into existence. In the ensuing decade the first prohibition convention was held (Wisconsin), and the Anti-Saloon League formed.

The drys continued to agitate with tremendous vitality, not only politically but through propaganda as well. Schools, churches, public forums and the press bore witness to their activities—as did the saloons, which were invaded by temperance women who knelt in prayer and sang psalms.

By 1900, seven states had gone dry, and the movement continued to gain strength. Prior to World War I, two-thirds of American citizens lived in areas governed by dry laws. Most of these areas were rural; progress of the drys in the cities was slow.

In 1913, the Webb-Kenyon Act banned the shipment of liquors from wet states to dry states. In the same year members of the WCTU and the Anti-Saloon League marched to Washington and jointly proposed a national prohibition amendment. The outbreak of the war provided the drys with a more favorable climate, and while they did not immediately obtain their amendment, they succeeded in getting several wartime prohibition measures passed.

Pressing their advantage, however, they finally triumphed. A national prohibition amendment was at last submitted to the states. On January 16, 1919, Nebraska became the thirty-sixth state to ratify the amendment, and it became effective one year later. Subsequently all states ratified it with the exception of Connecticut and Rhode Island. This, the famous 18th Amendment, reads as follows:

ARTICLE XVIII

1. After one year from the ratification of this article the manufacture, sale, or transportation of intoxicating liquors within, the importation thereof into, or the exportation thereof from the United

States and all territory subject to the jurisdiction thereof for beverage purposes is hereby prohibited.

2. The Congress and the several States shall have concurrent power to enforce this article by appropriate legislation.

3. This article shall be inoperative unless it shall have been ratified as an amendment to the Constitution by the Legislatures of the several States, as provided in the Constitution, within seven years from the date of the submission hereof to the States by the Congress.

In October, 1919, Congress passed the Volstead Act (over President Wilson's veto). The act, which became effective January 16, 1920, defined the "intoxicating liquors" phrase of the amendment as referring to all alcoholic beverages containing more than one-half of one per cent of alcohol by volume.

2. The Prohibition Era

It took no more than a year or two for the American public to realize that their "noble experiment" was not working out very well. As the twenties progressed, it became more and more apparent that effective control rather than Prohibition was the answer to problems which had occupied the limelight in pre-Prohibition days. A distinction began to be drawn between the intelligent sale and consumption of liquors and indiscriminate sale and alcoholism, between moderate drinkers and alcoholics.

The nation had made a mistake. It took more than thirteen years to rectify it. During this period, social evils developed which made those of the past look like virtues by comparison.

The bootlegger had existed in pre-Prohibition days, and as the Prohibition movement gained momentum, had begun to thrive and prosper. This is evidenced by the fact that raids on illicit stills were common long before the WCTU and the Anti-Saloon League proposed their prohibition amendment. When the nation went dry in 1920, the bootlegger was ready and waiting. Organized crime took over and methodically went about the business of illegal production, smuggling, bribery of government representatives and the establishment of speakeasies. Moreover, the bootlegger set ridiculously high prices and peddled liquors which were not only inferior but often poisonous. Blindness and deaths from the bootleg product became prevalent enough to deteriorate in news value, as did raids on stills and speakeasies.

Lawful competition between distillers gave way to criminal competition between bootleggers, who won front page publicity by machine-gun solutions of their differences. The "St. Valentine's Day Massacre" in Chicago in 1929, when gangsters lined up six rivals and shot them down in cold blood, typified the bootleggers' way of doing business.

It might be presumed that the consumer, who had to pay exorbitant prices for liquors which might blind or kill him, would decide to stay away from them or at least use them sparingly. The opposite is true. Authoritative estimates show an increase during Prohibition over per capita consumption in wet regions prior to Prohibition. Legally, the United States was dry. In actuality, it was not only wet, but wetter. Prohibition, as the saying went, did not prohibit.

As the public woke up morning after morning to fresh news of crime, illness and death, statisticians were tallying up the costs of prohibition. Dollar-wise, it was estimated that enforcement was costing federal, state and local governments an average of 50 million dollars a year. The loss in annual revenue to these governments was estimated at a billion dollars. At the same time the consumer was himself suffering a dollar loss. It was estimated that he was paying the bootlegger about a billion a year more than he would have paid for legal liquors, taxes included. Estimates were also made as to the loss suffered by those who had been employed in the legitimate liquor and allied industries. This added several hundred million dollars to the yearly bill being rendered by Prohibition.

Some items on the bill were not to be stated in terms of dollars—disease and death, the sensational growth of organized crime, plus overall deterioration in moral and social welfare.

The nation had had enough. As prohibition societies had once sprung up, repeal societies now began to spring up. Among these, the Association Against the Prohibition Amendment proved to be especially influential. In the midst of this agitation, the Wickersham Report made it clear that Prohibition had failed.

It was now only a matter of time. In February, 1933, Congress sent an amendment for repeal of the 18th amendment to the states for ratification. The temper of the times was demonstrated when, in the following month, Congress passed a law legalizing the manufacture and sale of wines and beers containing 3.2% alcohol. Meanwhile, the states were acting quickly. Before the end of the year (December 5, 1933), Utah became the thirty-sixth state to ratify the amendment, and Prohibition bowed itself out. Thus, the United States joined the list of nations which had adopted and then abolished Prohibition during the present century (the others are Iceland, Norway, Finland, Sweden, Russia, Turkey, Newfoundland, and nine provinces of Canada).

The 21st Amendment reads as follows:

ARTICLE XXI

1. The eighteenth article of amendment to the Constitution of the United States is hereby repealed.

2. The transportation or importation into any State, Territory, or Possession of the United States for delivery or use therein of intoxicating liquors, in violation of the laws thereof, is hereby prohibited.

3. This article shall be inoperative unless it shall have been ratified as an amendment to the Constitution by convention in the several States, as provided in the Constitution, within seven years from the date of the submission hereof to the States by the Congress.

3. The Post-Repeal Period

The 21st Amendment set the general pattern in which the newborn liquor industry was to operate. As with other industries, it was to be subject to federal, state and local legislation. Some of this legislation was specifically to concern liquors; other legislation had already been enacted (or was in the future to be enacted) and included the liquor industry along with other industries. In accordance with Section 2 of the new amendment, control was left to the individual states. This meant that a state could maintain total state-wide prohibition if it so desired; it could permit the operation of the industry with no specific state liquor legislation; or it could legislate to effect a situation somewhere between these two extremes.

This was a clear-cut pattern, and remains so to the present. It marked a sharp advance over pre-Prohibition years.

Immediately after Repeal, governmental units proceeded to enact liquor laws and regulations. Much of this legislation answered the need, for the first time in the nation's history, for intelligent and comprehensive treatment of the industry's sociological problems and trade practices.

At first, Codes of Fair Competition were set up under the National Industrial Recovery Act (June, 1933) and were administered by the Federal Alcohol Control Administration (FACA). In May, 1935, the Supreme Court declared the Act unconstitutional. The FACA was abolished and was replaced by the Federal Alcohol Administration (FAA). In August, 1935, the Federal Alcohol Administration Act was passed. This act, with subsequent amendments and with regulations relating to it, is in force today. Basically, it contains the primary features of the Codes of Fair Competition under the NIRA.

In 1940, the FAA was superseded by the Alcohol Tax Unit of the Treasury Department's Bureau of Internal Revenue (redesignated, in 1953, as the Internal Revenue Service). Eventually authority was vested in the Alcohol and Tobacco Tax Division of the Internal Revenue Service. Sharing in authority over the liquor industry today is the Bureau of Customs, which also operates out of the Treasury Department.

In the individual states, too, administrative and enforcement units were established after Repeal. In addition, state liquor legislation was enacted. In some states, prohibition was retained; other states set themselves up as monopolies in the liquor business; a third group put the liquor business on a basis of private enterprise. Within the states, many counties and municipalities also took action.

In anticipation of Repeal, lawful distillers (who had spent their time during Prohibition in the production of industrial alcohol, and of alcoholic beverages for medicinal and sacramental use) banded together in 1933 and formed a trade association, which they named the Distilled Spirits Institute. There had been no trade association composed solely of distillers prior to this time. When the NIRA was declared unconstitutional, DSI became immediately active, and contributed substantially to the formulation of regulations under the Federal Alcohol Administration Act, and to the revision and expansion of regulations of the Bureau of Internal Revenue. At hearings conducted on the foregoing regulations, DSI presented the industry viewpoint. In addition, DSI adopted resolutions for industry self-regulation in the field of advertising. Members of DSI bound themselves to observance of these resolutions, which set up standards for the industry above and beyond those required by law. These resolutions, plus some additions, have been followed faithfully and remain in effect today.

So much for the development of the general administrative, legislative and regulatory environment in which the industry operates. What about the operation itself? What has been happening in the industry since Repeal?

The largest distilling organizations which were prepared to serve the American public at the time—and they continue to remain the largest—were the Distillers Company, Ltd. (DCL), controlling most of the world's supply of Scotch whiskies; two American companies: National Distillers Products Corporation and Schenley Distillers; and two Canadian companies: Distillers Corp.-Seagrams, Ltd. and Hiram Walker-Gooderham and Worts, Ltd., both of which opened plants in the United States at the time of Repeal. National, Schenley, Seagram and Hiram Walker, as they are popularly called, are generally known in the industry as "the Big Four."

Along with these giants of the liquor world, scores of other domestic distillers went into operation. Meanwhile the nation's ports were opening to cargoes of distilled spirits from overseas.

Stores of aged whiskies were low, and distillers went into all-out production. Before long it was common to see advertisements proclaiming 6-months-old whiskey, then 8-months-old whiskey, and so on. But while some whiskey was put on the market for immediate sale, a certain portion was kept in warehouses for a longer period, and was earmarked for withdrawal only after it had reached two, three and four or more years of age. Grain neutral spirits, which require no aging, were produced in quantity and were blended with straight whiskey in order to increase the marketable supply.

Other types of distilled spirits were also finding their way to the marketplace. Gin had become popular during Prohibition. Homemade "bathtub gin" had familiarized the public with the product, and when distillers now placed legally distilled gin in stores and bars, it met with wide acceptance and demand. Concurrently, brandies, rums, cordials and other distilled spirits were joining whiskies and gins on shelves and back-bars.

As liquors became available in ever-increasing quantity, as older straight whiskies replaced younger straights, and as distillers began to feel the pinch of competition more keenly, price reductions became frequent. In some cases, distillers were able to announce a price reduction for a brand at the same time as an increase in age.

In time the bubbling cauldron of post-Repeal marketing and advertising began to simmer down. Supply was meeting and adjusting to demand, distillers were finding fewer competitive product differences to talk about, and markets were stabilizing. This was the situation in the late thirties, prior to World War II.

In looking back over these few years of post-Repeal and pre-war liquor history, other significant facts are to be noted.

During the Prohibition period, American marketing and advertising had come into its own. The food, tobacco, drug, automotive and other industries had grown tremendously in size and importance. Advertising agencies and marketing and market research organizations had been perfecting their techniques. Whereas in the past, years of patient effort were required to establish a brand name nationally, this now could be accomplished seemingly overnight.

The world which the liquor industry woke up to, Rip Van Winkle fashion, in 1933, was thus quite different from the world to which it shut its eyes in 1920. Finding itself, as a new industry, suddenly thrust into a society in which advertising and marketing methods had been revolutionized, it faced the problem not only of utilizing these methods with no background of experience, but of doing so under laws which were more restrictive than those for any other major industry. Within a short time, however, the industry succeeded in adjusting itself, and was eventually able to match others in the scope of its achievement.

This last point may be illustrated by the fact that most of the largest-selling brands in America today were unknown during Prohibition and pre-Prohibition days. The man in the street had never heard, for example, of the names Seagram, Calvert, or Schenley. There were no such brands as Seagram's 7 Crown, Calvert Reserve, Schenley Reserve, Imperial or PM, all of which rank among the top-selling brands in America today. Modern marketing and advertising skill helped to establish these brands in positions of leadership. Traditional brands received equal benefit, of course, from modern marketing and advertising methods. Old Crow and Old Sunny Brook are examples. Many other traditional brands belong on the list with them.

The new industry was not quite six years old when, in September, 1939, Hitler invaded Poland, thus precipitating World War II. Two years later Japan bombed Pearl Harbor and the United States found itself directly involved in the war. Preparations for this eventuality had already been started, and included a complete overhaul of the nation's economy. Along with other industries, the liquor industry "went to war." In fact, it had offered its facilities to the government a year before Pearl Harbor, and was already partially engaged in war production by November, 1941. In October, 1942, the War Production Board asked for the industry's entire output. Total conversion followed, with most plants operating twenty-four hours a day, seven days a week, in the production of alcohol for the manufacture of synthetic rubber, smokeless powder, chemical warfare materials, medical supplies and other wartime products. The call from the War Production

Board was motivated by wartime requirements, and not by any desire to bring back Prohibition.

Though devoting their manufacturing facilities to war alcohol, distillers kept one eye on the future. Realizing that they would be back in the beverage business when the war was won, and realizing also that brand names were their most valuable equity, they decided upon a twofold policy. First it was decided to keep liquor products on the market as long as possible, however short the supply. There was just so much whiskey and other spirits in barrels and in bottles. At an unchecked rate of consumption, this supply might disappear in a relatively short time. It was decided to cut down the distribution and sale of these liquors. Stocks were rationed and brands put on an allocation basis. In order to stretch out supplies even further, many brands of straight whiskey were converted into blends through the use of grain neutral spirits. More whiskey was thus made available.

As a second major step in keeping brands and brand names before the public, producers and importers maintained consistent advertising campaigns, despite shortages. These campaigns sounded the same note: "We are now devoting our facilities to war production. If you cannot get X Brand at your favorite store or bar, be sure to ask for it again later on. Supplies, though short and rationed, are shipped periodically."

This policy of keeping brand names alive was not only sound but successful, as post-war years demonstrated.

After the surrender of Germany and Japan, total beverage production was resumed. As supplies became available again, the industry experienced a top year with the sale in 1946 of 230 million gallons of distilled spirits. Consumption fell off after 1946, but the industry continued to go along in high gear. The sellers' market which had developed during the war gave way to a buyers' market. Normal competitive patterns emerged again.

After a few peacetime years, the industry was able to assess with accuracy the changes wrought by the war. The policy of maintaining brand names had proved itself. Major pre-war brands had come back to assume major post-war sales positions. Unknown brands, particularly West Indies and South American rums, which flooded the country during the period of the war shortages, had all but disappeared. Also, the industry noted, drinking habits had undergone changes. Before the war, bars had accounted for about two-thirds of total sales; after the war, purchases for home consumption increased, with stores doing two-thirds of the business. The store—bar ratio was thus reversed. Taste preferences, too, had changed during the war. Whereas straight whiskies had dominated the market prior to 1942, wartime conversion of straights to blends had turned the picture around. Tastes which the public acquired during the war stayed with them. More people continued to prefer blends, which kept outselling straights even after the latter began returning to the market in quantity in 1949, 1950, and 1951. Changes in taste preferences were noted in connection with other types of distilled spirits as well.

Price-wise, liquors had gone up since Repeal. Increased wartime and post-war federal taxes, plus state and municipal taxes, were accounting for about 50% of retail bottle prices. The industry protested, stating that rising prices served only to swell the ranks of the sizable minority which patronized the bootlegger. Meanwhile, however, the majority of the public remained loyal to major advertised brands, despite increased prices. Within the category of advertised brands, in fact, there was a shift from lower-priced toward middle and upper-priced items. To put it another way, a trend had begun toward concentration of more business in fewer brands, and in higher-priced brands. The nation's middle-income group became entrenched as the backbone of the industry's consumer market.

What has been happening on the wet-dry front since Repeal? The drys have continued to agitate, and while they offer a serious and constant threat to the existence of the industry, have succeeded only in winning minor local victories. Through federal and state control, and through the self-policing activities of the industry itself, liquors have at last become respectable members in the family of American products. No longer do the drys have the same sort of targets which they shot at before Prohibition. And no group has become more conscious than the industry itself that observance of the law, self-regulation, and regard for social welfare are the most effective safeguards against a return to Prohibition. This realization, plus astute management, and the utilization of modern production science and modern marketing and advertising methods, have advanced the industry tremendously. From its small beginnings in New England, Pennsylvania and Kentucky, and despite over a decade of Prohibition, it has grown to become one of America's economic giants.

CHAPTER THREE

Aspects of the Liquor Industry

We will observe now some of the important aspects and characteristics of the liquor industry.

1. Size and Importance

As already noted, the industry is one of America's economic giants. Annual production, bottled output and consumption are each measured in terms of hundreds of millions of gallons. Moreover, millions of gallons of distilled spirits are exported each year to every part of the globe, and about ten times as much gallonage imported.

Dollar-wise, the industry is also a giant. Billions of dollars are collected annually by federal, state and local governments in taxes, import duties, permit and license fees. More billions go each year into the pay envelopes of millions of persons employed by the industry and by its suppliers. Additional billions are paid by the industry to these suppliers for grains, fruits, plants, equipment, barrels, bottles, cartons, transportation, fuel, electricity, advertising, marketing, merchandising, sales promotion and other goods and services. Still more billions are paid out yearly by the consumer in the retail purchase of distilled spirits.

The size and importance of the industry may also be measured in terms of business units. Producers, importers and wholesalers are numbered in the thousands, and retailers in the hundreds of thousands.

2. Federal, State and Local Law

FEDERAL LAW. A few pages back we briefly traced the development of federal liquor legislation. We will now examine this legislation as it affects the liquor industry today. The government has enacted more laws and regulations for liquors than for any other product. These laws and regulations may be considered under two main classifications: revenue legislation, and legislation controlling the operation of the industry.

The Internal Revenue Service collects excise taxes on both domestic and imported spirits. In addition, the Bureau of Customs collects duties on imports (it will be observed that imports pay both excise taxes and customs duties). Further revenue is derived from rectification taxes; special or occupational taxes; floor taxes; container, case and export stamps. Excise taxes usually account for about 90% of total distilled spirits revenue.

Liquor taxes and duties are paid directly to the government by producers and importers. As a result, they are "hidden taxes" as far as the consumer is concerned. In this respect, liquors differ from many other products—jewelry and cosmetics, for example—which are subject to federal excise taxes. On such products, the consumer pays the tax at the time of purchase as a percentage of the retail price, in the same manner that he pays many sales taxes. The vast majority of consumers have no idea of the actual excise tax they pay when purchasing liquors.

In addition to specific liquor taxes, the industry, like other industries, is also subject to taxes (both federal and state) including the following: corporation and income taxes, capital gains taxes, capital stock taxes, mercantile license taxes, special gross business income taxes, social security taxes, unemployment insurance taxes.

Federal laws and regulations concerning the operation of the industry cover every conceivable aspect of it—importing, distilling, rectifying, standards of product identity, cooperage, warehousing, bottling, labeling, wholesaling, retailing, credit, advertising, etc. In this connection it is worth observing that distilling, rectifying, warehousing and bottling must be conducted under the supervision of federal representatives (called storekeeper-gaugers), who have keys to the producer's equipment and warehouses. Without these storekeeper-gaugers, equipment cannot be used, or premises opened and entered.

The Federal Alcohol Administration Act, together with regulations relating to it, concerns itself only with certain specified subjects regarding industry control. The purpose of this law, as stated in the Act itself, is "to further protect the revenue derived from distilled spirits, wine, and malt beverages, to regulate interstate and foreign commerce and enforce the postal laws with respect thereto, to enforce the twenty-first amendment, and for other purposes."

The law sets forth provisions, with respect to liquors in interstate and foreign commerce, under the following main headings:

a. *Permits.* Importers, distillers, rectifiers, warehousemen, bottlers and wholesalers are required to obtain basic permits issued by the Secretary of the Treasury.

b. *Unfair competition and unlawful practices.* Specifically outlawed are exclusive retail outlets, the "tied house," commercial bribery and consignment sales. Moreover, the law provides for detailed regulations with respect to bottling, labeling and advertising. The purpose of these regulations is to prevent deception of the consumer, to provide him with accurate and adequate information, to prevent disparagement of competitive products, and to prevent statements which are "false, misleading, obscene or indecent." We will have occasion, in a later chapter, to explore carefully these marketing and advertising aspects of federal liquor law.

c. *Bulk spirits.* The law defines the phrase "in bulk" as referring to containers with a capacity of more than one wine gallon. Provisions are set forth concerning bulk sales and bottling of distilled spirits, and warehouse receipts used in connection with them.

d. *Penalties.* The Act gives jurisdiction to specified courts for suits brought by the United States Attorney General "to prevent and restrain violations of any of the provisions of this Act." Anyone who operates without a basic permit, or who violates any of the provisions concerning unfair competition and unlawful practices, is guilty of a misdemeanor and subject to a fine.

e. *Interlocking directorates.* These are prohibited if they "substantially restrain or prevent competition in interstate or foreign commerce in distilled spirits." Fines up to $1000 may be imposed for violations.

f. *Disposal of forfeited alcoholic beverages.* The Secretary of the Treasury receives all forfeited alcoholic beverages. He may destroy them or turn them over for medicinal purposes to government agencies and to charitable organizations. Government agencies may also receive forfeited alcoholic beverages for scientific and other uses.

In addition to specific liquor legislation under the authority of the Treasury Department, the industry, like other industries, is subject to the authority vested in other federal administrative bodies and laws. For example, the Federal Trade Commission is empowered to act against unfair trade practices, price discrimination, and false and deceptive advertising. As another example, products, including liquors, which are adulterated or misbranded may be seized by the government when shipped in interstate or foreign commerce. As to prices, Fair Trade legislation provides for the establishment of fixed prices on trademarked brands in interstate commerce, in accordance with individual state laws.

STATE AND LOCAL LAW. Inasmuch as the states have power to legislate on liquors within their individual borders, they have provided for administrative and enforcement liquor units, and have enacted specific legislation concerning liquors.

Some states have established exclusive state liquor administrations. In others, villages, boroughs, municipalities and counties have liquor-governing bodies.

As in the case of federal legislation, state laws provide for the collection of liquor revenue and for the control and regulation of the industry. In addition, states have legislated on the wet-dry question. Two states maintain state-wide prohibition. About two-thirds of the states have both wet counties and dry or partially dry counties. Other states are completely wet. Most wet or partially wet states provide for local option (the privilege of political units within a state, varying in size from precincts to counties, to vote themselves from dry to wet or vice versa).

In the matter of revenue, the main sources of state liquor income are license fees, excise taxes and sales taxes. In states which are in the liquor business for themselves ("monopoly states") an additional source of revenue is derived from the retail sale of liquors in state-owned stores. To arrive at net liquor revenue, states deduct administrative, enforcement and collection costs. Monopoly states also deduct the cost of liquors and the cost of the retail sales operation. In many states, revenue is also collected by counties and smaller political units.

With respect to control and regulatory legislation, wet states have their own laws on licenses, production, warehousing, bottling, labeling, wholesaling, retailing, Fair Trade, advertising, etc.

Many counties and other political units have also enacted control and regulatory legislation.

3. Important Industry Problems

ENEMIES OF THE INDUSTRY. Unlike any other industry in the United States today, the distilled spirits industry has as its sworn enemy a nation-wide, organized opposition which devotes itself to death-to-the-finish tactics. The reference is of course to the drys, whom we met in the previous chapter. Thus, a primary problem of the industry is one of existence itself. The drys today are not only well-organized, but intelligent, vigorous and zealous. Their attempts to destroy the industry take many forms. Aside from direct propaganda concerning alcoholism and other sociological problems, the drys keep up a steady barrage against federal, state and local legislative bodies. Almost every year, for example, an attempt is made to have Congress pass a law which would prohibit interstate transportation of distilled spirits advertising. In states where local option obtains, the drys attempt to keep dry areas dry, and to convert wet areas to dry areas. It is clear, therefore, that the drys make frontal attacks and also operate in indirect and subtle ways.

Also threatening the existence of the industry, if less obviously, is the bootlegger. Crime, illness and deaths which are attributable to bootleg liquors serve to furnish drys with ammunition against lawfully produced spirits. Furthermore, it is estimated that sales of bootleg liquors run about 25% of legitimate sales. To this extent, the market for legitimate liquors is reduced. It will be noted that dry victories and bootleg operations both combine to shrink liquor markets (by dry victories in local option elections and by bootlegging in any form, or in any locality).

SOCIOLOGICAL PROBLEMS. Alcoholism, bootlegging, teen-age drinking, drunken driving, and retailing which is either unprincipled or in bad taste constitute the main sociological problems of the industry.

a. *Alcoholism.* Medical science has demonstrated that alcoholism is a disease, either physical or mental, or both. One type of alcoholic has a physiological imbalance which results in a craving for excessive amounts of alcohol. Another type of alcoholic suffers from a psychological imbalance and calls upon alcohol to furnish an adjustment. Alcoholics account for only a small percentage of all users of spirits. Although the industry is not responsible for the abuse of its products by any individual drinker, the existence of alcoholism itself is construed by some as a reason for wholesale prohibition of liquors.

b. *Bootlegging.* Crime and racketeering are the bedfellows of bootlegging. Today, raids on illicit stills, of which over 10,000 are seized yearly, continue to make important news. The fact that injurious and deadly spirits are produced unlawfully does not remove the indictment in the minds of some against legitimate spirits produced in strict accordance with strict law.

c. *Teen-age drinking.* Drinking by minors has also been blamed on the industry, despite scrupulous avoidance of any appeal to minors, and despite a campaign by the industry against those retailers who, deliberately or unknowingly, sell to minors. Laws prohibit sales to minors. It has been nevertheless considered by some that it is the fault of the industry at large that a small percentage of teen-agers and a small percentage of retailers break these laws.

d. *Drunken driving.* This is another case of abuse of liquors by a small percentage of drinkers. Yet accidents from drunken driving constitute a sociological problem which the industry cannot ignore.

e. *Retailing evils.* The liquor retailer has a special responsibility. Along with advertising, he represents the point of contact between the industry and the consumer. If he obeys the law and conducts himself in his own best interests, he keeps his establishment clean and in order, refuses to sell to minors and to intoxicated persons, and promotes but does not force sales. Most retailers operate in this way. Those who fail to do so wind up with stores or bars which are eyesores in the community, breeding places for vice, or both. As long as retailers of this type persist, they are to be numbered among the sociological problems with which the industry must contend.

TAXES. The industry is always alert to the problems created by high taxes, and has always been quick to combat them. It takes the following stand: Liquors should most certainly be taxed. However, when taxes climb too high, sales of legitimate liquors are reduced, the purpose of the tax collector is defeated, and other evils arise. High taxes result in high retail prices which induce consumers to either discontinue purchase of liquors, or to patronize the bootlegger. As a result, profits are lost by distillers, and revenue by government units. Furthermore, inasmuch as liquor taxes are hidden, the consumer cannot be blamed if he concludes that high retail prices represent price-gouging. As a result, the industry is a victim of ill-will and resentment arising from a situation which it not only did not create, but which it actively opposed.

PUBLIC RELATIONS. It will be noted from the foregoing discussion of drys, bootlegging, sociological problems and taxation, that the industry is faced with a series of vital problems in public relations. The fact that the industry is not responsible for them does not alter the fact that they exist. Great strides have been made in meeting these problems. Two national public relations associations are vigorously active: Licensed Beverage Industries, Inc. and the Women's Association of Allied Beverage Industries. In addition, the Distilled Spirits Institute continues the fine public relations job which it began at the time of Repeal.

It is considered that if the public is completely informed, the industry will cease to be threatened. Primarily, therefore, the industry attempts to convey the following ideas to the consumer: Alcoholism is a disease which the industry deplores rather than embraces; the industry preaches moderation (not only for reasons of social welfare, but because the moderate drinker is the mainstay of the consumer market); bootlegging is illegal, against industry interests, and is not to be compared with the operation of legal distillers; the industry tries to prevent rather than promote teen-age drinking; the industry cannot be blamed for motor accidents caused by any individual who is foolish enough to become intoxicated and then take the wheel; disreputable retailers are as much of a headache to the industry as to their communities; dry statistics and propaganda are often distorted and not in accordance with the facts; high retail prices are the result of high taxes.

Aside from its information campaign to the public, the industry has attempted to solve these various problems at their source, with the hope that this will eventually contribute to better public relations. In connection with alcoholism, for instance, the industry has made substantial grants to hospitals and research organizations, to the end that a cure for alcoholism may be found.

As far as bootlegging is concerned, the industry keeps up a constant battle against this enemy, and campaigns for a reduction in taxes, which would be immediately reflected in a reduction of retail prices to the point where the low prices of the bootleg product would become less attractive.

In connection with teen-age drinking, the industry puts pressure on retailers to become increasingly conscious of the age of their younger patrons, and to eliminate sales to minors.

Also, the industry has cooperated with the National Safety Council, and has contributed funds for an educational program designed to prove the need for reliable tests for intoxication when reckless driving or automobile accidents are attributed to drinking.

Finally, realizing that the retailer is the showcase of the industry, pressure has been put on recalcitrants to keep their premises attractive, and to conduct their businesses in good taste and in accordance with the law.

PROBLEMS CREATED BY AGING REQUIREMENTS. Some spirits, particularly whiskey, are aged. When the aging period stretches on into a period of four or more years, which is the usual case with whiskey, the distiller finds himself saddled with several problems:

a. *Forecasting the market.* Every distiller of whiskey or other spirits which undergoes aging must possess some talent for clairvoyance. Before he can manufacture his product, he must prophesy the state of the market at a time which may lie many years in the future. The market may remain the same, it may expand with prosperity, it may shrink with a depression. In addition, the distiller must forecast the future popularity of his particular class and type of spirits, and the price at which it is likely to sell (a sudden sharp rise or fall in the excise tax, for example, may markedly change patterns of consumption).

If the distiller is wrong in his forecast, he will find that he has produced either too much or too little. In such cases, particularly when blended or unbonded straight whiskies are involved, a possible solution to his problem may lie in the sale or purchase of bulk whiskies on the open market. However, bulk prices at the time he is forced to sell or buy may be unfavorable, and the available bulk may not be of exactly the type or quality desired.

As a very extreme solution, and it must be emphasized that this has been done only in periods of acute shortage, such as wartime, when a distiller has under-produced, he may adjust his supply by employing other methods. For example, a straight-whiskey marketer, under-produced, may desire to increase his available marketable supply by converting his product into a spirit blend. Or a spirit blend producer may attempt to stretch his stocks by decreasing the percentage of straight whiskey and increasing the percentage of grain neutral spirits. Such methods, as indicated above, are used only in periods of great stress, for they call for a product change which may damage the all-important consumer equity which has been built up for the brand name.

If a distiller is unable to adjust his supply to demand, he of course finds himself in a difficult position. If his supply exceeds demand, merchandise begins piling up in his warehouse. This merchandise represents not only money spent for production, but a substantial federal tax liability which must eventually be paid. If the supply falls short of demand, he can sell only what he has, and thus lose profits which increased sales would bring.

b. *Taxation.* We have noted that the distiller pays federal excise taxes. He incurs an obligation to pay these taxes at the time that spirits are distilled. In fact, even prior to distillation, he must post bond with the government, guaranteeing to pay the tax when due. Thus, aging requirements put a tax obligation on the distiller for a substantial period of time before his brands can be marketed.

c. *Inventories.* The products of most industries usually require anywhere from one to three months to pass from the raw material stage to the stage of the finished, marketable product. As a result, inventories can turn over quickly. In the case of distilled spirits aged for four or more years, however, warehouse facilities must be able to accommodate the production of that many years. As aged whiskey leaves the warehouse, newly distilled whiskey arrives to join whiskey which has been aging but which has not reached the withdrawal age. Hence, the problem of inventories and warehouse space becomes one of major proportions.

RE-SALE PRICE MAINTENANCE. Retail price-fixing ("Fair Trade") has been a bone of contention in the liquor industry, as in other industries. In 1951, the dispute reached sufficient proportions to reach the U. S. Supreme Court (*Schwegmann Brothers, et al., vs. Calvert Distillers Corporation*). The retailer who opposed Fair Trade won the case. Aside from repercussions in the liquor industry itself, the decision of the Court was followed by a price war among major retailers, primarily in New York City, on many types of trademarked merchandise which had been Fair-Traded until that time. In 1952 Congress passed the McGuire Act, which brought Fair Trade back. Today, provided that supporting Fair Trade legislation is in effect in any given state, manufacturers may fix retail prices of branded, trademarked products (and copyrighted articles) which are in free and open competition with similar items.

MULTIPLICITY OF STATE LAWS. An examination of state liquor laws reveals a lack of uniformity which has consistently hampered operations within the industry. In the matter of state advertising laws and regulations, for example, variations are so wide that the advertiser is forced to alter his copy from state to state, and in some instances so drastically that he must abandon the basic copy theme of his campaign.

Variations in state laws constitute a problem which administrators are not only aware of, but which they attempt to solve. However, it is to be expected that, considering individual state problems, progress must necessarily be slow.

RE-USE OF CONTAINERS. Although federal law prohibits the re-use of liquor bottles, unscrupulous retailers re-fill bottles bearing famous labels with inferior liquors, both legal and bootleg, thus cheating the consumer and injuring brand reputation. This is an extremely difficult problem to solve. Some attempts have been made to invent a non-refillable bottle.

4. National Associations

All branches of the industry are represented by national associations. In addition, as we have learned, two national public relations associations have been formed. Moreover, open state administrators and monopoly state administrators each have their own associations.

STATE ADMINISTRATORS AND COMMISSIONERS

a. *Open states.* The National Conference of State Liquor Administrators was founded in Chicago in 1934. With a membership consisting of administrators in open states, NCSLA has the following purposes: "to devise and promote the enactment of state liquor laws; to devise and promote the use of such methods and devices of administration and interstate cooperation as will serve to enforce and to make effective the particular liquor laws of each state." NCSLA holds a yearly convention, in which members of the industry are invited to participate. In addition, NCSLA holds an annual executive meeting, at which member states discuss problems of alcoholic beverage control.

b. *Monopoly states.* The National Alcoholic Beverage Control Association was founded in Des Moines in 1938. Membership consists of administrators in monopoly states. Its purposes are as follows: "to devote time and study to the problems of monopoly state liquor control; to require open and ethical practices on the part of all vendors of alcoholic beverages; to cooperate with all state and federal agencies charged with the control, sale or taxation of alcoholic beverages." NABCA meets semi-annually to discuss problems of each of the monopoly states. At regional meetings from time to time, recommendations are made to members on strengthening and improving enforcement.

NABCA regularly issues a report on alcoholic beverage prices, and in addition issues a comprehensive monthly report of sales by vendor, class, type and brand for each monopoly state.

NCSLA and NABCA have together formed the Joint Committee of the States to Study Alcoholic Beverage Laws. The purpose of this committee is to study and improve liquor laws in both open and monopoly states.

PRODUCERS

a. The nature of the Distilled Spirits Institute, Inc., and its contribution since Repeal to the industry, to government and to public relations has already been outlined. Members of DSI do approximately 90% of the total distilled spirits business in the United States. Purposes of DSI are as follows:

1. to cooperate with federal and state authorities in the promotion of proper distribution systems and observance of laws relative to the manufacture and sale of alcoholic beverages throughout the United States

2. to maintain the industry upon a high and ethical basis to the end that it will command public respect

3. to work for the prevention of practices within the industry which are contrary to sound public policy

4. to oppose improper methods and illegitimate practices inimical to the proper conduct of the industry

5. to compile statistical, legal and other information for general publication and for use by members of the Institute.

DSI has a Board of Directors which functions as its governing agency. Meetings are held eight or nine times a year. An executive committee meets on call between regular meetings of the Board.

DSI activities are as follows:

1. A statistical reporting service issues regular reports on public revenues, production, bottling, apparent consumption, etc. These reports are models of reliability and accuracy.

2. A legislative reporting service issues information on federal and state legislative proposals, and circulates current governmental orders, regulations, bulletins, and notices.

3. A local option division prepares literature, statistics and general local option information which is made available to the industry, to the press and to areas where local option elections are proposed or called.

4. DSI's Washington department keeps in close contact with the Internal Revenue Service in order to present industry recommendations when changes are contemplated in federal liquor laws and regulations. Occasionally DSI also contacts the Federal Trade Commission, the Department of Justice, and other government departments and agencies.

5. A member of DSI is registered under the lobbying act and presents the industry viewpoint on pending legislation to Senators and Representatives. At hearings on proposed bills, industry members present the industry viewpoint to Congressional committees; on bills agreed upon after consultation with the Internal Revenue Service, the DSI representative attempts to facilitate consideration and passage through discussion with Congressmen.

6. The DSI press relations department serves press associa-

tions, press and radio commentators, magazine writers and other newsmen and news organizations. The press relations department also prepares speeches and trade paper articles.

7. DSI field representatives are assigned to various sections of the country and keep abreast of local matters which affect the industry. Each DSI man enjoys wide personal contacts among the trade, liquor officials, the press, local associations and other groups. One of his aims is to cement good relationships with liquor administrators, and to cooperate with them in fulfilling their duties. Another important function of the DSI representative is to assist at local option elections. He is an expert in organizing campaigns and planning strategy.

b. The Puerto Rican Rum Institute is also a producers' trade association. Organized in San Juan, Puerto Rico in 1943, the Institute has a membership consisting of Puerto Rican rum distillers and rectifiers. Its purpose is to "regulate, promote, protect, and encourage the development of the rum industry in Puerto Rico, and to function as liaison between the industry and the insular and federal governments and agencies." One of the important accomplishments of the Institute has been sponsorship of a substantial advertising and promotion campaign for Puerto Rican rums marketed in the United States.

IMPORTERS. The National Association of Alcoholic Beverage Importers, Inc. was organized in New York City in 1934. Its members handle approximately 85% of all imported alcoholic beverages. Among the activities of NAABI is presentation of the importers' viewpoint to governmental and other authorities, and the circulation regularly of import information to members and trade papers. Among other efforts, NAABI has helped achieve the elimination of individual import quotas, adoption of standardized import bottle sizes, reduction of tariffs, and the establishment of lower freight rates on shipments from the United Kingdom.

WHOLESALERS. The Wine and Spirits Wholesalers of America has a membership of hundreds of wholesale distributors of wines and spirits. The broad purpose of WSWA is to represent the interests of wholesalers within the industry and, in a larger sense, to promote increased recognition of the economic importance of wholesalers in general. Among the activities of WSWA are the following: WSWA brings wholesaler views before federal authorities; keeps its membership informed of federal legislative trends; serves as a clearing house for the exchange of information among members; provides a meeting-place for the formulation of national wholesaler policies; gathers and disseminates statistics and other information on alcoholic beverage wholesaling; publishes annually a list of members and their respective beverage lines.

BROKERS. The Whiskey Brokers of America, Inc. was organized in 1938 at White Sulphur Springs, West Virginia. The purpose of this association is to stimulate business in bulk whiskey, in accordance with rules which it has drawn up for ethical trade practices to be observed by its members.

RETAILERS

a. *Off-premise retailers.* The National Retail Liquor Package Stores Association, Inc. was founded in 1934, and has a membership consisting of more than fifty state and local retail package store associations. Its purpose is to operate in the interests of package stores in particular and of the industry in general. Among its functions are the promotion of retailer services to the public, establishment of uniform trade practices, reform of abuses, and furtherance of good relations among its members. In addition, NRLPSA fights legislation which it considers detrimental.

b. *On-premise retailers.* The National Licensed Beverage Association has a membership consisting of approximately thirty-five tavern associations which represent 40,000 on-premise retailers. Its purpose and functions for on-premise retailers generally correspond with those of NRLPSA for off-premise retailers. By means of a monthly bulletin, NLBA keeps its members posted on matters concerning on-premise retailing.

PUBLIC RELATIONS. Reference has already been made to the industry's two national public relations associations:

a. Licensed Beverage Industries, Inc. was organized in 1946 and has several hundred members representing every branch of the industry. The purpose of LBI is "to merit, assure and safeguard favorable public opinion for the industry." To accomplish this is, of course, to gain support for the industry in eliminating its difficulties. As already noted, LBI conducts a broad and intensive campaign with respect to taxation, alcoholism, bootlegging and other public relations problems. In the conduct of its operations, LBI maintains among other organizational units a research and statistical division, a media relations division, a division of field activities and a women's division. It also enlists the services of a publicity counsel and an advertising agency.

LBI gathers and analyzes pertinent material, translates it into news articles and other informational matter, then transmits this to national publications, news services, newspapers, trade papers, and to radio and television networks and local stations. Clippings of news stories and editorial opinion are later collected, digested and circulated throughout the industry. Supplementing its publicity effort, LBI utilizes advertising campaigns and point-of-sale material as a means of reaching both the consumer and the trade.

Through its division of field activities, LBI places regional representatives throughout the country. These men carry out LBI policies and goals in their areas, maintaining a close watch on public opinion. In addition to steady local contact with all levels of the industry and with liquor authorities, LBI men keep in constant touch with chambers of commerce, civic leaders, military authorities and other groups and persons. Moreover, LBI men maintain active memberships in local press associations, and see to it that local news outlets are supplied. When local option elections are in the offing, or when there is a movement to curtail private enterprise in favor of a monopoly system, LBI men go into immediate action.

The women's division of LBI is particularly active with clubwomen, business women and professional women outside the industry, and acts as liaison with the Women's Association of Allied Beverage Industries.

b. The Women's Association of Allied Beverage Industries is the only women's organization in the industry. Through its headquarters and through chapters from coast to coast, WAABI contributes importantly to industry public relations. WAABI conducts an educational campaign to the public, particularly to women, on alcoholic beverages; acts as social ambassadors for the industry through participation in national and local civic and philanthropic campaigns; maintains personal contact with other types of women's groups and organizations.

5. Industry By-Products

Of the nation's total grain crop, 75% or more is used on the farm. The remainder goes to market. Less than 1% of the total crop is used by beverage distillers, who return approximately one-third (by weight) of their grain to the farm in the form of concentrated food for poultry and livestock. This food is known as "distillers feeds." Hundreds of thousands of tons of distillers feeds are produced annually. Additional by-products, including fusel oil and corn oil, are manufactured as well. Distillers feeds, however, constitute the bulk of the by-product operation.

After alcohol is distilled from grain, a wet mash containing grain particles remains. This mash, which is unusable for alcoholic beverages, is called stillage. From this are manufactured three types of distillers feeds: distillers dried grains, distillers dried solubles and distillers dried grains with solubles.

Distillers dried grains consist of grain particles which have been filtered out of the stillage and then dried.

The remaining liquid portion of the stillage is run through vacuum evaporators and reduced to a syrupy substance. This syrup, which also contains food matter, is processed in two ways. Most of it is used to produce distillers dried solubles, which consist of the solid matter remaining after the syrup has been subjected to intense heat and drying. Syrup which is not used in this way is added to undried grain particles which have been filtered out of the stillage. The finished product in this instance is known as distillers dried grains with solubles.

About 85% of total stillage is used in producing distillers dried feeds. An additional 14%, which remains in liquid form, is also used for animal and poultry feeding, usually at farms near distilleries. The remaining 1% is unrecovered.

Stillage differs in one important respect from the original grain mash used for distilling alcoholic beverages. When malt is added to the original grain, the starch content of the grain is converted into sugar which is then fermented. Thus the stillage, and hence distillers feeds, do not contain the starch of the original grain. However, distillers feeds are high in proteins, vitamins and minerals (higher in fact, as a result of yeast action, than the original grain). From this viewpoint, therefore, distillers feeds are enriched concentrated products which are valuable as supplements to original grain (corn, oats, etc.) in livestock and poultry feeding. Original grain is available in such quantity on the farm, of course, as to provide the starch necessary for such feeding.

The nation's major distillers have formed an association known as the Distillers Feed Research Council. Originally sponsored by the Distilled Spirits Institute, it operates today as an independent organization. Its function is to sponsor research projects concerning distillers feeds, and to disseminate information to farmers, feed manufacturers, universities and other individuals and organizations.

CHAPTER FOUR

Products, Production, Warehousing and Bottling

How are liquors produced? How are they aged? When are they bottled? What are they called? In what respects do they differ from each other? Which are commercially important?

We will concern ourselves in this chapter with answers to these and related questions.

1. Definitions

The following terms are among those most frequently used in connection with liquors, liquor production and warehousing and bottling.

DISTILLATION. The process by which alcohol is separated from a fermented substance.

STILL. The apparatus which is used in the distilling process. There are two types of stills:

a. *Pot still.* This is the original type of still. It consists of a pot-shaped vessel with a tapering neck which connects to a tube in which vaporized alcohol is collected. Two distillations are usually required when pot stills are used. The first distillation produces a liquid of low alcoholic strength called low wines. These low wines are placed in another, usually smaller, pot still. The second distillation produces the desired spirit at the required alcoholic strength. Pot stills are little used in this country. Their primary use is for the production of Scotch and Irish whiskies, cognac and other foreign brandies, and Jamaica rum.

b. *Continuous still.* Also called the column still and the patent or Coffey still, after Aeneas Coffey, who patented it in 1832. The continuous still is cylindrical in shape and often rises several stories in height. The complete distilling operation is conducted in this still, from the mash to the finished liquor, which is obtainable at any desired alcoholic strength. Distillation is accomplished by bringing steam into contact with the fermented mash. In the United States, continuous stills are used almost exclusively.

CISTERN. A tank.

PROOF. The alcoholic content by volume of distilled spirits is usually stated in terms of "proof." To arrive at the percent of alcoholic content, the proof is divided by two. Thus, the alcoholic content by volume of a 100 proof whiskey is 50%. Most distilled spirits are bottled at 86 proof. Other popular bottlings are at 86.8 proof, 90 proof, 93 proof and 100 proof. The law defines proof as "the ethyl alcohol content of a liquid at 60° Fahrenheit, stated as twice the percent of ethyl alcohol by volume." The symbol ° is sometimes used when indicating proof, e.g., 86° proof.

Spirits may be distilled at different proofs, usually in excess of 100 proof, and are reduced in proof by the addition of distilled water.

DISTILLED SPIRITS. Sometimes referred to simply as spirits. Federal law defines distilled spirits as "ethyl alcohol, hydrated oxide of ethyl, spirits of wine, whiskey, rum, brandy, gin, and other distilled spirits, including all dilutions and mixtures thereof, for non-industrial use." Among non-industrial uses, in addition to beverage use, are the following: "Uses . . . in the manufacture, rectifying or blending of alcoholic beverages; or in the preparation of food or drink by hotel, restaurant, tavern, or similar establishment; or for sacramental purposes; or as a medicine." The law cites the following as for industrial use: tax-free alcohol used by governmental agencies, colleges and universities, research laboratories, hospitals and sanatoria; denatured alcohol or denatured distilled spirits; distilled spirits used for experimental purposes and in the manufacture of flavoring extracts, syrups and food products; scientific, chemical, mechanical and industrial products; toilet products; medicinal, pharmaceutical or antiseptic products, including druggists' prescriptions.

The law further states that distilled spirits in containers of one wine gallon or less are considered to be for non-industrial use.

a. *Rectified spirits.* Distilled spirits whose natural composition has been altered by processing which follows original and continuous distillation through closed pipes and vessels.

b. *Neutral spirits.* Spirits which have been distilled at or above 190 proof. This proof may subsequently be reduced, but according to legal definition, the product continues to be designated as neutral spirits. Neutral spirits are usually named for the commodity from which they are distilled, e.g., "grain neutral spirits."

c. *Proof spirits.* 100 proof distilled spirits.

d. *Bulk spirits.* Distilled spirits in containers which have a capacity exceeding one wine gallon.

AGE. The period between distillation and bottling when spirits are stored in wood containers.

STANDARDS OF IDENTITY

a. *Class.* The general classification to which any liquor belongs. The following are the main classes of distilled spirits: whiskey, gin, cordials (liqueurs), brandy, rum, vodka.

b. *Type.* One of the varieties of distilled spirits belonging to a specific class. For example, straight bourbon whiskey is a type of whiskey; London dry gin is a type of gin; New England rum is a type of rum.

GALLON

a. *Wine gallon.* The standard United States gallon of 231 cubic inches (128 fluid ounces). Quarts, fifths, pints and half-pints are the important subdivisions of the gallon with respect to distilled spirits.

b. *Proof gallon.* A wine gallon of 100 proof distilled spirits.

c. *Original proof (entry) gallon.* A proof gallon of whiskey or other spirits at the time it is placed into a wood container for aging.

d. *Tax gallon.* Defined by federal law as "the unit of distilled spirits upon which the rate of tax prescribed by law is imposed." Domestic spirits are taxed on the basis of the proof gallon. Assuming a federal excise tax of $10.50 per proof gallon, the excise tax, and the number of proof and tax gallons for each wine gallon of spirits at 100 proof, below 100 proof, and above 100 proof are illustrated by the following examples:

	Wine Gallons	Proof Gallons	Tax Gallons	Excise Tax
86 proof	1	.86	.86	$ 9.03
100 "	1	1.00	1.00	10.50
120 "	1	1.20	1.20	12.60

Bottled imported spirits pay federal excise taxes and customs duties based on the proof gallon if 100 proof or higher. If under 100 proof, regardless of what the proof may be, the federal excise tax is equivalent to the number of wine gallons multiplied by the excise tax per proof gallon; the duty is equivalent to the number of wine gallons multiplied by the duty per proof gallon. Assuming a federal excise tax of $10.50 per proof gallon and an import duty of $1.50 per proof gallon:

	Wine Gallons	Proof Gallons	Tax Gallons	Excise Tax	Customs Duty	Total Tax and Duty
86 proof	1	.86	1.00	$10.50	$1.50	$12.00
100 "	1	1.00	1.00	10.50	1.50	12.00
120 "	1	1.20	1.20	12.60	1.80	14.40

e. *Imperial gallon.* 1.2 wine gallons.

INTERNAL REVENUE BONDED WAREHOUSE. A warehouse, under federal government supervision, for storing and aging distilled spirits.

CUSTOMS BONDED WAREHOUSE. A warehouse, under federal government supervision, for storing imported spirits, or for storing domestic spirits earmarked for export.

BOTTLING HOUSE. A place in which spirits are bottled.

BOTTLING IN BOND DEPARTMENT. That part of an internal revenue bonded warehouse which is maintained for the bottling of spirits which are designated as "bottled in bond."

2. Production, Warehousing and Bottling

All spirits are distilled; some are aged; some are rectified. Some go through all three processes. We will examine now each of these processes, along with the warehousing and bottling of spirits.

THE DISTILLING PROCESS. Essentially, the process of distilling spirits is as follows: a fermented liquid, mash or other substance is heated in a still until the alcohol vaporizes. The alcohol, having thus been separated from the mash, is cooled and condensed into liquid form. Great advances have been made over the years in the science of distillation, and today huge plants utilize complex apparatus. Fundamentally, however, the distilling principle as just outlined underlies all operations.

Different types of raw materials are used in manufacturing distilled spirits. Broadly speaking, spirits are produced from raw materials containing either sugar or starch.

Grapes and sugar cane are examples of raw materials containing sugar.

Examples of raw materials containing starch are cereal grains, e.g., corn, rye, barley and wheat. In the manufacturing process, the starch content is converted by malt into sugar.

Thus, in the case of all distilled spirits, either raw or processed materials must contain sugar as a basic substance. This sugar is fermented through the action of yeast. The alcohol which is thus produced is then distilled, and carries with it distinctive properties of the substance.

Examples of distilled spirits made from raw materials containing sugar are rum, which is made from sugar cane, and brandy, which is made from fruit.

Examples of distilled spirits made from raw materials containing starch are whiskey, gin and vodka, all of which are customarily produced from cereal grains.

When spirits are distilled, the distillate (which is always colorless) contains not only alcohol but matter called "congeners." These congeners, which consist of fusel oil, acids, esters, aldehydes and other substances, give to each liquor, depending upon the raw material from which it is produced, its distinctive taste, aroma and other characteristics.

The higher the proof at distillation, the lower the congeneric content, the less distinctive the taste and aroma, and the lighter the body of the distillate. For example, neutral spirits, which must be distilled at 190 proof (95% alcohol) or higher, are light in body, and devoid of flavor and aroma to the point of being indeed "neutral."

The lower the proof at distillation, the higher the congeneric content, the more distinctive the taste and aroma, and the heavier the body of the distillate. For example, whiskies, which are ordinarily distilled at less than 160 proof (80% alcohol), retain sufficient congeners to possess the distinctive qualities which are characteristic of whiskey.

Although congeners create the specific character of different kinds of spirits, not all are desirable. Some are responsible for the rawness and other unpleasant qualities of newly distilled spirits. These undesirable qualities can be removed, up to a point, by processing other than aging. Leaching is an example of such processing. In leaching, undesirable substances are removed by passing spirits through charcoal. The aging process, however, which is utilized in producing most whiskies, brandies, and rums, is all-important as a method for smoothing out rough edges.

AGING. Following distillation, spirits are usually reduced in proof by the addition of water. If they are to be aged, they are placed in wood containers, usually barrels. Domestic whiskey affords a good example of the aging process. According to law, most domestic whiskies must be placed in new oak barrels which are charred on the inside. As the whiskey remains in the barrels, chemical action takes place with the charred wood. This action mellows the whiskey (during the process, incidentally, whiskey acquires its distinctive amber color from the charred wood). The aging process is usually continued for many years. As might be expected, it takes less time to age a whiskey which was distilled at a high proof, and which therefore contains a smaller quantity of "raw" congeners, than it does to age a whiskey distilled at a lower proof, and which therefore contains a larger quantity of "raw" congeners. From this it may be deduced that different whiskies will properly mature over varying periods of time. It may further be deduced that indefinite aging does not necessarily keep improving a whiskey. In fact, beyond a certain age, whiskey may deteriorate in the barrel. Generally speaking, most whiskies reach their peak of maturity between four and eight years.

It should also be noted that age is not synonymous with quality. Although age improves spirits, it cannot change inferior spirits into good spirits.

The aging process ceases when spirits are removed from wood containers. Spirits do not age in bottles.

RECTIFICATION. Let us refer to our definition of rectified spirits: "Spirits whose natural composition has been altered by processing which follows original and continuous distillation through closed vessels and pipes." Now, let us round out our concept of rectification by quoting from the definition of a rectifier as given by federal law. A rectifier is anyone who "rectifies, purifies or refines distilled spirits or wines by any process other than by original and continuous distillation from mash, wort or wash, through continuous closed vessels and pipes, until the manufacture thereof is complete... Provided ... that nothing... shall be held to prohibit the purifying or refining of spirits in the course of original and continuous distillation through any material which will not remain incorporated with such spirits when the manufacture thereof is complete."

The following are examples of rectification and rectified spirits:

a. *Spirit blends* (whiskies consisting of a blend of straight whiskey and neutral spirits). The whiskey in this product is distilled and aged. Blending with neutral spirits constitutes rectification.

b. *Re-distilled spirits.* Many gins are examples of spirits which have been re-distilled.

c. *Compounding* (mixing) neutral spirits with flavoring materials.

Straight whiskies, bottled in bond whiskies and continuously distilled gin are examples of spirits which are not rectified.

Filtration of extraneous material during distillation, or the addition of water to reduce proof, do not in themselves constitute rectification.

Whether or not a liquor is classified as rectified spirits is important to its producer, inasmuch as such spirits pay a rectification tax in addition to other taxes.

WAREHOUSING AND BOTTLING. For purposes of storage and aging, domestic spirits are transferred from distilleries or rectifying plants to internal revenue bonded warehouses, which are under the joint custody of the federal government and the proprietor. Imported spirits, most of which are bottled before shipment, are placed in customs bonded warehouses upon arrival in this country.

Spirits which are ready for consumption are transferred to bottling houses for bottling, labeling and the affixing of red strip stamps. The latter indicates that federal excise tax has been paid. Red strip stamps are also affixed to bottles of imported distilled spirits, either in a foreign country or in a customs bonded warehouse.

Bottling procedure differs for bottled in bond spirits. Bottled in bond whiskies and brandies are required by law to be bottled under federal government supervision at an internal revenue bonded warehouse. Hence the phrase, "bottled in bond." Strip stamps must also be affixed to bottles of bonded liquors. These stamps are green in color, and thus distinguish bonds from other spirits.

3. Whiskey

More whiskey is produced in the United States than all other classes of beverage spirits combined. More than 90% of domestic whiskey is produced in four states—Kentucky, Illinois, Maryland and Indiana, with well over half the production coming from Kentucky alone. Other whiskey-producing states are California, Massachusetts, Missouri, Ohio, Pennsylvania, Tennessee and Virginia. Scotland, Ireland and Canada constitute the main sources of supply of imported whiskies.

Corn, rye, wheat, barley, malt and rye malt are the grains used in making whiskey in this country. Of these, corn is used in greatest volume, with rye next. At the distillery, grain is ground into a meal. To this meal is added a small amount of malt, which is itself a grain, usually barley, which has been moistened in order to make it sprout. Along with malt, water is added to the meal. The resulting mixture is cooked. During the cooking, the starch content of the mixture is converted into sugar by the malt. The mixture (mash) is now cooled and removed to fermenting vats. Here yeast is added, and serves to ferment the sugar, producing an alcoholic liquid which is called "distiller's beer." This is not the beer we know as a beverage, of course, but does bear some resemblance to it.

We now have a fermented grain mash. This is pumped into the still. Here the alcohol is distilled into whiskey, i.e., separated from the mash by vaporization and condensation (according to law, whiskey must be distilled at less than 190 proof). Next, the newly distilled whiskey is transferred to tanks in the cistern room of the distillery. Here water is added to reduce the proof to anywhere from 80° to 110°. Before the whiskey leaves the distillery it is put into barrels. These barrels, which are usually made of new white oak, and usually charred on the inside, are delivered to an internal revenue bonded warehouse. After storage and aging in bonded warehouses, whiskey is ready either for bottling or for further processing, e.g., blending. When bottled, whiskey must be at least 80 proof.

A variation in the method of production yields sour-mash whiskey. In the sour-mash method, the mash is cooked for a longer period. In the process of fermentation, which is also continued for a longer

PRODUCTION SPECIFICATIONS–

Product	Grain	Minimum % Specific Grain in Fermented Mash	Distilling Proof	Proof on Leaving Cistern Room
Grain Neutral Spirits	no particular	---	190° or higher	---
Whiskey	" "	---	under 190°	80°-110°
Rye	rye and other	51% rye	160° or lower	"
Bourbon	corn and other	51% corn	" " "	"
Corn	" " "	80% corn	" " "	"
Straight	no particular	---	" " "	"
Straight Rye	rye and other	51% rye	" " "	"
Straight Bourbon	corn and other	51% corn	" " "	"
Straight Corn	" " "	80% corn	" " "	"
Bonded Rye	rye and other	51% rye	" " "	"
Bonded Bourbon	corn and other	51% corn	" " "	"
Bonded Corn	" " "	80% corn	" " "	"
Blend of Straights	no particular	---	" " "	"
Blend of Straight Ryes	rye and other	51% rye	" " "	"
Blend of Straight Bourbons	corn and other	51% corn	" " "	"
Blend of Straight Corn	" " "	80% corn	" " "	"
Blend (spirit)	no particular	---	---	---
Blended Rye	rye and other	---	---	---
Blended Bourbon	corn and other	---	---	---
Blended Corn	" " "	---	---	---
Blended Scotch Type	a. malt b. no particular	a. 100% malt b. 100% any	a. 160° or less b. over 180°	---

(1) Must be product of one distillery and one season; must be bottled in internal revenue bonded warehouse under federal government supervision.
(2) Specifications are for each straight whiskey in the blend.
(3) Specifications are for each straight rye (or bourbon or corn) whiskey in the blend.
(4) The designation 'a' refers to one component of the blend, and 'b' to the other.
*Not required to be straight whiskey.

PRINCIPAL DOMESTIC WHISKIES

Minimum % Straight Whiskey by Volume	Maximum % Grain Neutral Spirits	Wood Container	Minimum Age (years)	Minimum Bottling Proof	Remarks
---	100%	---	---	---	---
---	---	---	---	80°	---
---	---	charred new oak	---	"	---
---	---	" " "	---	"	---
---	---	uncharred or re-used charred oak	---	"	---
100%	---	charred new oak	2	"	---
"	---	" " "	"	"	---
"	---	" " "	"	"	---
"	---	uncharred or re-used charred oak	"	"	---
"	---	charred new oak	4	100°	(1)
"	---	" " "	"	"	(1)
"	---	uncharred or re-used charred oak	"	"	(1)
"	---	charred new oak	2	80°	(2)
"	---	" " "	"	"	(3)
"	---	" " "	"	"	(3)
"	---	uncharred or re-used charred oak	"	"	(3)
20% at 100°	80%	---	---	"	---
51% rye	49%	---	---	"	---
51% bourbon	"	---	---	"	---
51% corn	"	---	---	"	---
a. 20% malt* b. 80% whiskey*	---	a. new plain or re-used oak b. " " " " "	a. 3 b. 3	"	(4)

period, material from a previous run is used in the mash along with fresh yeast. Many famous brands of bourbon are sour-mash whiskies.

Thus far we have noted the basic processes which are involved in the production of all types of domestic whiskies. Legally, whiskey which is reduced to no less than 80 proof in the cistern room after distillation may be immediately bottled. However, very little whiskey of this kind is marketed. Such whiskey is colorless, raw and unpalatable. Moreover, its identification as a product is confined to the one word "whiskey." No reference to bourbon, rye, or to any other grain is permitted; nor may the terms "straight" or "blend" be used.

In order to be designated by the name of a grain, and in order to be designated as a straight or blend, the first requirement which whiskey must meet is distillation at 160 proof or less (compare this with the requirement of less than 190 proof for just "whiskey"). As in the case of "whiskey," proof after distillation must be reduced to between 80° and 110°, and bottling must be at 80° or higher. Most whiskies are distilled at anywhere from 115° to 140°, and are bottled at anywhere from 86° to 100°.

What additional requirements must be met in order for whiskey to be entitled to a grain designation and/or the designation "straight" or "blend"?

To merit a grain designation such as "rye whiskey," "bourbon whiskey" (made from corn), "wheat whiskey," "malt whiskey" (made from malted barley) or "rye malt whiskey," at least 51% of the fermented mash must consist of the specified grain. Moreover, the product must be stored in charred new oak containers. In the case of "corn whiskey" (not the same product as "bourbon whiskey," although both are made from corn), requirements differ. For this, at least 80% of the fermented mash must be corn, and storage must be in uncharred oak containers or in re-used charred oak containers (corn whiskey is "white whiskey").

Whiskies of these types, although entitled to carry the name of the grain, still have not met the requirements which permit them to be called "straight" or "blended." As factors on the market, these non-straight and non-blended whiskies are unimportant.

We come now to the types of domestic whiskey which are the popular favorites in this country. These may be classified as straight whiskies, bottled in bond whiskies, blends of straight whiskies and spirit blends.

STRAIGHT WHISKEY. In addition to distillation at 160 proof or less, reduction to 80 to 110 proof in the cistern room, and bottling at 80 proof or higher, further requirements must be met in order for a whiskey to be called "straight." The all-important additional requirements concern age. Straight whiskey must be aged at least two years and, except for corn whiskey, must be aged in new charred oak containers. To be called "straight," a whiskey need not have any specific percentage of any one grain in the fermented mash. However, if a whiskey is to be called "straight" and is also to carry the name of a grain, it must meet all specifications for straight whiskey plus the added specification that the fermentated mash contain at least 51% of the grain in question. Whiskies of this type are designated as "straight bourbon whiskey," "straight rye whiskey," "straight wheat whiskey," etc.

Although the aging requirement for straight whiskey is two years, in actual practice today most straights are aged a minimum of four years.

The requirements for "straight corn whiskey" differ from those for other grain-designated straights. At least 80% of the fermented mash must be corn. In addition, the product must be aged for at least two years in uncharred or in re-used charred oak barrels. Neither "corn whiskey" nor "straight corn whiskey" may be subjected to treatment with charred wood at any time.

We have mentioned "straight whiskey" and several types of grain-designated straights. Of all of these, only two are commercially important: straight bourbon whiskey and straight rye whiskey. Straight bourbon is by all odds the nation's overwhelming straight whiskey favorite. Although a fair quantity of straight rye is sold, it does not begin to compare in sales volume with straight bourbon.

Straight bourbons and straight ryes are often identified by the states in which they are distilled, e.g., Kentucky straight bourbon, Pennsylvania straight rye, Maryland straight rye. Among straight bourbons, Kentucky whiskey is by far the most popular. Fine straight bourbon is also produced in other states, e.g., in Illinois and Indiana. These "northern straights," so-called, are usually light in body and light in color as compared to Kentucky bourbons.

BOTTLED IN BOND WHISKEY. Strictly speaking, bottled in bond whiskies (also popularly called "bonded whiskies" and "bonds") belong under the classification of straight whiskies which may be designated by the name of the grain. Bottled in bond whiskies must not only meet all the requirements of such whiskies, but must meet other requirements as well. A bottled in bond whiskey must be:

a. the product of one distillery and one distilling season.

b. aged a minimum of four years.

c. bottled at 100 proof.

d. bottled at an internal revenue bonded warehouse under federal government supervision.

Only two types of bonded whiskey are commercially important: bottled in bond straight bourbon whiskey and bottled in bond straight rye whiskey. Popularity follows the same pattern as that of straight whiskies which are not bottled in bond. In other words, bonded bourbon sells much more heavily than bonded rye, and Kentucky bonded bourbon sells more heavily than bonded bourbons produced in other states.

The designation "bottled in bond" cannot be considered a symbol of quality in itself. Federal law does not require that special grains be used, or that a special method of distilling be followed. A fine four-year-old straight which is "free bottled" or "bottled out of bond" (not bottled under government supervision at a bonded warehouse) may very well be superior to an average bonded whiskey. The idea of quality became associated with bonded whiskey, of course, because some of the finest and oldest brands on the market today, e.g., Old Grand-Dad, are bonds.

Blends of straight whiskies. When two or more straight whiskies are blended, they are designated as "blended straight whiskies" or "a blend of straight whiskies." The straight whiskies which go into this product may vary considerably from each other. For example, they may have been distilled at different proofs, from different grains, and may have been aged for different periods of time. If a blend of straights is to be designated by the name of a grain, each of the straight whiskies which are blended together must be entitled to the designation of the specific grain. For instance, "blended straight rye whiskies" must consist of a blend of straight rye whiskies only. Similarly, "blended straight bourbon whiskies" must consist of a blend of straight bourbon whiskies only.

Blends of straight whiskies enjoy a limited popularity today. Compared to non-blended straights, they hold a small segment of the market.

SPIRIT BLENDS. Most blended whiskies are produced from straight whiskey and grain neutral spirits. In order to be designated as "blended whiskey" ("whiskey—a blend"), a product must contain at least 20% by volume of 100 proof straight whiskey, and must be bottled at not less than 80 proof. Most spirit blends are bottled at or near 86 proof and contain 35% straight whiskey and 65% grain neutral spirits.

If a spirit blend is to carry the name of a particular grain, at least 51% by volume must be straight whiskey which is itself entitled to the grain designation. Thus, "blended rye whiskey" (also called "rye whiskey—a blend") must contain 51% by volume of straight rye whiskey; "blended bourbon whiskey" must contain at least 51% by volume of straight bourbon whiskey.

This figure of 51% was mentioned earlier in our discussion of straight whiskies which are permitted to bear the name of a grain. These references to 51% should not be confused. In the case of grain-designated straight whiskies, 51% refers to the amount of the specific grain in the fermented mash. In the case of grain-designated spirit blends, 51% refers, as just stated, to the percentage by volume of grain-designated straight whiskey in the blend; the remaining percentage is accounted for, of course, by grain neutral spirits.

In most spirit blends, the straight whiskey content is comprised of two or more straight whiskies. These are selected by the blender for differences in body, flavor and other characteristics.

Grain neutral spirits serve a particular purpose in producing blended whiskey. Inasmuch as they are distilled at 190 proof or higher, they are extremely light-bodied. As a result, they contribute to the lightness which is a particular characteristic of spirit blends.

When grain neutral spirits are mixed with straight whiskey (whiskies), a blending agent such as sherry is usually added (blending agents may not exceed 2½% of total volume).

Prior to bottling, the components of a blend are often permitted to "marry" for an indefinite time.

Spirits blends, e.g., Seagram's 7 Crown, Calvert Reserve and Schenley Reserve, outsell all other types of whiskey. Unlike straight whiskies, which are most popular in the grain-designated category, e.g., straight bourbon, spirit blends sell most heavily in the blend category which is not entitled to the grain designation ("whiskey—a blend" or "blended whiskey"). However, some individual grain-designated brands account for volume sales, e.g., Bourbon de Luxe, a blended bourbon whiskey (also bottled as a straight). Reference to the state of distillation is not featured by most volume spirit blends. Notable examples of blend volume brands which feature their state are Old Sunny Brook and Hill & Hill, both of which are Kentucky spirit blends (also bottled as straights). Bourbon de Luxe, mentioned a moment ago, is also a Kentucky whiskey.

Before concluding our discussion of domestic blended whiskey, reference should be made to "blended Scotch type whiskey" ("Scotch type whiskey—a blend"). This product is neither a blend of straights nor a spirit blend.

As its name indicates, blended Scotch type is a whiskey which is like Scotch but which is not made in Scotland. Federal law makes certain that the product has the principal characteristics of Scotch by setting forth specific requirements which correspond to those observed by Scottish distillers. Blended Scotch type whiskey must consist of a blend of two kinds of whiskey. It is composed of "not less than 20% by volume of 100 proof malt whiskey or whiskies distilled in pot stills at not more than 160 proof... solely from a fermented mash of malted barley dried over peat fire and aged for not less than three years in new plain, or re-used oak containers; and not more than 80% by volume of whiskey distilled at more than 180 proof... aged for not less than three years in new plain, or re-used oak containers."

A close examination of this definition reveals similarities to the production process used for spirit blends. Note the reference to 20% by volume of 100 proof whiskey distilled at 160 proof or less, and the reference to 80% by volume of whiskey distilled at over 180 proof (the latter corresponds to grain neutral spirits, which are also distilled at a very high proof). Marked differences from the production process used for spirit blends are also readily apparent. Note the insistence on malt whiskey, pot stills, "malted barley dried over peat fire"; also note the minimum three-year aging requirement, the fact that both components of the blend must be aged, and the fact that "new plain, or re-used oak containers" must be used instead of charred new oak containers.

Blended Scotch type whiskey accounts for only a minute part of whiskey volume in this country.

The many types of whiskies which we have discussed thus far are domestic whiskies. We will proceed now to a discussion of imported whiskies.

There are three types of imported whiskies—Scotch, Irish and Canadian. Of these, Scotch is not only the largest seller, but accounts for more volume than any other imported liquor. In fact, Scotch sells more heavily than any category of distilled spirits with the exception of domestic whiskey and gin.

Of the other types of imported whiskey, Canadian accounts for substantial volume; Irish whiskey, on the other hand, accounts for very little volume.

SCOTCH WHISKY. Only whisky produced in Scotland in accordance with British law may be called Scotch whisky. According to our own law, no Scotch may be labeled as "straight." If it contains a blend of whiskies, it is labeled "blended Scotch whisky" or "Scotch whisky—a blend." The fact is that the overwhelming majority of Scotches sold in this country are blends. There are two principal components: a blend of malt whiskies; and grain whisky. None of these whiskies may be less than three years of age, and if less than four years, the age must be stated on the label.

There are four areas in Scotland which produce malt whisky. Highland and Lowland malt whiskies are produced in northern and southern Scotland, respectively. Islay malt whiskies are produced on the island of Islay, which lies off the southwest coast. Campbeltown malt whiskies are distilled on the peninsula which lies to the east of Islay. Each of these whiskies has its own distinctive characteristics. Two or more of these types are usually combined when producing the blended malt whisky component of Scotch.

Although producers of famous brands have their own distilleries in Scotland, most of the malt whiskies which go into the average Scotch (and some Scotches contain up to thirty varieties) are made in small independent distilleries, of which there are approximately one hundred. Generally speaking, these independents do no bottling or brand marketing, but simply supply their product in bulk to owners of specific labels.

How is malt whisky produced?

Every Scotch malt whisky is made exclusively from Scottish barley. This barley is soaked in warm water for two or three days. Next it is placed on stone floors. Here it is turned over continuously until it germinates. The malted barley is then spread out over large screens. Beneath these screens, peat (partially decayed plant matter from Scottish moors) is burned. While heat from the peat fires dries out the malt, smoke passes up through the screens and permeates it. It is this action of peat smoke on malt which gives Scotch its characteristic smoky taste.

After drying and storage, the malt is ground into a meal and thoroughly mixed with warm water. The liquid portion (wort) is drawn off and cooled. Yeast is added to it and, following fermentation, the liquid (now called wash) goes to a pot still. The distillate (low wines) is low in proof, and goes to another, smaller pot still, which produces the whisky at the desired higher proof. Next, the whisky is reduced to approximately 120 proof, and is transferred to used sherry casks or to uncharred oak casks for aging.

We have discussed the production of Scotch malt whisky. Although some Scotch malt whisky is marketed, it is too heavy to suit popular taste.

As we have noted, up to thirty malt whiskies may be blended for a single brand. Each blender has his own particular combination of malt whiskies, which he selects on the basis of their individual characteristics. These blends are aged in casks, following which they are ready to be combined with the grain whisky component of the finished blend.

Production of this grain whisky is similar to the production of grain neutral spirits in this country. Scottish distillers use corn and barley, the fermented mash of which is distilled in continuous stills instead of in pot stills. Distillation is at 180 proof or higher, thus yielding a very light-bodied spirit. This grain whisky is aged for at least three years.

At this point, the Scottish distiller has on hand a supply of aged and blended malt whiskies, and a supply of aged grain whisky. The malt and grain whiskies are now mixed, with malt whiskies comprising from 25% to 50% of the total blend. This new blend goes into casks for additional aging before bottling.

Most brands of Scotch are marketed in this country at 86 and 86.8 proof.

IRISH WHISKEY. Federal law has established a pattern of requirements for Irish whiskey which is similar to that for Scotch whisky. Thus, only whiskey made in Ireland, in accordance with Irish law, may be designated "Irish whiskey." Moreover, all spirits in Irish whiskey must be at least three years old, and if less than four years, the age must be stated on the label. In addition, Irish whiskey may not be called "straight." When a mixture of spirits, it is designated "blended Irish whiskey" or "Irish whiskey—a blend."

There are two kinds of Irish whiskey. One is produced in northern Ireland, the other in the Irish Free State.

The whiskey of northern Ireland is made in accordance with a method similar to that used in producing Scotch. There are two components: a blend of malt whiskies; and grain whiskey. Each of the malt whiskies is distilled in pot stills at approximately 171 proof from a fermented mash of barley malt. The grain whiskey is distilled in continuous stills at over 180 proof. The blend of malt whiskies and the grain whiskey are combined.

The whiskey of the Irish Free State is a blend of whiskies, each of which is similarly produced. Distillation is in pot stills at not more than 171 proof from a fermented mash of small cereal grains. At least 50% of the mash is malted barley. The remainder of the mash consists of unmalted barley, wheat, oats or rye.

Unlike Scotch, Irish whiskies do not have a smoky flavor. When Irish malt is kilned, smoke is not permitted to reach it.

Most Irish whiskies are aged for seven years or longer, and are bottled at 86 proof.

CANADIAN WHISKEY. Canadian whiskey may be produced only in Canada in accordance with Canadian law. It may not be called "straight whiskey." When a mixture of spirits, it is designated "blended Canadian whiskey" or "Canadian whiskey—a blend."

All spirits in Canadian whiskey must be aged at least two years. It will be recalled that three years is the minimum for Scotch and Irish whiskies. However, as in the case of Scotch and Irish, the age, if less than four years, must be stated on the label.

Canadian whiskies which are marketed in this country are primarily blends, and are characterized by a flavor and lightness of body which give them a marked resemblance to American spirit blends. Wheat and rye are the principal grains used.

Most Canadian whiskies are bottled at 86, 86.8 and 90.4 proof.

4. Gin

America's most popular liquor next to whiskey, gin is a spirit which does not require aging, is generally colorless, and has as its distinguishing characteristic the flavor of the juniper berry (juniper is an evergreen of the pine family.) Sloe gins, fruit-flavored gins and mint-flavored gins are more logically classified as cordials than as gins, despite their designations, and will be discussed later.

Most Americans drink domestic gins. Chief imports are from Holland and England.

There are two types of gin: distilled gin and compound gin.

In the production of distilled gin, two methods are used—the method of original distillation and the method of re-distillation. In original distillation, a fermented mash (usually grain) is distilled. The distillate passes through a "gin head" which contains juniper berries and other aromatic botanicals, e.g., aniseed, coriander seed, cassia bark. The flavor of the botanicals is absorbed by the distillate which, upon condensation, becomes gin.

In the method of re-distillation, neutral spirits are produced from the fermented grain mash. These neutral spirits are placed into another still and re-distilled. At this point, the production process becomes identical with that in original distillation. The distillate passes through a gin head containing botanicals and emerges as the finished product.

In some instances, the gin head is not employed. Instead, the botanicals are placed in the still, and their flavor is in this way extracted during the distilling process.

Differences in flavor among gins are accounted for by differences in the quality and variety of the botanicals.

Gin which is made by either the process of distillation or re-distillation, which has the juniper berry flavor, and which is bottled at 80 proof or higher, is designated as "distilled gin." Most of the gins on the market are distilled gins.

Compound gin, as distinguished from distilled gin, is a product, according to federal law, "obtained by mixing neutral spirits with distilled gin or gin essence or other flavoring materials customarily used in the production of gin, and deriving its main characteristic flavor from juniper berries and reduced at time of bottling to not less than 80° proof; and includes mixtures of such products." Any gin produced by compounding must be designated "compound gin." Very little compound gin is produced commercially.

The most common type of domestic gin is "distilled dry gin" (the word "dry," as applied to gin or to other spirits, means "not sweet"). Distilled dry gin is also called "distilled London dry gin." This designation is permitted for American-made gins, because the name is considered to have become generic. Other gin names of foreign origin which are considered generic are Geneva, Hollands, Old Tom, Tom and buchu gin. Each of these gins must be designated as either distilled or compound.

Federal law prohibits any statement of age for gin. "Golden" gins are "aged," however, even though they may not claim age. Their color is derived from storage in charred barrels.

Domestic gins are usually bottled at 90 proof.

England and Holland supply us with most of our imported gins. However, the quantity sold in this country is almost negligible.

England's London dry gin is generally produced by the method of re-distillation and is somewhat heavier-bodied than American gins. Old Tom, another English gin, and almost unknown here, is distinguished by its sweet taste.

Dutch gins are distinctly different from American and English gins. They are usually distilled at a low proof from a fermented mash containing not only the grain (barley malt) but juniper berries and other botanicals as well. As a result, these gins are heavy-bodied and strongly flavored.

Dutch gins are best known under the names of Hollands, Geneva and Schiedam.

5. Cordials

The terms "cordials" and "liqueurs" are synonymous.

Most of the cordials consumed in the United States are domestically produced. A small quantity is imported from France, Denmark, Great Britain, Greece, Italy and other countries. In terms of sales volume, as a class of spirits, cordials rank directly after whiskey and gin.

Cordials are the candy product of the liquor industry. Every cordial has three components: a distilled spirits base, flavoring, and sweetening.

The distilled spirits base may be neutral spirits, brandy, gin, whiskey or other spirits. Of these, neutral spirits and brandy are used most frequently. If the proof of the finished product is 48° or less, the distilled spirits base must be at least 80 proof, and must account for more than 50% of the total volume.

The flavoring material may consist of one or more of the following: fruits, flowers or plants; the pure juices of fruits, flowers or plants; other flavoring material; extracts of the foregoing. Synthetic or imitation flavoring may not be used; every cordial must contain natural flavoring material only.

Sugar or dextrose or both must be added in an amount not less than 2½% by weight of the finished cordial.

Given the three components of every cordial—a spirits base, flavoring and sweetening—how are cordials produced? Two basic methods are in general use. In one method, finished cordials are produced from a distilled spirits base without utilizing the distilling process. In the second method, distillation is required.

Fruit cordials, e.g. blackberry, apricot, peach, afford a good example of the non-distillation method. In this method, the fruit is kept in direct contact with the spirits base until the latter absorbs flavor and color. Transference of flavor and color may be accomplished in several ways. One way is to repeatedly percolate the spirits base through the fruit. Another way is to steep the fruit in the spirits base until the process is completed; the liquid cordial is then drawn off.

Cordials which are made from plants, flowers, seeds, etc., are produced by the distillation method. Usually, the flavoring material is soaked (macerated) in the spirits base; thereupon the mixture is distilled. There are variations on this method. For example, the flavoring material may be removed following maceration; the liquid may then be vaporized and passed through the flavoring material prior to condensation.

Like any distillate, a distilled cordial is colorless. As a result it is sometimes necessary to add coloring matter. For example, of two varieties of crême de menthe, white and green, the former is colorless, the latter artificially colored. When artificially colored, a statement to this effect must appear on the label.

Following the processing of the spirits base and flavoring material, sweetening is added. In some instances, thereafter, cordials are set aside to "age" for several months (federal law, however, does not permit age statements for cordials).

Despite the production methods employed, cordials may not be legally designated as "distilled" or "compound." They may, however, be described as "dry" if the sugar or dextrose content is less than 10% by weight of the finished product.

Federal law makes a special point of setting forth provisions concerning the production of "rye liqueur," "bourbon liqueur," "rock and rye," "rock and bourbon," "rock and rum" and "rock and brandy."

Rye liqueur—at least 51% of the spirits content must be rye whiskey (or straight rye, or whiskey distilled from a rye mash). Rye liqueur must possess a rye flavor and must be bottled at 60 proof or higher.

The specifications for bourbon liqueur are the same as those for rye liqueur except, of course, that bourbon whiskey is used instead of rye whiskey.

Rock and rye and other "rock and" spirits must contain rock candy (or sugar syrup) and may (but need not) contain fruit, fruit juices or other flavoring materials. Proof must be 48° or higher. In addition, the following requirements must be met:

Rock and rye—at least 51% of the spirits content must be rye whiskey (or straight rye whiskey, or whiskey distilled from a rye mash).

Rock and bourbon—same specifications as for rock and rye, except that bourbon whiskey is used instead of rye whiskey.

Rock and rum—100% of the spirits content must be rum.

Rock and brandy—100% of the spirits content must be grape brandy which has been distilled at 170 proof or less.

There are a great many varieties of cordials. Among them are the following (the primary flavoring material is given in each case when not identical with the name):

Anisette—aniseed
Apricot
Blackberry
Bourbon
Cherry
Crême d'ananas—pineapples
Crême de bananes—bananas
Crême de cacao—cocoa beans (2 varieties: brown and white)
Crême de cassis—black currants
Crême de fraises—strawberries
Crême de framboises—raspberries
Crême de menthe—mint (2 varieties: green and white)
Crême de noyaux—fruit stones
Crême de vanille—vanilla beans
Crême de violette—violets
Curacao—orange peel
Kummel—caraway seed
Maraschino—cherries
Parfait amour—violets
Peach
Peppermint schnapps—mint
Rock and rye—rye whiskey, rock candy, fruit
Rye—rye whiskey
Sloe gin—sloe berries
Triple sec—orange peel

These cordials, together with other varieties, are produced both in this country and abroad. Some spirits of the cordial type are not readily classified among the best known standard varieties. Such products are more easily recognized by brand name or by other names. Among them, together with country of origin, are the following:

Amer Picon—an aperitif cordial (France)
B & B—Benedictine and brandy (France)
Benedictine D. O. M.—made from herbs and other ingredients in accordance with a secret formula; cognac base (France)
Chartreuse—made from plants and other ingredients in accordance with a secret formula. Two varieties, green and yellow (France)
Cointreau—a type of triple sec (France)
Cherry Heering—cherry liqueur (Denmark)
Danziger Goldwasser—orange peel, spices, herbs, plants; contains flecks of gold leaf (Germany)
Drambuie—honey, Scotch whisky base (Scotland)
Forbidden Fruit—grapefruit, brandy base (U.S.)
Grand Marnier—a type of curacao (France)
Irish Mist—honey, Irish whiskey base (Ireland)
Ouzo—a type of anisette (Greece)
Pernod—a type of anisette (France)
Pimm's Cup No. 1—made from distilled dry gin, grain neutral spirits, fruit flavors, sugar, caramel; used in making gin slings (England)
Southern Comfort—peaches, peach liqueur, bourbon base; secret formula (U.S.)
Strega—plant liqueur (Italy)
Swedish Punch—sweetening and flavor added to a base of arrack (Dutch East Indies) rum (Sweden)
Van der Hum—tangerine flavor (South Africa)
Vielle Cure—plant liqueur (France)

Cordials, both domestic and imported, are marketed in a wide range of proofs, in a wide variety of bottle designs.

"Flavored brandies" and "flavored gins" are closer in character to cordials than to regular gins and brandies. Federal law requires that brandies and gins be bottled at no lower than 80 proof. Flavored brandies and flavored gins are bottled at 70 proof.

Apricot-flavored brandy, blackberry-flavored brandy, cherry-flavored brandy, ginger-flavored brandy and peach-flavored brandy are the popular varieties of flavored brandies.

Orange-flavored gin, lemon-flavored gin and mint-flavored gin are the popular varieties of flavored gins.

Inasmuch as the name of a particular fruit may be applied both to brandies and to flavored brandies, confusion sometimes arises. For example, peach brandy is sometimes confused with peach-flavored brandy. Peach brandy is distilled from peach juice, mash or wine, and is bottled at 80 proof or higher. In the finished product, peach flavor is not pronounced. Peach-flavored brandy, on the other hand, consists primarily of a brandy base to which peach flavoring is added, and is bottled at 70 proof. In the finished product there is a pronounced peach flavor.

6. Brandy

Approximately 90% of all brandy produced in the United States is made from grapes (including raisins), and approximately 95% of the entire production is accounted for by California alone. Other brandy states are Florida, which produces citrus-fruit brandies, and New York, New Jersey, Virginia, Oregon and Washington, all of which produce apple brandies. Other fruits commonly used for making brandy are peaches, prunes, dates, pears, plums, figs, cherries, apricots, blackberries and elderberries.

In addition to production for direct beverage purposes, brandy is manufactured for use in fortifying wines. As we have noted, brandy is also used as a base for cordials and fruit-flavored brandies.

Cognac comprises the great bulk of imported brandies, thus making France, which also ships to us Armagnac, Calvados and other brandies, the leading foreign source. Spain runs a poor second to France, with Italy, Hungary, West Germany, Greece, Yugoslavia and Portugal trailing in that approximate order. Some dozen or so additional countries ship their brandies to this country.

In order to earn the designation "brandy," spirits must be distilled solely from the fermented juice, mash or wine of fruit or its residue, and may consist of a single distillate or a blend of distillates. In addition, proof at distillation must be under 190°. However, if the product is not to be designated as "neutral brandy," the proof at distillation must be 170° or less. Following distillation (continuous stills are used almost exclusively in this country), brandies go through a period of aging. Some are then bottled; some are blended with other brandies. Such blends are often set aside to "marry" prior to bottling.

Age may be claimed for brandy, but age statements are not mandatory unless the product is less than two years old.

The minimum bottling proof for brandies is 80°. However, there is one exception to this general rule. A brandy may be bottled at a proof as low as 72° if it has been aged for at least 50 years, and if its low proof is the result only of evaporation during the aging process. The federal government had Cognac in mind when making this exception. Cognacs over 50 years of age may drop below 80 proof. Without a special ruling, they could not be marketed in this country as brandy.

If a liquor is to be designated as "fruit brandy," or if it is to be designated by the name of a specific fruit, it must meet requirements in addition to those stated above.

The government definition for fruit brandy is highly technical. Basically, however, fruit brandy must be distilled solely from the juice or mash of whole, sound, ripe fruit, or from standard grape, citrus or other fruit wine (provisions are also set forth as to the amount of volatile acidity and the use of pomace, lees and lees brandy).

In order to be designated by the name of a specific fruit, e.g. "peach brandy," a fruit brandy must be made exclusively from one variety of fruit. If it is made from more than one variety, the designation is "fruit brandy," plus a statement of its composition.

Brandy made from grapes (white grapes are generally used) may be designated either as "grape brandy" or simply as "brandy." Brandy made from apples may be designated as "apple brandy," or as "applejack."

Requirements for the designation "dried fruit brandy," and for the designation of a specific dried fruit, e.g., "dried apricot brandy," correspond to those for fruit brandies. However, brandy made from raisins or raisin wine must be designated as "raisin brandy."

Other types of brandy are lees brandy, pomace (marc) brandy and residue brandy.

Lees brandy is made from the lees (sediment) of standard fruit wine and is designated by the name of the fruit, e.g., "peach lees brandy."

Pomace brandy, also called marc brandy, is made from the pomace (pulp and skin) of fruit, and is designated by the name of the fruit, e.g., "peach pomace brandy." Brandy made from the pomace of grapes may be designated as "grape pomace brandy," or as "grappa brandy," or simply as "grappa."

Residue brandy is made wholly or in part from the residue of fruit or wine, and is designated by the name of the fruit, e.g., "peach residue brandy."

If a brandy does not meet the requirements for any of the above designations, it may be designated only as "brandy"; moreover, in direct conjunction with the word "brandy" there must appear a complete statement concerning its composition.

Of the types of brandy mentioned above, only grape brandy and apple brandy sell in substantial volume.

Many domestic brandies are identified by the name of the state of origin, e.g., "California brandy." A few domestic brandies have borrowed the names of their imported counterparts when these names may legally be used, e.g., kirsch or kirschwasser (cherry brandy); slivovitz (plum brandy).

Aside from bottled in bond brandies, which are few in number, domestic brandies are generally bottled at 84 proof.

Among imports, our federal law takes special notice of Cognac, defining it as "grape brandy distilled in the Cognac region of France, which is entitled to be so designated by the laws and regulations of the French Government."

In 1909, the French passed a law which delimited the Cognac region in western France. Only brandy produced in this region, and nowhere else in the world, may be designated as "Cognac." This Cognac district is sub-divided into smaller districts called *Grande Champagne, Petite Champagne, Borderies, Fins Bois, Bons Bois, Bois Ordinaires* and *Les Bois communs dits à Terroir.* The *Grande Champagne* district, in which the town of Cognac is located, is the central area around which the other districts are located. Sometimes a Cognac is designated by the district in which it originates. For example, a "fine Champagne Cognac" is a fine Cognac made either in the Grand Champagne or in the Petite Champagne.

Cognac is produced primarily by independent farmer-distillers, of whom there are several thousand. These men grow their own grapes (principally the Folle Blanche, a white grape), make wine from them, and distill the wine into brandy in pot stills. This new colorless brandy is delivered to Cognac shippers. For aging purposes, brandies are placed in Limousin casks (casks made of white oak from the forest of Limoges). Following the aging period, which may exceed a half-century, Cognac, which draws its amber color from the casks, is readied for blending. Aged Cognacs, which may have been produced in different years and in different parts of the Cognac region, are "married" for several months.

Most Cognacs are bottled at proofs in the 80's.

Many Cognac labels show stars and letters of the alphabet. The stars represent gradations of quality among the brands of any one shipper. However, they do not represent equal standards of quality for all brandies. Thus, one shipper's five-star Cognac will be superior to his three-star Cognac, but this three-star Cognac may be superior to another shipper's five-star Cognac. Despite popular belief, a star on a Cognac label is not the equivalent of a year of aging.

The letters on a Cognac label represent specific words. For example, the letters "VSOP" represent the words "very special old pale."

Some American brandies also use the symbols of stars and letters as an indication of quality, as do other classes and types of distilled spirits.

Armagnac is another famous French brandy. A grape brandy, Armagnac is made, like Cognac, principally from the Folle Blanche. It is produced in the region of France southeast of Bordeaux.

Other French brandies include Calvados, an apple brandy made in Normandy, and Quetsch, a plum brandy made in Alsace.

A few fine Spanish brandies are shipped from Jerez, the center of Spain's sherry and brandy industry.

7. Rum

Most of the rum marketed for beverage purposes in the United States is produced in Puerto Rico. Rums produced in this country are next in sales volume. Other important sources of supply are the Virgin Islands, Cuba, Jamaica and British Guiana.

Within our borders, Massachusetts is the largest producer, followed by Kentucky, Pennsylvania and Louisiana. The major portion of this American rum is used as flavoring, particularly by the tobacco industry.

Rum may legally be distilled only from the fermented juice of sugar cane, sugar cane syrup, sugar cane molasses or other sugar cane by-products. It must be distilled at less than 190 proof and must be bottled at 80 proof or higher. It may consist of a single distillate, or a mixture of distillates.

Although all rums must meet these general requirements, New England rum (the only rum recognized as a specific "type" under federal standards of identity) must meet additional requirements. It must be made in the United States, and must be distilled not only at less than 190 proof, but at less than 160 proof. Moreover, it may not be a mixture or a blend of rums; it must be straight rum. New England rum is flavorful and somewhat heavy-bodied.

If New England rum is the only type of rum, what about other rums which have a geographical designation, e.g., Puerto Rico, Cuba, Demerara, Barbados, Virgin Islands, St. Thomas, St. Croix, Jamaica, Martinique, Trinidad, Haiti, San Domingo?

Each of these rums must conform to the basic standard of identity. However, the law makes it clear that no rum may bear a geographical designation unless it is in fact produced in the place for which it is named.

Rum is made both in continuous stills and in pot stills. Following distillation, it is usually aged and blended, then aged again before bottling. Age claims may be made, but statements of age are not mandatory, no matter how young the rum may be. The majority of rums are between four and seven years old.

Two methods are primarily used in the production of rum, most of which is made from molasses. One method is used in the production of Puerto Rican, Cuban and other light-bodied rums. Jamaica rum, which is heavy-bodied, provides a good example of the second method.

In the light-bodied method, a mixture of water and molasses is fermented. This mixture then goes to a continuous still. Distillation will be nearer the 190-proof mark in some instances, and nearer the 160-proof mark in other cases. Thus, two kinds of rum are produced, one very light in body, the other somewhat heavier in body. The latter gives flavor to the rum; the former provides the quality of lightness.

Following distillation, the product is placed in uncharred oak casks for aging. After the aging period, it is leached and caramel is added. Next, it is readied for blending with other rums. After blending, the product is again stored in casks prior to bottling.

Most light-bodied rums are marketed as "Gold Label" and "White (Silver) Label," and are bottled at either 84 or 86 proof. Gold Label rums are darker and sweeter than the White Label variety.

Molasses is also used in the production of Jamaica rums. As in the case of Puerto Rican and Cuban rums, molasses is mixed with water. In the production of Jamaica rums, however, a sugar-cane by-product called "dunder" is added to the mixture. After fermentation, the mixture is pot-stilled. Distillation is at a comparatively low proof, thus producing a rum which is heavier bodied and more highly flavored than Puerto Rican or Cuban varieties. Jamaica rums are aged in oak puncheons, then blended and bottled. Caramel gives them their sweetness and distinctive golden mahogany color.

Some Jamaica rums are called London Dock rums. These rums are aged in warehouses located on the docks of London, prior to exportation to the United States and other countries.

Jamaica rums are bottled at anywhere from 86 proof to 151 proof.

Among sweet, dark, heavy-bodied rums, Demerara is best known next to Jamaica rums. Demerara rum is produced in British Guiana.

8. Vodka

Prior to 1950, so little vodka was sold in this country that government statistics were not published. Beginning in 1950, however, vodka began to skyrocket in sales and quickly became an important class of spirits along with whiskey, gin, cordials, brandy and rum.

Only domestic vodka has any commercial importance.

Unlike other classes of spirits, which must be so produced as to have distinctive flavor, aroma and other qualities, vodka is required by law to be devoid of any distinctive properties.

Essentially, vodka is grain neutral spirits treated with charcoal. Neutral spirits have very few distinctive qualities to begin with. Treatment with charcoal removes most, if not all, the congeners which account for any slight individuality which the neutral spirits may possess. Thus, vodka is free of taste and aroma. In addition, it is colorless.

Grain neutral spirits used in making vodka must be reduced to not more than 110 proof and not less than 80 proof. At this point, either of two methods of treatment with charcoal may be employed.

In one method, the product is filtered through charcoal contained in tanks. There must be at least 1½ pounds of charcoal to each gallon of neutral spirits. Charcoal and neutral spirits must be in contact at least eight hours. Every 40 hours, at least 10% of the charcoal must be replaced by new charcoal; at least six pounds of new charcoal must be used for every 100 gallons of neutral spirits.

In the second method, grain neutral spirits are kept in constant movement by mechanical means when placed in contact with charcoal. This process must go on for at least eight hours, and at least six pounds of new charcoal must be used for every 100 gallons of neutral spirits.

Following treatment with charcoal, the finished product emerges as vodka. If flavoring material is added, the designation must be "flavored vodka."

Prior to bottling, vodka may be stored only in metal, porcelain or glass containers or in paraffin-lined tanks.

Vodkas are marketed at 80 proof and also at 100 proof.

9. Bottled Mixed Drinks

There is a market, but a comparatively small one, for bottled cocktails and other mixed drinks. Manhattans, martinis and eggnogs account for the great bulk of sales. The rest of the market is shared primarily by the following: the old-fashioned, daiquiri, Gibson, Tom Collins, rum collins, side car, stinger, vodka martini, whiskey sour.

Imports are insignificant. Advocaat, a Dutch eggnog, is known to some extent.

10. Bitters

Although bitters are produced domestically, imported bitters dominate the market, with one brand, Angostura, accounting for the bulk of sales. Angostura Bitters are imported from Trinidad and Tobago.

Bitters, which are used primarily as ingredients in mixed drinks, consist of a spirits base combined with other materials which provide distinctive taste properties. There are two types of bitters used in preparing mixed drinks: aromatic bitters and flavoring bitters.

Aromatic bitters, to which category Angostura belongs, consist of a spirits base with which aromatic materials are combined.

Orange bitters, lemon bitters and lime bitters are the three types of flavoring bitters. Orange, lemon and lime flavoring, respectively, are combined with a spirits base in the manufacture of these products.

11. Other Distilled Spirits

Other than the spirits which have already been discussed, there are few of any commercial significance. Among these few, mention may be made of aquavit (akvavit), the Scandinavian national drink, and tequila, the Mexican national drink. A small quantity of aquavit and tequila finds its way to the American market.

CHAPTER FIVE

Package, Carton and Case

Most brands of distilled spirits are packaged in glass bottles, although earthenware containers are used to a limited degree. In some instances, the bottle is placed within a carton, which is usually a cardboard box bearing appropriate copy and illustrative material. As will be pointed out, bottle containers other than cartons are also sometimes used.

From the viewpoints of merchandising and advertising, the case in which brands are packed for shipment must also be considered, inasmuch as it may serve both as a vehicle for advertising and as a foundation for point-of-sale display.

1. The Package

In liquor marketing and merchandising, the package is particularly important. In many other package goods industries, it is not uncommon to find brands which have distinct product advantages over their competition. Such brands may be markedly superior in quality, or may contain ingredients which competitive brands lack. In the liquor industry one rarely finds a brand of a specific type of spirits, in a particular price class, which differs strikingly, productwise, from competitive brands. The reason for this is clear. Considering the strict formulae which must be observed in the manufacture of each type of spirits, product variations are seldom substantial. Even when this is the case, however, such variations may usually be described only in technical language which is either over the head of the consumer, or of little interest to him. Age differences are among the few product variations among distilled spirits which the consumer readily understands.

Thus, lacking a strong competitive product story with which to woo the consumer, the average producer or importer of spirits must suggest brand superiority in other ways. One of these methods—along with such selling tools as merchandising, advertising, point-of-sale material, and trade support—is package design. An examination of the many intelligently designed liquor packages on the market today indicates the close study which marketing and advertising men have given to this matter.

In package design, as in the production of distilled spirits, the industry must operate within the framework of federal law. Elements of federal liquor packaging law will be included in the discussion which follows.

The package consists of the container, closure, federal strip stamp and labels. Sometimes decorative and other material is used.

CONTAINERS. Distilled spirits may be packaged either in glass bottles or in earthenware containers.

a. *Glass bottles*

1. *Indicia.* Certain information must be blown into the bottom or the body of the bottle. For domestic liquors, this information consists of the permit number of the manufacturer; the year of production (indicated by the last two numerals, e.g., 55 for 1955); and a symbol and number which have been assigned to the bottler. In addition, the following legend must be blown into the shoulder of the bottle: "Federal Law Forbids Sale or Re-use of this Bottle." The symbol and number of the bottler may be omitted from bottles of distinctive shape or design which are used for cordials, liqueurs, bitters, cocktails and other specialties.

For imported liquors, the following information must be blown into the body or bottom of the bottle: the name, and city or country, of the producer or exporter abroad, or the name and city in the United States of the importer. As with domestic spirits, the phrase prohibiting sale or re-use of the bottle must appear on the shoulder. Cordials and some specialties which are imported in distinctive bottles need not carry the foregoing indicia.

2. *Sizes.* Both domestic and imported spirits are bottled in accordance with the following standards of fill:

1 gallon (128 oz.)	⅘ pint (12.8 oz.)
½ gallon (64 oz.)	½ pint (8 oz.)
1 quart (32 oz.)	⅛ pint (2 oz.)
⅘ quart (25.6 oz.)	⅒ pint (1.6 oz.)
1 pint (16 oz.)	1/16 pint (1 oz.)

Only Scotch whisky, Irish whiskey, blended Scotch type whiskey, brandy and rum may be bottled in the 4/5 pint size.

Only brandy may be bottled in the 1/16 pint (1 oz.) size.

Cordials, as well as cocktails, highballs, and some other specialties are not bound by the above standards of fill. In addition to the above sizes, they may be found, for example, in 3/4 pint and 3/4 quart sizes.

The 4/5 quart is popularly called a "fifth" (one-fifth of a gallon).

The 4/5 pint is popularly called a "tenth" (one-tenth of a gallon).

1/8 pint, 1/10 pint and 1/16 pint sizes are popularly called "miniatures."

Most spirits are sold to the consumer in fifths, pints, and half-pints, with the fifth the leading volume size.

Although all of the above sizes are legal from the federal point of view, not all sizes are permitted by state laws in all states.

Failure by a bottler to observe standards of fill constitutes misbranding under federal law.

3. *Standard liquor bottles.* A standard liquor bottle is one which is manufactured and filled in such a way as not to mislead the consumer. A bottle is considered not to be a standard bottle, and hence misleading to the consumer, if its contents are other than one of the standards of fill; if its headspace (when 1/2 pint or larger) exceeds 8% of the total capacity of the bottle after closure; if the bottle gives the impression of containing more spirits than is actually the case (even if the correct net contents are stated on the label). Failure to use standard bottles constitutes misbranding.

Cordials and some specialties are not required to use standard bottles.

4. *Shapes, designs and colors.* Liquor bottles are produced in all conceivable shapes: cylindrical, globular, rectangular, triangular, square, flat, round, pear-shaped, concave, etc. Designs are often effected in the glass and may consist of anything from simple fluting to decorative symbols or figures.

The bottle itself is sometimes a design. For example, a "fiddle bottle" simulates the shape of a violin. Some bottle designs simulate non-commercial containers of spirits. For example, "flask bottles" in pint or smaller sizes simulate flask containers and have a functional use in that they fit into the pocket. Decanter bottles, which are especially popular during the holidays, simulate decanters ranging from old-fashioned traditional types to those in the forefront of modern glassware design.

Among the important commercial sizes, quarts and fifths are primarily sold in simple cylindrical bottles, plain or fluted. These bottles vary mainly in height, diameter and the proportion of the body to the neck. Pints and half-pints are primarily sold in flask-shaped bottles.

Liquor bottles are produced in a variety of colors, including amber, green and gray, in addition to the colorless (flint) variety. Colorless and amber bottles comprise the majority.

In the field of cordials and specialties, bottles are produced in an especially large and ingenious variety of shapes, designs and colors.

b. *Earthenware containers.* In addition to glass containers, distilled spirits may be packaged in earthenware containers. Domestic distilled spirits which are packaged in earthenware containers of distinctive shape or design must carry on the container, in underglaze coloring, the symbol and number of the bottler, plus the phrase prohibiting sale or re-use of the container. Earthenware containers for domestic cordials and some specialties need not be so marked.

Distinctive earthenware containers for imported spirits must carry, in underglaze coloring, the same indicia as spirits imported in glass. Earthenware containers for imported cordials and some imported specialties need not be so marked.

CLOSURES. There are many devices for closing the mouth of the bottle. Among them are the following:

a. A screw-on metal or plastic cap. This simple closure is in common use.

b. A threaded metallic cap which locks over the mouth and neck of the bottle, with the lower part fitting into, and held in place by, a narrow groove in the bottle neck. The cap snaps into two parts when turned. The lower part, in the shape of a narrow ring, remains on the bottle, caught by the groove. The top part becomes a simple cap which unscrews easily.

c. Plastic or wood top cork. This consists of a cork to which is affixed a wood or plastic disc which rests on the top of the bottle when the cork is inserted. Simple corks are seldom used for distilled spirits.

d. A cap with a hinged lever, which, when pressed down, locks the cap, and releases the cap when pressed up.

e. Jigger caps. Some caps are produced in the shape of jiggers, and are used as such.

In addition to the cap itself, sealing material is often used. Usually this is not affixed until the government strip stamp is gummed over the cap. One type of sealing material is a film-like plastic—transparent, translucent or opaque—which is applied wet and shrinks tightly into place. When dry, it peels off readily. Copy and art may be impregnated into this sealing material in a variety of colors.

STRIP STAMPS. All spirits, both domestic and imported, must carry a federal strip stamp over the cap of the bottle. Strip stamps are approximately ⅝-inch wide and 6 inches long, are gummed down over the cap, down the sides of the neck, and on short-necked bottles extend on to the shoulders. Stamps of smaller dimensions are used for bottles containing less than ½ pint.

Strip stamps are available in all denominations, corresponding to standards of fill. However, all sizes under ½ pint carry the same stamp, on which appears the phrase, "Less than ½ pint."

As we noted in the previous chapter, there are two types of strip stamps:

a. *Red strip stamps.* These are affixed to containers of all types of spirits, both domestic and imported, with the exception of bottled in bond spirits. In addition to denoting content (quart, ⅘ quart, etc.), which notation appears on both ends, the stamp carries the following wording: "Bottle Stamp," "U.S. Internal Revenue" [repeated], "Tax Paid Distilled Spirits" and the bottle serial number. Red strip stamps affixed to bottles of imports usually carry the name and address of the importer.

b. *Green strip stamps.* These are affixed only to bottles of bottled in bond spirits. At one end of the stamp appears the notation of contents; at the other end, the notation "100 proof." In addition, the stamp carries the following phrase, "Bottled in Bond under the Supervision of the U.S. Government in Internal Revenue Bonded Warehouse." The season and year of both distillation and bottling are also set forth, together with the name of the distiller and the serial number.

LABELS. There are usually two labels on a bottle of distilled spirits—a front label and a back label. Some brands also have one or more additional labels on the shoulder or neck of the bottle; by their positions, such labels attract the eye, and are useful for a trademark, slogan or other selling device.

From the viewpoint of design, most labels belong to one of two general categories. One type of label represents the school of modern design. Such labels have a smart appearance. Many of the large-selling spirit blends have labels of this type. The other type of label conveys the impression of tradition and age. Such a label may be the original, as used for generations for a historic brand, or may be a comparatively new label, designed along traditional lines, for a more recent brand.

In addition to modern and traditional labels, there are labels which achieve other effects. For example, some labels for domestic products, e.g., brandy and vodka, simulate foreign labels; other labels suggest the product from which the spirits are made, e.g., a peach-colored label for a peach cordial.

The government has set forth highly detailed labeling regulations under the Federal Alcohol Administration Act. Failure to observe these regulations constitutes misbranding. Among the important requirements are the following:

a. *General requirements*

1. All mandatory statements on labels must be legible and must appear on a contrasting background. Type or lettering must be no less than 8 point Gothic caps (except for bottles smaller than the half-pint size).

2. All statements must be in English except as follows: Brand name, place of production and producer's name may be in a foreign language provided the label carries the phrase "product of" followed by the name of the country in which the spirits were produced. Additional statements in a foreign language may appear on the label provided they do not conflict with labeling requirements as set forth by federal law.

3. In addition to statements which are mandatory on all labels, additional statements may appear if they do not conflict with federal law.

b. *Mandatory information.* There are two types of labels—the brand label (front label) and the Government label (back label). The brand label states the brand name, the class and type of the product, and the name and address of the producer, rectifier, importer or bottler. In the case of imported spirits, the name and address of the importer may appear on either the brand label or the Government label. On the Government label appears the alcoholic content; net contents; artificial or excessive coloring or flavoring (if any); percentage of neutral spirits (if any) and name of the commodity from which distilled, e.g., "grain neutral spirits"; the name of the commodity in the case of continuously distilled gin, e.g., "distilled from grain"; a statement of the percentage and the age of whiskey or whiskies in a product, plus the percentage of grain neutral spirits, if any; the state in which domestic whiskey and straight whiskey (except blends) are distilled.

Any information which appears on the Government label may be restated on the brand label. Moreover, the Government label need not be used if all mandatory information appears on the brand label.

1. *Brand name.* The brand name must not give erroneous impressions as to age, origin, identity or other characteristics of the product. If the word "brand" is used in conjunction with the name, it may legally be considered to have removed an otherwise erroneous impression. For example, if a young straight whiskey (less than four years old) were to be named *Veteran,* it may be presumed that the word "brand" would be required to appear next to the name so that the name does not convey a misleading idea as to age.

2. *Class and type.* These must be stated on the brand label in conformity with federal standards of identity, e.g., "straight bourbon whiskey," "apple brandy"; or in conformity with trade understanding and usage, e.g., "Manhattan Cocktail." If standards of identity or established trade designations do not exist, a distinctive or fanciful class name must be created, e.g., "Aprikeen" (a name which might be invented for apricot-flavored spirits which do not conform to any standard of identity or to trade understanding and usage).

A cordial need not be labeled as a cordial when the type name clearly indicates that the product belongs to this class of spirits. For example, anisette, kummel and crême de menthe need not be labeled as cordials, but fruit cordials, such as blackberry or peach, must be so labeled.

In some cases, a label for a product with a distinctive or fanciful name, or with a name in accordance with trade usage, must contain a statement of its composition.

3. *Name and address.* Labels must carry the name and address of distillers, rectifiers, importers and bottlers as follows (street address may be omitted):

On labels of domestic spirits, the phrase "bottled by" must appear, followed by the name of the bottler, and the place of bottling. This is not mandatory, however, when domestic spirits are bottled by or for the distiller or rectifier. In this case, the phrase "distilled by," or "blended by," followed by the name and address of the distiller or rectifier, may be used instead.

In place of the phrase "blended by," one of the following is used, if appropriate to the type of rectification which is involved: "made by," "prepared by," "manufactured by," "produced by."

The above statements for domestic spirits, if applicable, may (but need not) appear on labels of bottled imported spirits. They are required to appear only if so specified by state or foreign law.

The following statements are mandatory with respect to imported spirits:

If distilled spirits are imported in bottles, the label must carry the phrase, "imported by," "imported exclusively by," or some similar phrase. This must be followed by the name and address of the importer, exclusive agent or sole distributor.

If distilled spirits are bottled after importation, they must carry the same information as just described for bottled imports, plus the phrase "bottled by," followed by the name and address of the bottler. If the importer is also the bottler, the phrase preceding name and address is "imported and bottled by."

In the case of both domestic and imported spirits, the following may be stated, in addition to mandatory requirements: the name and address of the person, e.g. a retailer, for whom the spirits are bottled, immediately preceded by the phrase "bottled for," "distributed by," or some other similar phrase.

Labels for domestic whiskies other than blends must give the name of the state where the whiskey was distilled, if the name of the state is not the same as that in the address on the label. In such cases, the phrase "distilled in" must be used, followed by the name of the state.

4. *Alcoholic content.* A statement of alcoholic content must appear on the Government label. This statement must be in terms of proof, except for cordials and specialties, which must be labeled in terms of either proof or percentage by volume, e.g., "60 proof" or "30% alcohol by volume."

5. *Net contents.* Net contents must be stated as follows: 1 pint, 1 quart, 1 gallon.

If less than a pint, in fractions of a pint, e.g., "½ pint."

If more than a pint, but less than a quart, in fractions of a quart, e.g., "⅘ quart."

If more than a quart, but less than a gallon, in fractions of a gallon, e.g., "½ gallon."

All fractions must be stated in lowest denominators.

Net contents need not be stated on the label if they are blown into the bottle on the brand label side, and if they are at least ¼ inch high (a smaller size is permissible for bottles of less than ½ pint).

6. *Neutral spirits.* When liquors (except cordials and specialties) contain neutral spirits, the label must state the percentage of neutral spirits, together with the name of the commodity from which distilled. The label statement must read substantially as follows: "...% grain (or fruit, or cane products) neutral spirits." The statement may also be phrased in this way: "...% neutral spirits distilled from grain (fruit, cane products)." The following phrase appears on the labels of most spirit blends: "65% grain neutral spirits."

7. *Continuously distilled gin.* Only the name of the commodity from which the gin is distilled need be stated, e.g., "distilled from grain."

8. *Coloring, blending, smoothing and flavoring materials.* If materials of this kind exceed 2½% by volume (except in the case of cordials and certain specialties), the name and percentage by volume must be stated on the label, e.g., "contains 4% sherry blending material."

When coloring materials (other than caramel) are used, the label must say "artificially colored." This phrase must also be used if the label suggests a source of color other than that actually used. When caramel is the only coloring matter used, the phrase "colored with caramel" or a similar phrase may be used instead of "artificially colored." However, neither phrase need be stated when caramel is used in brandy, in rum, or in whiskey other than straight whiskey.

When natural, as distinguished from synthetic, coloring materials are used, the phrase "artificially colored" may be replaced by a phrase stating the actual source of color, e.g., "color derived from blackberries."

If beading oil is used, this fact must be stated on the label as follows: "contains beading oil."

9. *Age statements.* Statements or representations of age are prohibited on the labels for neutral spirits, gin, cordials, vodka, bitters and specialties.

Age statements are optional for bottled in bond whiskies, for four-year-old (or older) straight whiskies, blends of straights, Scotch whiskies, Canadian whiskies and Irish whiskies, and for rum, irrespective of its age. An age statement is optional for brandy only when it is two years old or older.

Age statements are mandatory for all spirits not previously mentioned.

Age must be stated as follows for straight whiskies and imported whiskies which contain spirits aged for less than four years: "This whiskey is __ years old."

For blends of straights which contain whiskey under four years of age, the age of the youngest straight must be stated. The statement must be phrased as follows: "The straight whiskies in this product are __ years or more old." In addition, the percentage and age of each straight whiskey in the blend may (but need not) be stated. If stated, the phrasing must be as follows: "__% straight whiskey, __ years old; __% straight whiskey, __ years old; __% straight whiskey, __ years old."

An age statement for the product itself is prohibited for spirit blends. However, the age of the straight whiskey in the blend must be stated, together with the percentage of straight whiskey and percentage of grain neutral spirits. The statement must be phrased as follows: "The straight whiskey in this product is __ years old; __% straight whiskey, __% grain neutral spirits." If more than one straight whiskey is in the blend, the age of the youngest must be stated. The statement must be as follows: "The straight whiskies in this product are __ or more years old; __% straight whiskey, __% grain neutral spirits."

In addition, the percentage of each straight whiskey in a spirit blend may (but need not) be stated, as follows: "__% straight whiskey, __ years old; __% straight whiskey, __ years old; __% straight whiskey, __ years old."

The percentage and age of the youngest malt whiskey and the percentage and age of the youngest grain whiskey must be stated for blended Scotch type whiskey: "The malt whiskey in this product is __ years old; __% malt whiskey, __% other whiskey, __ years old."

In the case of any domestic whiskey, other than blended Scotch type whiskey, which is stored in re-used cooperage (rather than in new charred oak barrels), the following statement must be made in place of a standard age statement: "Stored __ years in re-used cooperage," or "stored __ years or more in re-used cooperage."

Brandy which is less than two years old must carry the following statement: "This brandy is __ years old."

In any of the above cases, where an age statement is either permitted or mandatory, age may be understated, but may not be overstated.

References to, or visual representations of age (e.g., pictures of barrels), are not permitted on the labels of gins, cordials, vodkas, prepared mixed drinks, specialties or other spirits which are prohibited from carrying an age statement on the label. References to age or representations of age are permitted on products which must carry age statements, provided the mandatory age statement is equally conspicuous. Inconspicuous representations of age are permitted on the label, even though the age statement is omitted, for whiskies or brandies for which age statements are optional.

c. *Prohibited practices.* Federal law specifically prohibits certain types of statements and devices on labels. These include the following:

1. Statements which are false, misleading, or disparaging of competitive products; statements or devices which are obscene or indecent; misleading statements or devices (irrespective of falsity) which relate to analyses, standards, tests, or to any guarantee. An enforceable guarantee is permitted, however, if it appears on the label in substantially this form, "We will refund the purchase price to the purchaser if he is in any way dissatisfied with the contents of this package." This statement must be signed on the label by the permittee.

2. Also prohibited on labels are names of living persons or existing organizations used as brand names, if these falsely suggest an endorsement.

3. Simulations of United States or foreign stamps are prohibited.

4. The words "bottled in bond," "bonded," "bond" and "aged in bond" may not appear on labels except those for bottled in bond spirits.

5. The word "pure" may not appear on any label, except as part of the name of a permittee, or of a retailer for whom the spirits are bottled.

6. Neither gin nor any other spirits may be labeled "double distilled," "triple distilled," etc.

7. Neither in the brand name nor elsewhere on the label may there appear any statement or visual device which relates in any way to the flag or the armed forces of the United States, or to any emblem, seal, insignia, or decoration associated with them. Statements and visual devices (flags, seals, coats of arms, crests and other insignia) may not be used if they are related to a government, organization, or person in such a manner as to be misleading.

8. Curative and therapeutic effects may not be claimed on labels if untrue or misleading.

OTHER BOTTLE ATTACHMENTS. Ribbons, cord, seals, neckbands, capsules, foil, and other material are often attached to bottles for decorative and merchandising purposes.

2. The Carton

Containers for individual bottles of distilled spirits have become increasingly popular. However, most spirits are sold without such containers. A great many are packaged in special holiday containers for Christmas gift purposes. On the other hand, some are sold in containers the year round.

Most individual containers are rectangular cardboard boxes. Of these, some are die-cut, in order that the bottle label may show through. Other types of containers are wooden boxes, baskets, drawstring fabric "stockings," wooden shoes, etc.

Federal law requires that regulations concerning labeling also apply to cartons. Thus, full mandatory information must appear on the carton, and prohibited statements and prohibited visual devices must be excluded. There is only one exception to this rule. If, through die-cutting or other production design, the carton permits a clear view of mandatory information on the bottle label, this information need not be repeated on the carton.

In addition, the carton must not be of such a size as to give the impression that it contains a bottle larger than the actual bottle.

3. The Case

The case in which bottled spirits are packed is more than a shipping container. Usually a rectangular cardboard box, it is used to carry advertising material, and serves as a retail display piece. In its latter function, part is usually cut away in order to show the enclosed bottles, and an upright display card inserted or attached behind the last row of bottles.

The number of bottles and net contents of cases vary. Data on volume sizes are as follows:

Size	Number of Bottles	Number of Wine Gallons
½ Gallon	6	3
Quart	12	3
⅘ Quart	12	2.4
Pint	24	3
½ Pint	48	3

It will be noted that there are three gallons to a case for all of the above sizes except the fifth. This fact is important to bear in mind when analyzing statistics which are set forth in terms of cases. In order to determine the actual quantity of spirits in a certain number of cases, it is of course necessary to determine how many cases represent fifths and how many cases represent other sizes. When the number of cases in each size is not known, a fairly good estimate of total gallonage can usually be made by multiplying the total number of cases by 2.7.

Cases must be marked prior to shipment in accordance with federal law. Every case must carry a serial number; class and type; name and address of the distiller, rectifier or bottler; the number of wine gallons; number of proof gallons; proof; the date of filling; and the number of the bottler's warehousing and bottling permit. The words "distiller," "rectifier," or "bottler" may be used but are not required. Abbreviations are permitted.

For example:

Ser. No. 1
Straight Bourbon Whiskey
John Doe Company
Bottler
New York, N.Y.
BD-135
3.00 W.G.
90 proof
2.70 P.G.
Filled May 2, 1954

If the spirits are bottled for a retailer, then the phrase "bottled for" or "bottled expressly for," followed by the retailer's name and address, may be substituted for the bottler's name and address.

CHAPTER SIX

Marketing Channels

In the last two chapters we followed the production, warehousing and bottling of distilled spirits; we discussed the many different kinds of spirits on the market today; finally, we viewed the finished product as packaged and cased for shipment. Now we are ready to observe distilled spirits as they travel from producers and importers to the ultimate consumer.

Marketing channels differ between open states and monopoly states. In open states (license states), producers and importers sell directly, or through brokers, to wholesalers, who in turn sell to retailers. In some instances, producers and importers sell directly to retailers. In monopoly states, producers and importers sell directly, or through brokers, to the state liquor unit (called the commission, board, etc. depending upon the state). Most monopoly states operate state-owned and state-operated stores (usually referred to as state stores).

In both open and monopoly states, retailers sell liquors to the consumer for off-premise and for on-premise consumption. While there are many types of off-premise outlets, the usual overall designation is "package stores." There are also many types of on-premise outlets; in this case, the usual overall designation is "bars." Approximately 50% of all retail outlets are bars, approximately 25% are package stores, and approximately 25% are combination package stores and bars. Thus it may be seen that close to two-thirds of all retail outlets sell liquors for on-premise consumption, and over one-third sell liquors for off-premise consumption.

Off-premise outlets are in operation in all wet states and territories. On-premise outlets are in operation in all wet territories and in all but eleven wet states.

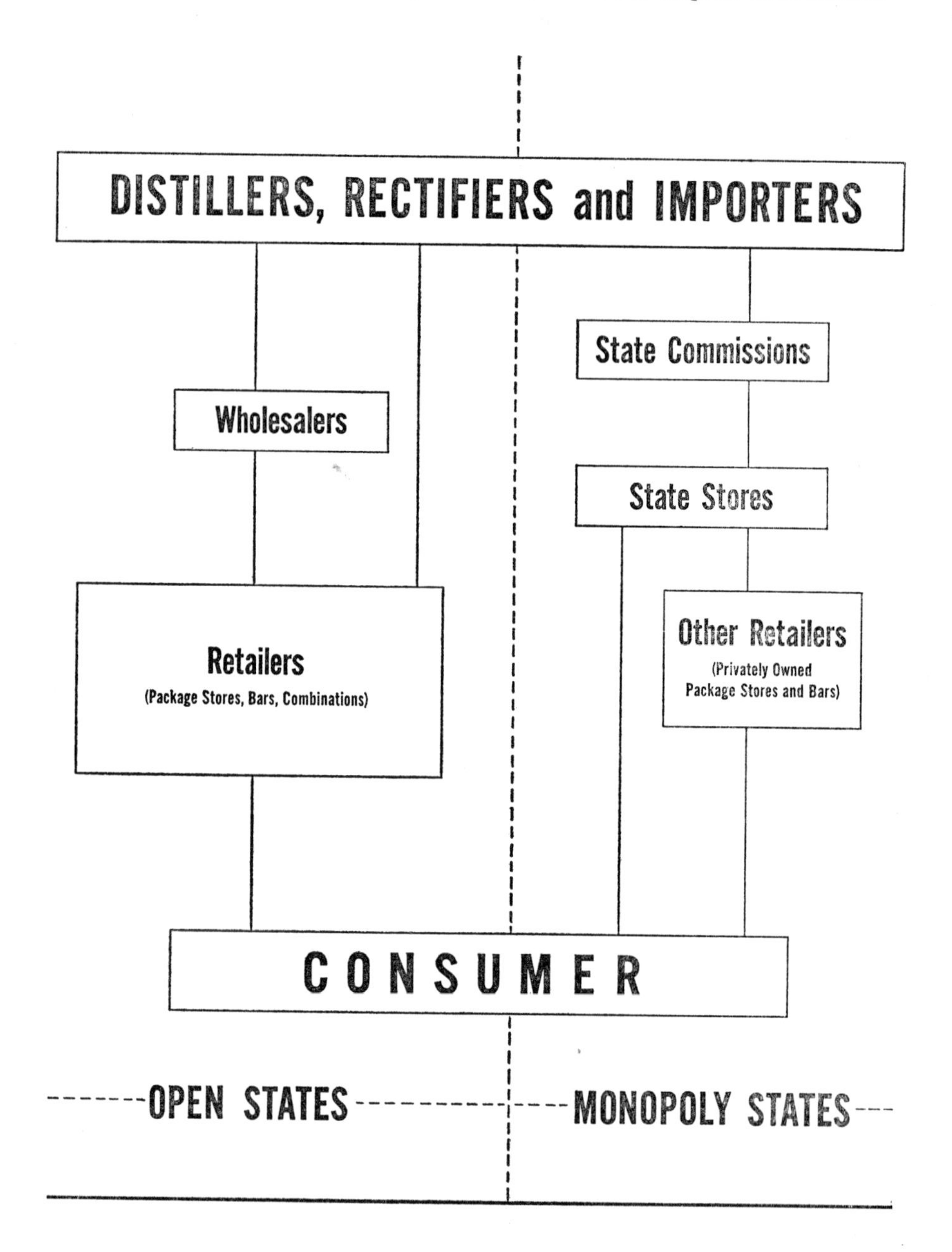

PRIMARY MARKETING CHANNELS

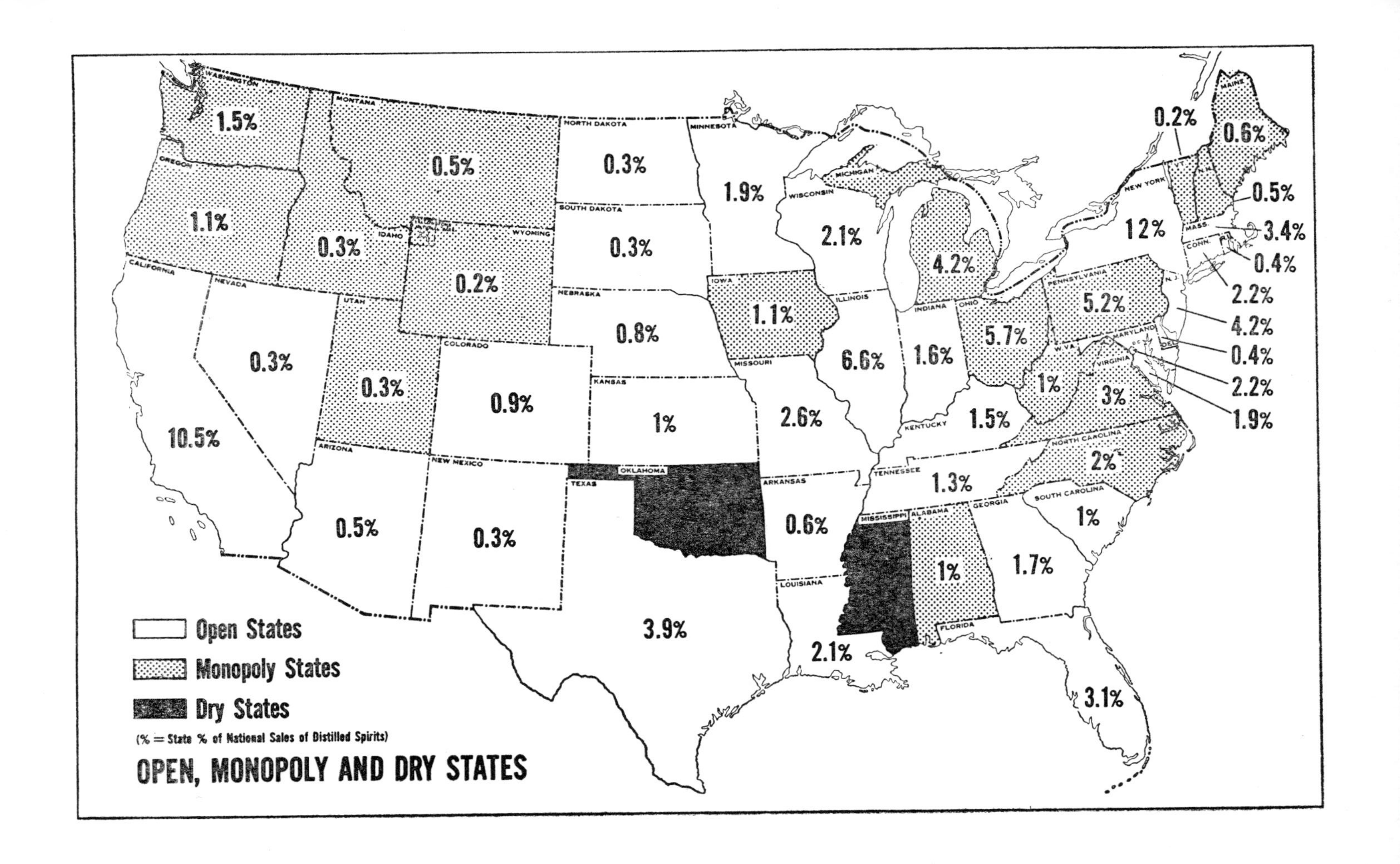
WASHINGTON
1.5%
OREGON
1.1%
CALIFORNIA
10.5%
NEVADA
0.3%
IDAHO
0.3%
MONTANA
0.5%
WYOMING
0.2%
UTAH
0.3%
ARIZONA
0.5%
COLORADO
0.9%
NEW MEXICO
0.3%
NORTH DAKOTA
0.3%
SOUTH DAKOTA
0.3%
NEBRASKA
0.8%
KANSAS
1%
OKLAHOMA
TEXAS
3.9%
MINNESOTA
1.9%
IOWA
1.1%
MISSOURI
2.6%
ARKANSAS
0.6%
LOUISIANA
2.1%
WISCONSIN
2.1%
ILLINOIS
6.6%
MICHIGAN
4.2%
INDIANA
1.6%
OHIO
5.7%
KENTUCKY
1.5%
TENNESSEE
1.3%
MISSISSIPPI
ALABAMA
1%
GEORGIA
1.7%
FLORIDA
3.1%
SOUTH CAROLINA
1%
NORTH CAROLINA
2%
VIRGINIA
3%
W. VA.
1%
MARYLAND
PENNSYLVANIA
5.2%
NEW YORK
12%
N. J.
DEL.
CONN.
MASS.
VT.
MAINE
0.6%
0.2%
0.5%
3.4%
0.4%
2.2%
4.2%
0.4%
2.2%
1.9%
Open States
Monopoly States
Dry States
(% = State % of National Sales of Distilled Spirits)
OPEN, MONOPOLY AND DRY STATES

1. Open States

There are 29 open states. Alaska, the District of Columbia and Hawaii are classified with them, making a total of 32 open markets, as follows:

Alaska	Illinois	New Jersey
Arizona	Indiana	New Mexico
Arkansas	Kansas	New York
California	Kentucky	North Dakota
Colorado	Louisiana	Rhode Island
Connecticut	Maryland	South Carolina
Delaware	Massachusetts	South Dakota
District of Columbia	Minnesota	Tennessee
Florida	Missouri	Texas
Georgia	Nebraska	Wisconsin
Hawaii	Nevada	

WHOLESALERS. Wholesale houses in open states may handle one line of distilled spirits exclusively, may handle the brands of competitive producers and importers, and may also handle, in addition to spirits, other types of alcoholic beverages and the products of other industries, e.g., wines, soft drinks, food. In major cities, dual or multiple distributorships are often set up, wherein two or more wholesalers handle the same brands in one market.

As in other industries, wholesalers maintain sales forces in order to sell and advise the retailer, place point-of-sale material, conduct sales drives, merchandise advertising campaigns, achieve distribution for a new brand, and so on.

RETAILERS. In all open states, spirits are sold by the bottle in package stores for off-premise consumption. In all but the following open states, spirits are also sold for on-premise consumption: Arkansas, Georgia, Kansas, South Carolina, Tennessee, Texas. Local law prohibits on-premise retailing in these states.

The primary types of off-premise outlets in open states are as follows: exclusive wine and liquor stores, drug stores, grocery stores, delicatessens, supermarkets, cigar and tobacco stores, confectionery stores, general merchandise stores. Sales are through both chains and independent stores.

Not all types of outlets are permitted in all states. In New York,

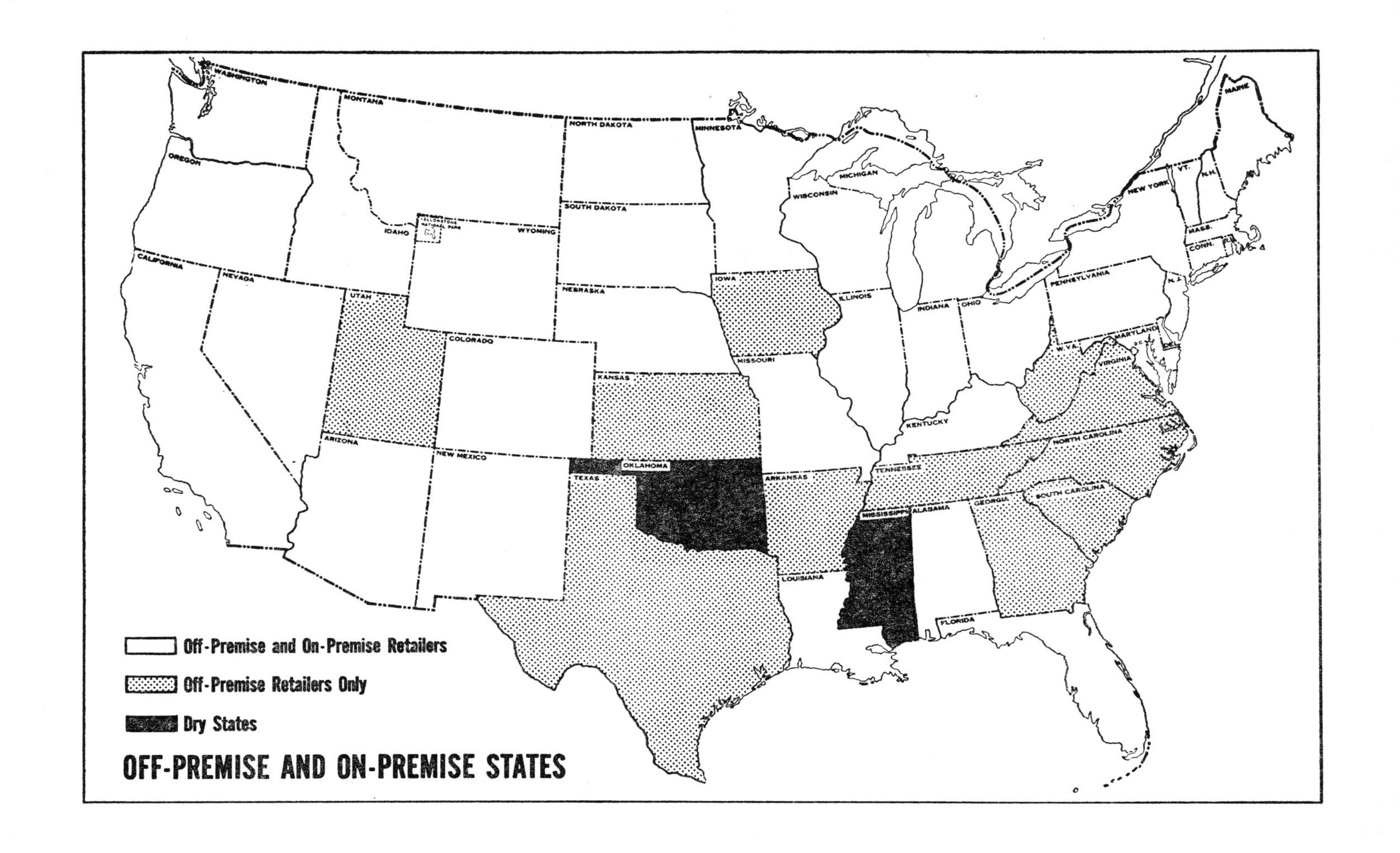

OFF-PREMISE AND ON-PREMISE STATES

for example, spirits for off-premise consumption may be sold only in stores which retail wines and liquors exclusively.

Taverns, hotels, clubs, restaurants and railroads comprise the bulk of on-premise outlets. Not all types of these outlets are permitted in all states. Moreover, state regulations are in effect as to how liquors may be served. For example, in some states drinks may be served only with food; in other states the customer may not be served unless he is seated.

PRODUCER AND IMPORTER BRANCH OFFICES. Producers and importers operate regional, state and local sales offices. It is the purpose of these branch offices to work with the home office in selling and servicing wholesalers, to assist wholesaler salesmen, to contact retailers, to report on local market trends and on company and competitive brand activity, to prepare sales quotas, to advise on local advertising and point-of-sale, and so on.

2. Monopoly States

There are 17 monopoly states. Montgomery County, Maryland, also operates on a monopoly basis (as do other but smaller counties). The 18 primary monopoly markets are as follows:

Alabama	Montgomery Co., Md.	Utah
Idaho	New Hampshire	Vermont
Iowa	North Carolina	Virginia
Maine	Ohio	Washington
Michigan	Oregon	West Virginia
Montana	Pennsylvania	Wyoming

STATE COMMISSIONS. There are no private wholesalers in monopoly states. The states themselves, through special liquor commissions, function as wholesalers. In having the state as a customer in the monopolies, as contrasted with the wholesaler as a customer in open states, the producer or importer is confronted with a different set of problems. For example, if he wishes to introduce a brand into a monopoly state, he must convince the state that the brand has a reasonable chance of succeeding. Before a listing is granted, a monopoly state will inquire into the success of the brand in other states, will compare the price to competitive listed items, will examine the quantity and quality of proposed advertising, and will ascertain whether there is a sufficient market for an additional item of the type of spirits under consideration. Sometimes a brand owner may have to wait for many months or even years for a listing in a given monopoly. Sometimes he may be required to have another of his brands de-listed in order to make room for a new label.

RETAILERS. With the exception of North Carolina and Wyoming, all monopoly states operate state-owned package stores. In North Carolina, package stores are owned and operated by individual counties. In Wyoming, package stores are privately owned, are licensed by counties and municipalities, and buy at wholesale direct from the state.

Many monopolies which sell through state stores also sell through privately owned off-premise outlets, e.g., grocery stores and drug stores. These outlets, which buy at a discount and which retail at the same prices as state stores, are located in Idaho, Michigan, Montana, Ohio, Oregon, Utah, Vermont and West Virginia. In all of these states except Michigan, private off-premise retailers are designated as "agencies" and are usually located in thinly populated areas where it would be unprofitable to conduct an independent state store operation. These agencies account for only a minor part of each state's total off-premise business. In Michigan, private off-premise retailers are called "S.D.D.'s" (Specially Designated Distributors), are located in areas of both large and small population, and account for the bulk of the state's off-premise business.

Except for newer stores in some monopoly areas, the typical state store is constructed strictly along functional lines and does not promote liquors to the consumer. No attention-arousing exterior signs are installed, no point-of-sale advertising is used, and no attempt is made to display merchandise attractively. A list of brands is posted which shows the price, together with a code number, for each size of each brand in stock. The customer is asked to consult the list, make his choice and give the code number to the sales clerk; the latter functions only as an order-taker.

It is obvious that state stores contrast sharply with open state package stores, which utilize personal salesmanship and all possible selling and display devices in order to promote sales and increase business.

With respect to on-premise outlets, these are in operation in all monopolies except Iowa, North Carolina, Utah, Virginia and West Virginia. Local law prohibits on-premise retailing in these states.

The primary types of on-premise outlets in monopoly states correspond to those in open states. Thus, taverns, clubs, hotels, restaurants and railroads all dispense liquors by the drink in the monopolies. As in open states, regulations specify as to how liquors may be served to the consumer. For example, Alabama permits on-premise consumption, but not sales by the drink. The consumer in this state buys by the bottle for either off-premise or on-premise consumption. Other regulations are in effect in other monopolies. For example, some monopolies prohibit sales to persons who are not seated, etc.

PRODUCER AND IMPORTER BRANCH OFFICES. As in open states, producers and importers maintain local offices.* These offices do not sell merchandise directly to either stores or bars. State stores receive their stocks from the state, while bars do their buying (at wholesale) from the stores. Company sales personnel are not permitted to call on state stores.** They are permitted to do so in the case of bars and privately owned package stores, however.***

In addition to retailer selling functions, local company offices cooperate with the home office in dealings with state commissions, e.g., in securing orders and new listings, and in obtaining approval of proposed local advertising. Other activities correspond to those of company branch offices in open states, e.g., preparation of sales quotas, reporting on company and competitive brand activity, advising on local advertising.

* Except in Iowa, Montana and Utah

** Except in Idaho and Vermont

*** Except in Montana, Oregon, Utah and West Virginia

CHAPTER SEVEN

Markets

The market for distilled spirits is comprised of adults who drink, who buy in legally wet areas and who patronize legitimate liquor retailers.

Thus it may be seen that the spirits market, compared to markets for many other products, is a restricted one. Additional restrictions are imposed by the industry itself. It is against industry principle to attempt to increase per capita consumption (annual per capita consumption has remained stable for many years, averaging between 1 and 1½ gallons in terms of total population, and between 1½ and 2 gallons in terms of adult population). Furthermore, it is against industry principle to convert non-drinkers into drinkers, or to sell to minors.

It is obvious that producers and importers, as a result of the restrictions just mentioned, cannot take action to increase the size of the market, which can grow only as adult population increases, as dry areas go wet, as taxes go down and as bootleggers go out of business. The individual brand owner may increase his sales only by winning a larger share of the existing market.

1. The Consumer Market

The market for distilled spirits may be classified in terms of frequency of individual drinking, urban vs. rural consumption, sex, age, income, race and nationality.

REGULAR AND OCCASIONAL DRINKERS. About two-thirds of the population of the United States is 21 years of age or older. Of this adult population, about 45% drink distilled spirits. Of this 45%, about 40% drink regularly (three or more times per week); the remainder drink once or twice a month or on special occasions. Hence it may be estimated that approximately 12% of the total population, or 18% of the adult population, constitutes the primary market.

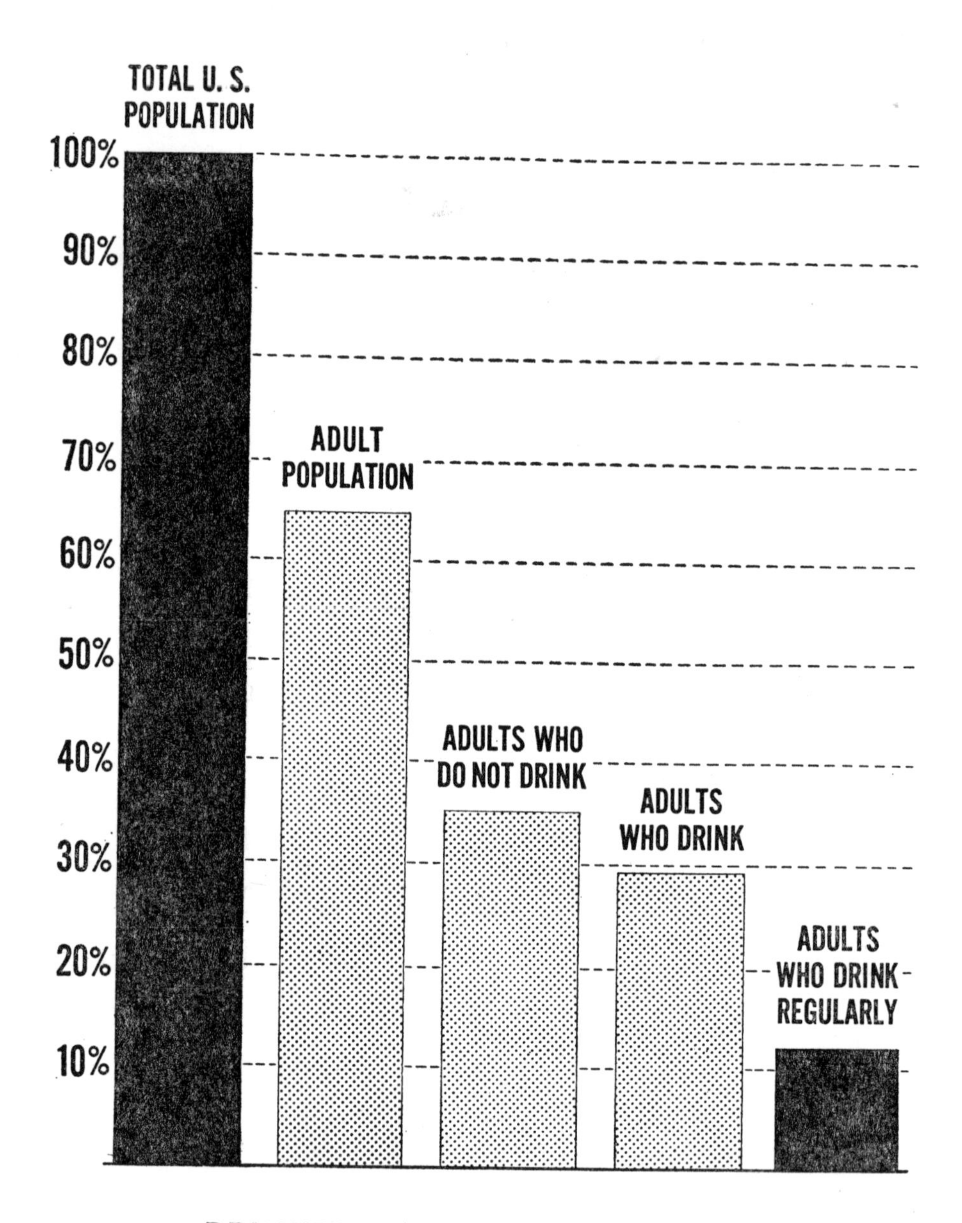

DRINKERS AND NON-DRINKERS

URBAN AND RURAL DRINKERS. The larger the city, the larger the percentage of those who drink. In major cities, approximately one out of five adults drinks regularly; three out of four drink occasionally. In rural areas, where dry strength is most heavily concentrated, approximately one out of twenty adults drink regularly, and one out of four drinks occasionally.

SEX. About 27% of men drink regularly and about 8% of women. Regular men drinkers outnumber regular women drinkers about three to one. In major cities, the percentage of women to men drinkers is higher than the national percentage. In the actual purchase of liquors, it is estimated that 75% of all customers are men.

AGE. Consumption of distilled spirits decreases with age. Approximately 50% of the adult population between 21 and 50 consume distilled spirits. In the segment of the population past 50, approximately 35% drink spirits. However, inasmuch as liquors are purchased for entertainment and gift purposes, as well as for personal consumption, the market consisting of men and women over fifty does not decrease in direct proportion to a decrease in personal drinking.

INCOME. Distilled spirits are used by consumers in all income brackets. Generally speaking, the individual consumer in higher-income brackets spends more for spirits than the consumer in middle-income brackets. The latter spends more for spirits than the lower-income consumer. The fact that the higher-income consumer spends more for spirits does not mean that he necessarily drinks more. Usually, he buys more expensive brands and entertains on a larger scale. However, the higher-income consumer does not buy expensive brands exclusively. Frequently he will purchase less costly brands for entertainment purposes.

Although the low-income consumer spends less for distilled spirits, this is not an indication that his consumption of alcoholic beverages as a whole is less, or that he buys only low-priced brands. He generally spends more than the middle or upper-income consumer for beer or wine; moreover, he is definitely in the market for high-priced spirits, since these may be purchased at low unit cost by the drink or in small sizes (pints, half-pints, miniatures).

In terms of total, rather than individual, expenditures in each income bracket, the picture changes. The middle-income group spends the most; the lower-income group ranks next; the upper-income group is last. One indication of the expenditure for spirits by income groups is the percentage of sales of low-, middle- and high-priced spirits.

These percentages are approximately 35%, 50% and 15%, respectively.

Of every dollar spent by the consumer for all goods and services, distilled spirits account for 1½% to 2%.

RACE. The Negro market is an important part of the total distilled spirits market. Negroes comprise about 10% of the national population, and purchase about 15% of all spirits.

Among southern states, Negro population ranges from approximately 15% to 40% of the population of individual states. Among northern states—in New York, Illinois, Pennsylvania and Ohio, for example—Negro population runs approximately 6% to 7%. Wet states with a Negro population of more than one-half million are listed below, in the order of size of Negro population:

Georgia
North Carolina
Alabama
Texas
New York
Louisiana
South Carolina
Virginia
Illinois
Pennsylvania
Florida
Tennessee
Ohio

Of the total Negro population, about two-thirds is in urban areas. Cities with a Negro population of more than one hundred thousand are listed below, in the order of size of Negro population:

New York
Chicago
Philadelphia
Los Angeles
Detroit
Cleveland
St. Louis
Washington, D. C.
San Francisco

Per capita consumption of Negroes exceeds that of whites. Moreover, a larger percentage of the Negro dollar is expended for spirits.

The Negro market as a whole has shown certain individual

characteristics. Preferences are for higher-priced brands, even though this may necessitate purchase in small sizes.

In addition, the Negro market has shown a tendency to shift from one brand to another with some frequency, giving one brand a play for a certain period of time, then dropping it in favor of another brand.

Another point worth noting is that Negroes, to a greater extent than whites, gravitate toward brands which are used by leaders in their individual social circles.

Many important brands today first rose to popularity in the Negro market.

NATIONALITY. Foreign-born residents of the United States account for approximately 7% of the total population. Of this 7%, about 70% were born in non-English speaking countries. Italian, Yiddish, German, Polish, Russian and Spanish are the languages most frequently spoken by foreign-born residents. Chinese and Japanese have some significance on the West Coast.

States with a foreign-born population of more than one-half million, in the order of size of foreign-born population, are as follows:

New York
California
Illinois
Pennsylvania
Massachusetts
New Jersey
Michigan

Of these states, percentage of foreign-born to total population ranges from approximately 9% in Illinois and Michigan to approximately 17% in New York.

States with a foreign-born population of 100,000 or more from any one country, together with the names of these countries, are listed below. Where more than one country is listed, order is according to the size of the foreign-born population:

New York—Italy, Germany, Poland, Ireland, Austria, Canada, England and Wales
California—Mexico, Canada, Italy
Illinois—Poland, Germany
Pennsylvania—Italy
Massachusetts—Canada, Italy
New Jersey—Italy
Michigan—Canada
Texas—Mexico

The foreign-born resident tends to consume the type of alcoholic beverage which is most popular in the country of his birth. For example, natives of England, Scotland, Ireland and Canada are usually whiskey drinkers (although not necessarily of Scotch, Irish and Canadian whiskies). As another example, natives of Italy and France tend toward wines as opposed to spirits.

A similar tendency to remain loyal to the home product may be noted among native-born drinkers who travel from one part of the country to another. For example, a blend drinker in New York, which is primarily a blend state, may move to Texas, which is primarily a straight state. Usually, the New York blend drinker will continue to drink blended whiskey; moreover, he will probably remain with his particular brand.

2. Wet and Dry Areas

The sale of distilled spirits is legal in all states except Oklahoma and Mississippi. In addition to wet states, the District of Columbia, Alaska and Hawaii are also (as we have noted) legal markets for distilled spirits.

Approximately 85% of the total population is wet.

Within the wet states, on the county level, the pattern varies. Any one state will belong to one of the following categories: (1) all counties totally wet; (2) totally wet and totally dry counties; (3) totally wet, totally dry and partially dry counties; (4) totally wet and partially dry counties; (5) totally dry and partially dry counties; (6) all counties partially dry. The majority of wet states have local option provisions, whereby dry counties may vote themselves wet, and wet counties may vote themselves dry.

The dry states, and the heaviest concentration of dry counties in wet states, are situated below and to the southwest of the Mason-Dixon line. Wet states with substantial dry territory are Alabama, Arkansas, Georgia, Kansas, Kentucky, North Carolina, Tennessee and Texas. There is, in addition, a fair amount of dry territory in Florida, Illinois, Louisiana, Maine, Vermont and Virginia.

Northeastern and midwestern states—Delaware, the District of Columbia, Illinois, Indiana, Maryland, Michigan, New Jersey, New York, Ohio, Pennsylvania and Michigan—are either totally wet or sufficiently wet in areas of large population to make them important markets. A wet band extends down the eastern coastline, cutting through state lines, with two states, Delaware and South Carolina, in the totally wet column. Geographically, the heaviest concentration of virtually unbroken wet territory is the area extending from the west coast to Kansas, Oklahoma and Texas, and continuing eastward, north of these states, to the Great Lakes.

States in the order of size of wet population are listed below.

	Wet % of State Population
1. New York	99
2. California	100
3. Pennsylvania	100
4. Illinois	88
5. Ohio	90
6. Michigan	100
7. New Jersey	97
8. Massachusetts	95
9. Texas	54
10. Missouri	100
11. Indiana	100
12. Wisconsin	95
13. Virginia	87
14. Minnesota	91
15. Iowa	100
16. Washington	99
17. Florida	83
18. Louisiana	82
19. Maryland	93
20. South Carolina	100
21. Connecticut	97
22. West Virginia	92
23. North Carolina	41
24. Alabama	52
25. Oregon	99
26. Kentucky	45
27. Nebraska	99
28. Georgia	38
29. Colorado	95
30. Tennessee	34
31. Arkansas	58
32. Kansas	56
33. District of Columbia	100
34. Rhode Island	99
35. Arizona	100
36. Utah	100
37. Maine	73
38. South Dakota	100
39. New Mexico	94
40. North Dakota	100
41. Montana	100
42. Idaho	100
43. New Hampshire	91
44. Delaware	100
45. Vermont	74
46. Wyoming	100
47. Nevada	100

3. Markets Lost to Bootleg Liquors

Statistics on illicit stills which are seized by government officers may be used to estimate the size and location of markets lost by legal distillers to the bootlegger. Approximately 75% of seized illicit stills are in the following southern states: Alabama, Florida, Georgia, Mississippi, North Carolina, South Carolina and Tennessee. Per capita consumption figures for these states (excluding Mississippi, which is legally dry) averages about 65% of the national figure. More than 50% of the total population of these states live in legally dry areas; this is well above the national average. Were it not for the fact that more illicit stills are discovered in these states than elsewhere in the country, it might be presumed that the area has more than its share of teetotalers. Under the circumstances, the conclusion must be drawn that the bootlegger is probably selling to about the extent that the area deviates from the national percentage.

Other states where seizures of illicit stills are significant are Indiana, Kentucky, Ohio, Virginia and West Virginia.

Based on the size of seized stills, and the estimated period of operation of each, it is calculated that total bootleg sales approximate 25% of legal sales.

CHAPTER EIGHT

Prices, Pricing and Profits

The purpose behind every marketing and advertising campaign for any brand of distilled spirits is, of course, to produce the largest possible net profit for the distiller, rectifier, importer or other vendor of the brand. It is equally obvious that correct pricing is vital to this purpose.

1. Pricing for Maximum Profit

When contemplating the introduction of a new brand to the market, the producer or importer must determine the retail price at the outset. In the case of a brand already established on the market, he must keep a watchful eye on the retail price, and stand ready to change it if marketing conditions so indicate. In calculating retail prices, producers and importers attempt to set those which will yield the largest net profit in terms of total sales volume.

Elementary economics tells us that total net profit does not necessarily increase as sales volume increases. Let us examine the following three examples in connection with a given brand of distilled spirits (in each case, the retail price is the same):

Annual Sales Volume (Cases)	Retail 5th Price	Gross Profit per Case	Total Gross Profit	Mktg., Adv. & Other Costs	Net Profit per Case	Total Net Profit
100,000	$4.50	$7	$ 700,000	$ 665,000	$ .35	$ 35,000
300,000	4.50	7	2,100,000	1,800,000	1.00	300,000
500,000	4.50	7	3,500,000	3,225,000	.55	275,000

In the above examples, the sale of 300,000 cases yields a smaller gross profit than the sale of 500,000 cases. However, the increased marketing, advertising and other costs which were necessary to achieve a sale of 500,000 cases result in a lower net profit.

Let us examine now the following examples, in which a given brand of spirits is retailed at different prices:

Annual Sales Volume (Cases)	Retail 5th Price	Gross Profit per Case	Total Gross Profit	Mktg., Adv. & Other Costs	Net Profit per Case	Total Net Profit
100,000	$4.50	$7	$ 700,000	$ 665,000	$ .35	$ 35,000
300,000	4.05	4	1,200,000	875,000	1.08	325,000
500,000	3.90	3	1,500,000	1,200,000	.60	300,000

In the above examples, the sale of 300,000 cases—at a lower retail price than the 100,000 case sale, but at a higher retail price than the 500,000 case sale—fails to yield the largest gross profit, but does yield the largest net profit. It also yields a larger net profit than the sale of 300,000 cases at a higher retail price, as given in the first of the above two tables.

These tables are not meant to indicate, of course, that any brand of spirits will begin to net a lower profit somewhere between 300,000 and 500,000 cases, but are simply meant to illustrate the possibilities inherent in the relationship between sales volume, retail price and net profit. Generally speaking, the greater the sales volume, the greater the net profit, but an effort to push sales volume upward in a highly competitive or resistant market may sometimes be accomplished only at a selling cost which will reduce net profit.

In attempting, therefore, to establish, or to review the merit of, a retail price for a given brand, the producer or importer must estimate the sales volume which may be achieved at varying retail prices, and decide finally upon the sales volume and retail price which promises to be most profitable. This is by no means a simple calculation. Factors other than price influence sales volume, and price is determined in accordance with factors other than volume. Among the important factors, other than price, which influence sales volume in connection with any brand are the following:

1. *Production and inventory.* The amount of the particular type of spirits which can be produced (or imported), together with the amount of spirits already on hand, will determine the quantity which can be placed on the market.

2. *Market potential.* The market may be able to absorb any

reasonable quantity of this type of spirits or, at the other extreme, may be at the saturation point.

3. *Sales trends.* The market for this type of spirits may either be shrinking or expanding. The brand may be climbing or falling.

4. *Competition.* The market may be highly competitive in all price classes, may be highly competitive in only some price classes, or may be open to increased volume in all price classes.

5. *Wholesalers.* The individual producer or importer may have insufficient wholesaler support to achieve a theoretical sales volume at a given price. His wholesalers may be weak or inefficient. Or they may be concentrating their efforts on competitive brands, either because these brands are strong consumer call items, or because the brand owner is discounting heavily, or both.

6. *Retailers.* As a result of deep discounting, competitive brands may be available to retailers at a substantially lower price than the brand in question, and the latter may therefore be expected to receive comparatively little retail support.

7. *Distribution.* The individual producer or importer may have insufficient distribution, and may lack the support necessary to increase it.

8. *Marketing and advertising funds.* The brand owner may be limited in the amount of money he can safely expend.

9. *Wholesaler and retailer inventories.* The status of middlemen inventories—whether normal, or above or below normal—will affect the sales volume for a given brand.

What are the factors, other than anticipated sales volume, which are observed in arriving at retail prices?

1. *Price classes.* Well-defined price classes exist in the liquor industry for different types of spirits. A given type of spirits, for example, may sell in low-, middle- and high-price brackets. The producer or importer will think twice before setting a price outside of standard price classes.

2. *Price trends.* The public may be shifting to higher-priced brands as against lower-priced brands, or vice versa.

3. *Consumer reaction.* If the indicated new retail price is higher than the present price, the producer or importer must determine whether the brand has the strength to withstand adverse reaction to a higher price. Such a reaction may well upset all calculations which are otherwise sound.

Also to be considered under the heading of consumer reaction is the establishment of retail prices at the odd penny, e.g., $4.49 rather than $4.50, $3.98 rather than $4.

At this point, let us assume that the brand owner has taken into account all the factors which affect sales volume and retail prices, and finds that he has narrowed his choice to one of two alternatives. Let us say, for example, that he can expect to achieve a certain volume at one retail price, but a larger volume and a larger gross profit at a lower retail price. Which retail price should he decide upon?

Since he is concerned with net profit, he will estimate the costs involved in achieving the volume at each price. He will then deduct this cost from gross profit, and thereby arrive at the method which will yield the greater net profit.

In calculating charges against gross profit, we are primarily concerned with marketing, advertising and related selling costs. However, it must be borne in mind that general administrative and other costs are also charged against gross profit.

Selling costs may be broken down as follows:

Sales expense—Salaries, sales offices, cost of sales meetings, cost of sales literature, general sales expenses, etc.

Marketing expenses—Allowances to wholesalers.

Advertising expenses—Magazine, newspaper, outdoor, car card, trade paper, direct mail and other advertising.

Sales promotion expenses—Point-of-sale material, novelties, give-aways, etc.

2. Price Control

We have spoken thus far in terms of the producer or importer deciding the retail price. It would be more accurate to state that, in many cases, he does not decide the actual price, but decides the price class in which he wants his brand to retail. He selects his price class when he establishes his price (F. O. B. price) to wholesalers and to monopoly states. Based on his knowledge of freight charges, state taxes, local taxes, and middlemen mark-ups, he can calculate the approximate price at which his brand will retail. Thus, in order to have his brand priced competitively at retail, he sees to it that his F. O. B. price is comparable to that of the competition.

Once having set his F. O. B. price, the brand owner has varying degrees of control over the establishment of actual retail prices. This control depends upon price laws, if any, in each state.

Under the McGuire Act, a manufacturer may fix retail prices in any state providing a retailer (only one in a state is required) signs an agreement which specifies a minimum price. In accordance with non-signer clauses of the Act, other retailers in the state need not sign in order to be bound by the provisions of the Act.

If these Fair Trade principles of the Act are to operate in a state, however, supporting state legislation must be in effect. Some states have not enacted such legislation. In these states, the brand owner has no control over retail prices. In other states, two types of Fair Trade laws have been passed.

One type, which may be called voluntary Fair Trade, permits the producer or importer to establish specific retail prices, but does not provide for automatic state enforcement. As a result, unless the brand owner sues, retailers can engage in price-cutting without state interference.

The second type of state Fair Trade legislation, referred to as mandatory Fair Trade, also permits prices to be fixed. In this case, however, the state automatically enforces Fair Trade without intervention by the brand owner.

In some states, prices are established through a mandatory mark-up system. Wholesaler and retailer mark-ups must conform to fixed percentages as specified by state law.

State Fair Trade laws are meaningful to the liquor industry only in open states. In the monopolies, each state fixes the retail price of each brand (in the case of monopolies with privately owned retail outlets, the state also fixes wholesale prices to these outlets). Although the brand owner cannot set the actual retail price, he can, in effect, accomplish this. Each monopoly state bases its prices on an established mark-up system. Knowing the particular mark-up system of each monopoly state, the brand owner can closely calculate retail price on the basis of his F. O. B. price and delivered price.

In open states with no Fair Trade legislation, or with voluntary Fair Trade, price-cutting and price wars are common. In these states, the per case charge against gross profit for allowances goes up sharply. In order to win trade support, brand owners and wholesalers discount (deal) as heavily as possible. In some instances, the brand owner provides an allowance to the wholesaler, who may pass it along to the retailer in the form of a discount. In other instances, the wholesaler not only passes along the discount, but adds to it. In still other instances, the wholesaler discounts to the retailer, without having received an allowance from the brand owner.

Discounting is legal in some states, but illegal in others. In mandatory Fair Trade states, discounts may not be passed along to the

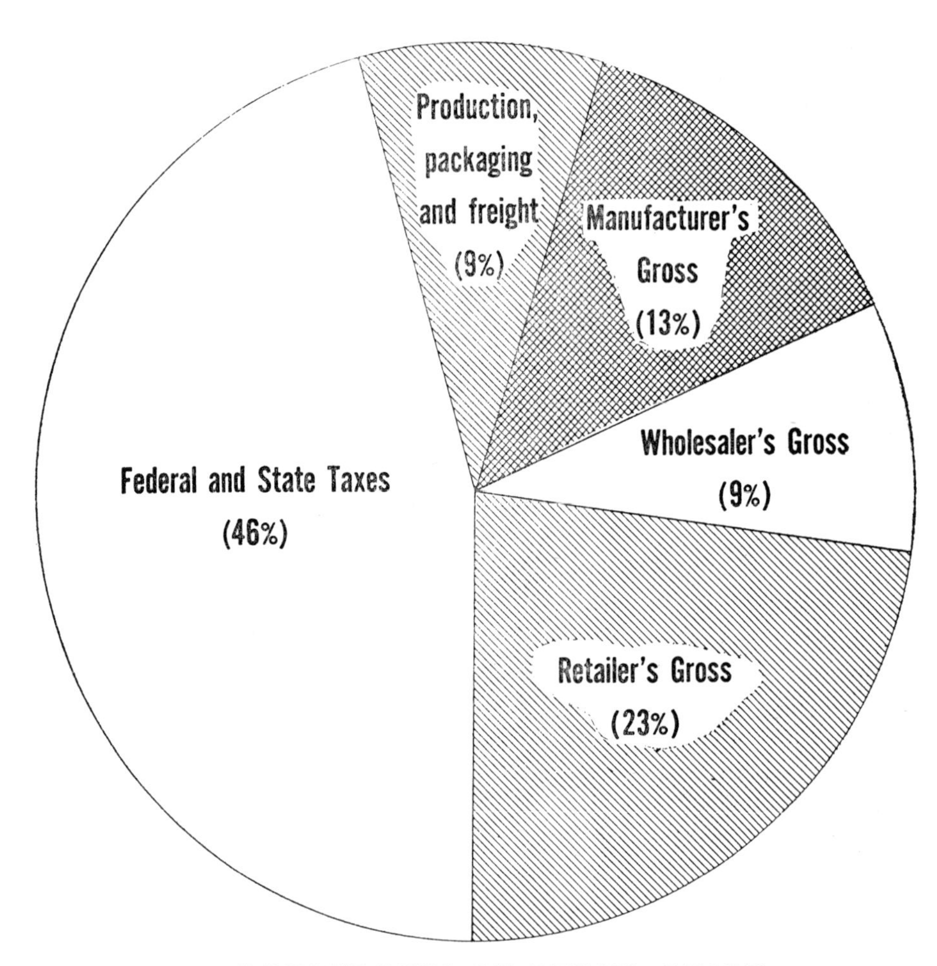

% BREAKDOWN OF RETAIL PRICE
('A' Blend Whiskey)

consumer, inasmuch as retail prices are fixed. In other open states, discounting usually results in reduced retail prices, and accounts for price-cutting practices and price wars in these markets.

In Fair Trade states and in monopoly states, only bottled spirits are price-fixed. On-premise retailers are not subject to price-fixing laws.

3. Price Structures

Price structures differ between open states and monopoly states and between domestic spirits and imported spirits.

OPEN STATES. The following are the components of price structures in open states: (1) manufacturer's cost (comprised of production cost, packaging cost and federal taxes) *or* the importer's cost (comprised of the cost of imported spirits, federal taxes and customs duties); (2) manufacturer's or importer's mark-up (gross profit); the addition of the manufacturer's (or importer's) mark-up to the manufacturer's (or importer's) cost gives the F. O. B. price; (3) freight costs; (4) state tax; (5) wholesaler's cost; the addition of freight costs and state tax to the F. O. B. price gives the wholesaler's cost; (6) wholesaler's mark-up; (7) retailer's cost; (8) retailer's mark-up; (9) retail price (plus local sales taxes, if any).

In order to arrive at a thorough understanding of open state pricing, we will build several price structures. By way of illustration and simplification, we will limit the discussion to a typical mandatory Fair Trade state, California, and will further limit the discussion to domestic whiskey. With respect to the latter, we will discuss the fifth price of a typical middle-priced straight bourbon (A straight), a typical middle-priced spirit blend (A blend), and a premium-priced bonded bourbon. Let us specify that our straight is 86 proof and 4 years old; that our blend is 86 proof and contains 35% four-year whiskey and 65% grain neutral spirits; and that our bond (100 proof) is 4 years old.

a. *Manufacturer's cost.* The cost of manufacture may be broken down into four parts: the cost of whiskey after aging, the cost of neutral spirits (if any), federal taxes and packaging costs.

A barrel of newly distilled whiskey contains approximately 50 proof gallons. However, after four years of aging, about 10 proof gallons are lost by evaporation. Thus, a barrel of 4-year-old whiskey ordinarily contains 40 proof gallons. Or to state it another way, to every barrel of whiskey there are 50 original proof gallons when made, and (after four years of aging) there are 40 regauge proof gallons when used. The cost of 4-year whiskey to the distiller is approximately $60 per barrel or $1.50 per proof gallon.

How many proof gallons go into a case containing 12 fifth bottles of the straight, blend and bond which are under discussion? Since the bond is 100 proof whiskey, 12 bottles of fifths contain 2.4 proof gallons (12 divided by 5). Since the straight is 86 proof whiskey, it contains 86% of 2.4 proof gallons, or 2.064 proof gallons. As for the 86 proof blend, 35% is whiskey; therefore the number of proof gallons of whiskey is 35% of 2.064 (the number of proof gallons in the 86 proof straight), or .7224 proof gallons. We have noted that the cost of whiskey per proof gallon is $1.50. Therefore, the case cost of the whiskey in each of our three types of distilled spirits is figured as follows:

	Proof gallons	Cost per Proof Gallon	Straight Whiskey Cost per Case
Blend	.7224	$1.50	$1.08
Straight	2.064	1.50	3.10
Bond	2.4	1.50	3.60

The straight and the bond contain straight whiskey only. The blend, however, also contains grain neutral spirits, and this cost must be determined before our calculations can be completed. We have noted that a case of our 86 proof blend fifths (35% whiskey and 65% neutral spirits) contains .7224 proof gallons of whiskey. How many proof gallons does it contain of neutral spirits? Just as we took 35% of 2.064 (proof gallons in the straight) to arrive at .7224 proof gallons of whiskey in the blend, we now take 65% of 2.064 to arrive at the number of proof gallons of neutral spirits in the blend. This figure is 1.3416. Grain neutral spirits cost approximately 50 cents per proof gallon. Therefore the cost of neutral spirits in a case of the blend comes to 67 cents. We add this to the cost of straight whiskey in the blend, $1.08, and arrive at a total cost for the blended whiskey of $1.75 per case. To recapitulate, the cost per case of our blend, straight and bond, is $1.75, $3.10 and $3.60 respectively.

We have now to add the federal excise tax and packaging costs to arrive at the total cost of manufacture. In the case of the blend, we must also add the federal rectification tax. The tax rates indicated below are currently in effect as this is written. Any change in the tax will affect the final figure, but the method of calculation will remain the same. In the event that 4-year-old whiskey varies from the cost of $1.50 per proof gallon, the final figure will of course also vary. But in this instance, too, the method of calculation will remain the same.

A completed table showing manufacturer's cost can now be drawn up:

	1 Case 86° Blend 5's	1 Case 86° Straight 5's	1 Case 100° Bond 5's
Cost of whiskey	$ 1.08	$ 3.10	$ 3.60
Cost of neutral spirits	.67	----	----
Federal excise tax @ $10.50 per proof gallon	21.67	21.67	25.20
Federal rectification tax @ 30¢ per proof gallon	.62	----	----
Packaging, etc.	2.00	2.00	2.00
	$26.04	$26.77	$30.80

b. *Manufacturer's mark-up.* As with manufacturers in other industries, the producer of distilled spirits must establish a mark-up over manufacturing costs which will cover selling, advertising, general administrative and other costs, and which will leave him a net profit. This mark-up is the distiller's gross profit per case. When added to manufacturing cost, the resulting figure is the F. O. B. price.

Let us now build up our price structure a bit further:

	Blend	Straight	Bond
Manufacturer's cost	$26.04	$26.77	$30.80
Manufacturer's mark-up	6.71	5.98	19.20
F.O.B. price	$32.75	$32.75	$50.00

It will be noted that the F. O. B. price is the same for blend and straight. The lower mark-up for the straight permits it to be retailed at the same price as the blend.

c. *Wholesaler's cost.* The per case cost to the wholesaler is determined by adding freight charges and state tax to the F. O. B. price. Let us take the case of a California wholesaler who buys from a

Kentucky distiller. The wholesaler's cost may be broken down as follows:

	Blend or Straight	Bond
F.O.B.	$32.75	$50.00
Freight	1.25	1.25
State tax	1.92	1.92
Wholesaler's cost per case	$35.92	$53.17

d. *Wholesaler's mark-up.* This is currently about 11% of the wholesale selling price.

e. *Retailer's cost.* This is of course the sum of the wholesaler's cost and the wholesaler's mark-up.

	Blend or Straight	Bond
Wholesaler's cost	$35.92	$53.17
Wholesaler's mark-up	4.53	6.95
Retailer's cost per case	$40.45	$60.12

f. *Retailer's mark-up.* Off-premise retailer mark-ups average 27% to 30% of the retailer's cost.

	Blend or Straight	Bond
Retailer's cost	$40.45	$60.12
Retailer's mark-up	12.11	17.88
Retail price (per case)	52.56	78.00
Retail price (per bottle)	4.38	6.50

On-premise retailer mark-ups are, of course, determined differently. Mark-ups by the drink will be discussed later.

A completed table, showing all elements of price structures as discussed on a case basis (for a California wholesaler buying from a Kentucky distiller or rectifier), shapes up as follows:

	Blend	Straight	Bond
Whiskey	$ 1.08	$ 3.10	$ 3.60
Neutral spirits	.67	---	---
Federal excise tax	21.67	21.67	25.20
Federal rectification tax	.62	---	---
Packaging, etc.	2.00	2.00	2.00
Manufacturer's cost	26.04	26.77	30.80
Manufacturer's mark-up	6.71	5.98	19.20
F.O.B. price	32.75	32.75	50.00
Freight	1.25	1.25	1.25
State tax	1.92	1.92	1.92
Wholesaler's cost	35.92	35.92	53.17
Wholesaler's mark-up	4.53	4.53	6.95
Retailer's cost	40.45	40.45	60.12
Retailer's mark-up	12.11	12.11	17.88
Retail case price	52.56	52.56	78.00
Retail bottle price	4.38	4.38	6.50

For other types of whiskey (of different proofs, ages, formulae); for gin, brandy, and other domestic spirits; and for sizes other than the fifth, the cost of manufacture will vary. Once the F. O. B. price is determined, however, the same method of calculation is used in arriving at the retail selling price.

It is interesting to note the approximate percentage of retail price of elements of the price structures discussed above:

	Blend	Straight	Bond
Production, packaging, freight	9%	12%	9%
Federal and state taxes	46%	45%	35%
Manufacturer's mark-up	13%	11%	24%
Wholesaler's mark-up	9%	9%	9%
Retailer's mark-up	23%	23%	23%
	100%	100%	100%

MONOPOLY STATES. In monopoly states, price structures differ from each other and from those in open states. Each monopoly has its own particular methods and percentages of mark-up. Some monopoly states, when computing mark-up, include only part of the federal excise tax, while others include the complete tax. As a result of differing methods and percentages of mark-up in the monopolies, retail prices for a brand may vary substantially from one state to another. In addition, they may vary from prices in open states. For instance, a brand may retail in different states as follows (fifth size):

Arkansas	$4.87
California	4.38
Connecticut	4.27
Pennsylvania	4.46
Virginia	3.45

In establishing prices to the monopolies, producers and importers are bound by each state to an agreement which provides that no vendor may sell a listed brand to any customer in the United States at a price lower than that to the state. The monopoly states take the position that, as state buyers, they are entitled to the vendor's lowest prices.

The following, which appears on a monopoly state purchase order, illustrates the idea of the agreement:

> "It is hereby warranted in consideration of this order that the above case price represents the lowest tax paid price f.o.b. distillery, or point of final shipment, offered any purchaser for this same merchandise. Provided, however, the vendor shall be deemed to have complied with this warranty notwithstanding any difference in net realized price on merchandise sold to different purchasers when such differences are due to state law or administrative requirements affecting such items as freight, handling or delivery charges, bailments or cash discounts."

Generally speaking, producers and importers set lower prices to the monopolies than to open state buyers. Thus a margin is created in open states for the establishment from time to time of vendor discounts to wholesalers. Without this margin, prices to monopolies would automatically drop whenever a vendor discounted to wholesalers in open states.

As an example of pricing under the agreement, let us take the case of a vendor who decides to provide a discount to wholesalers which is in excess of the margin which he has established. Let us suppose that the margin per case for his particular brand is 60¢. Let us further suppose that he decides upon a discount to wholesalers of 85¢ per case for a given period of time, e.g., one month. During the period of the discount, the price to monopolies is reduced by 25¢ per case. This price reduction remains in effect for the month that the discount to open state wholesalers is in effect. Monopoly retail prices will remain

The Medicinal Value of Whiskey

is admitted by the highest medical authorities. Indeed for many slight disorders it is a safe and certain cure. But to be effective, it must be the **genuine, pure, natural** article like

Sunny Brook
THE PURE FOOD
Whiskey

SUNNY BROOK is unsurpassed as a wholesome pleasant stimulant or an invigorating healthful tonic. **Every drop is distilled, aged and bottled under the direct supervision of U. S. Government Inspectors** and its absolute purity and mellowness make its use perfectly safe and free from harmful effects. The **"Green Government Stamp"** over the cork of each bottle states the correct age, proof and quantity

SUNNY BROOK DISTILLERY CO., Jefferson Co., Ky.

4—FULL QUARTS—$5

BY EXPRESS PREPAID

SEND YOUR ORDER TO

SHIPPED IN PLAIN BOXES. **SEND REMITTANCE WITH YOUR ORDER.**

NO GOODS SHIPPED C. O. D.

A pre-Prohibition whiskey advertisement

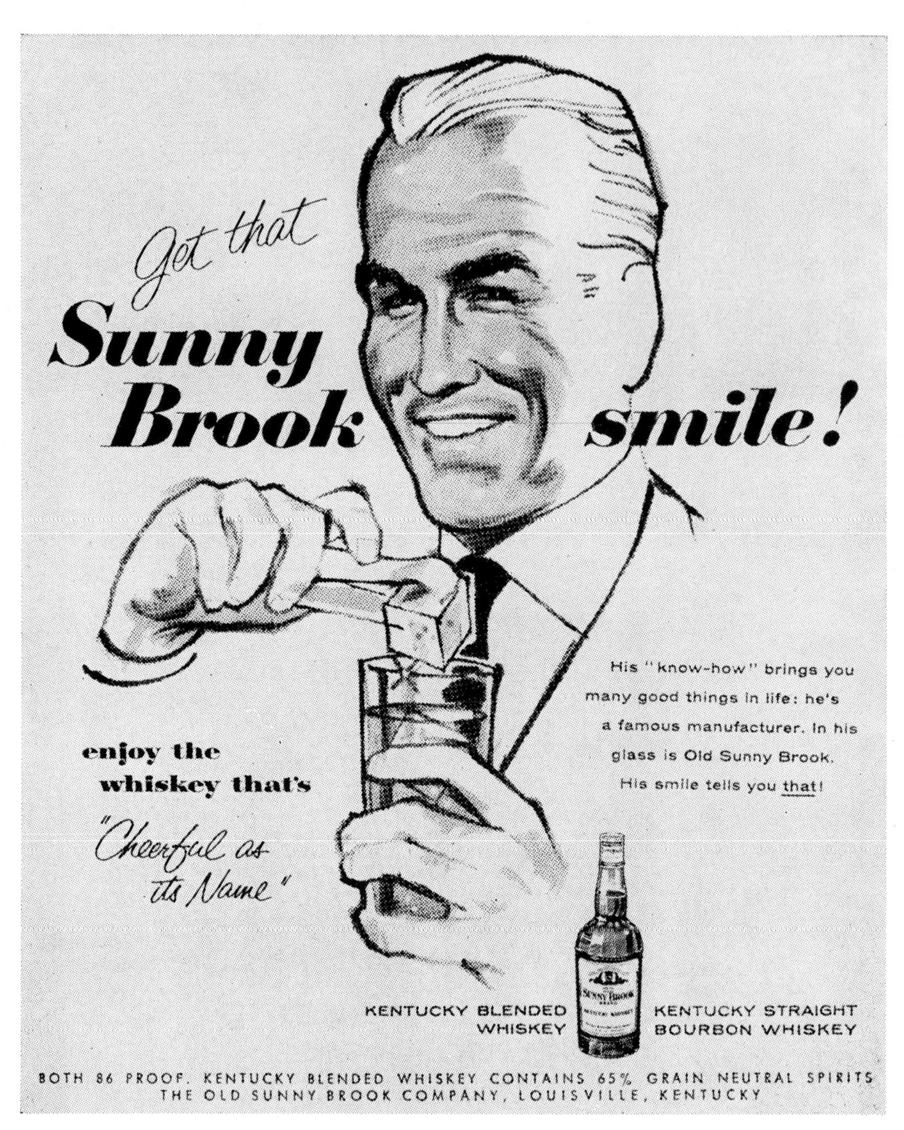

A current whiskey advertisement

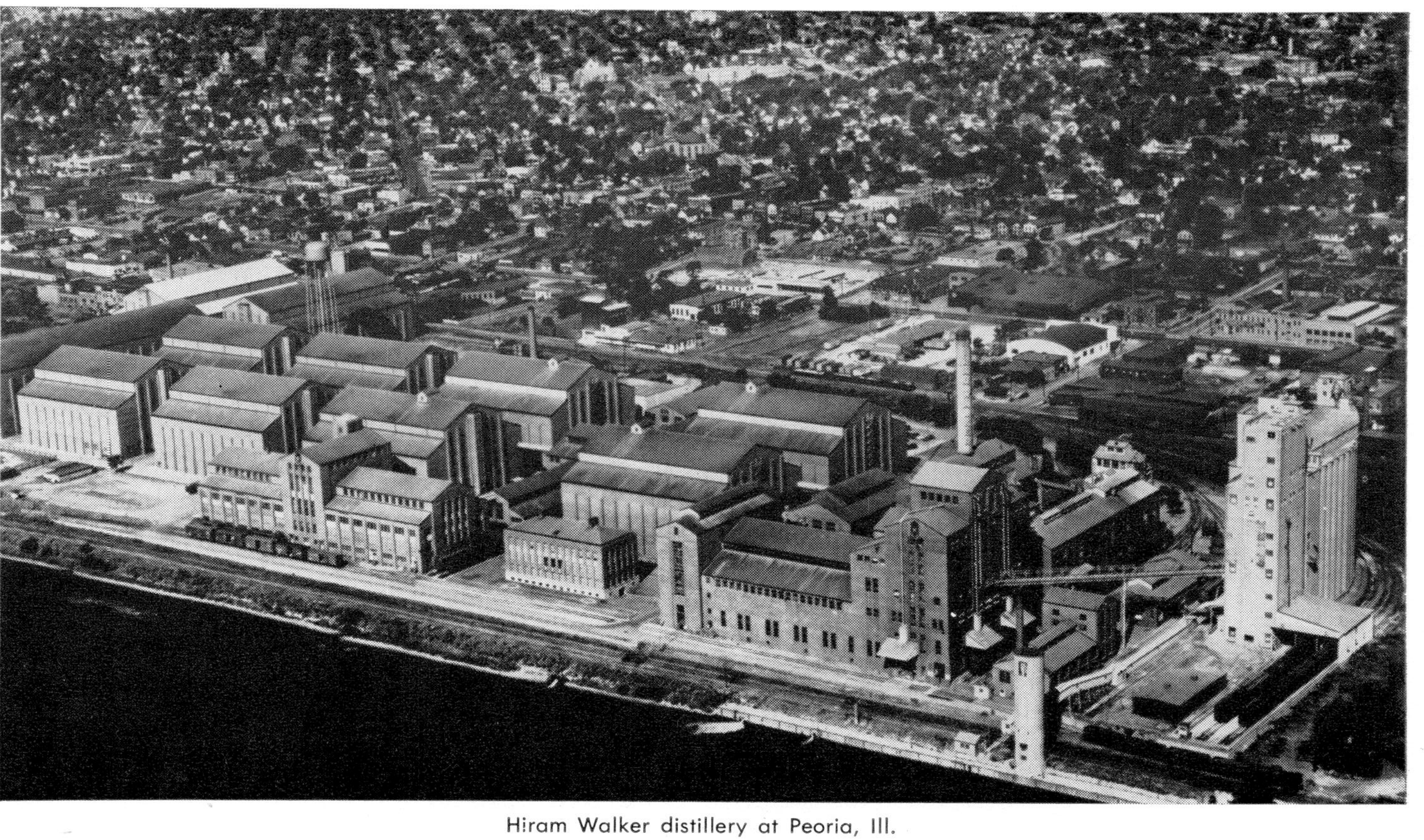

Hiram Walker distillery at Peoria, Ill.

James E. Pepper warehouse—Lexington, Ky.

Weighing barrels to compute gallonage

IT'S SMART TO SWITCH TO

Calvert

RESERVE

CALVERT DISTILLERS CORPORATION
Sales and Executive Offices Chrysler Building, New York, N. Y.

BLENDED WHISKEY
86.8 PROOF

The straight whiskies in this product are four years or more old. Thirty-five per cent straight whiskies, sixty-five per cent grain neutral spirits . . . Twenty-five per cent straight whiskies four years old, six per cent straight whiskies five years old, four per cent straight whiskies six years old.

Examples of front and back labels

Decanter and carton

"Super Liquor Store"—Decatur, Ill.

A self-service package store

Café de la Paix, Hotel St. Moritz—New York City

A well-designed bar and cocktail lounge

A Virginia State Store

State Store No. 195—Cleveland

Making a purchase at an Ohio State Store

Filling an order for mixed drinks

The taste that made Millions Sure made this drink famous!

Some call it "*over ice*"...some call it "*on the rocks*"...but by any name, it's now a nationwide favorite.

In a large measure, its success can be traced to the superb taste of America's finest whiskey, Seagram's 7 Crown.

It requires the smoothness and palatability of a whiskey like 7 Crown for an "over ice" drink to be fully enjoyed!

An advertisement for the world's largest selling brand of distilled spirits

unchanged throughout, with the result that the monopolies will automatically net a larger profit.

In monopoly states with privately owned retail outlets, we have noted a practice which indicates another difference from pricing in open states, i.e., that privately owned retail outlets in monopoly states purchase from state stores at a specified discount from the retail price.

4. Package Store and Bar Prices

PACKAGE STORE PRICES. The following are typical California retail prices for the blend, straight and bond as discussed in the preceding section:

	Quart	Fifth	Pint	½ Pint
Blend or straight	$5.40	$4.38	$2.75	$1.40
Bond	8.00	6.50	4.10	2.11

The following indicates the relationship between net contents and price for each size:

	Quart	Fifth	Pint	½ Pint
Blend, straight or bond				
% quart contents	100%	80%	50%	25%
% quart price	100%	81%	51%	26%

For other spirits, and in other states, the above relationships between prices and sizes prevail.

BAR PRICES. We have noted that the package store retailer, in order to arrive at retail price, adds a standard mark-up to his cost. In determining mark-up, the on-premise retailer must go through a somewhat more complicated process. First he must determine the cost per drink in the size in which he sells it. To this he adds his mark-up, which may range from 100% to 300% or more. The price is then usually rounded out to the nickel. Further calculations are required for mixed drinks.

Drink sizes vary, e.g., ¾, ⅞, 1, 1⅛, 1¼, 1½ and 2 ounces. Most bars pour from quart bottles, although fifths are also used. For purposes of simplification we will discuss only one-ounce drinks as poured from quart bottles of the A blend (or straight) and the premium-priced bond which we have been discussing.

A case of quarts contains 384 ounces. The retailer's cost per one-ounce drink therefore is as follows:

	Blend or Straight	Bond
Cost per case	$49.99	$74.15
Cost per drink	.13	.193

The retailer must now decide his mark-up. Let us look at 100%, 200% and 300% mark-ups on cost.

	Blend or Straight	Bond
Cost per drink	$0.13	$0.193
Selling price (100% mark-up on cost)	.26	.386
Selling price (200% mark-up on cost)	.39	.579
Selling price (300% mark-up on cost)	.52	.772

Since drink prices are usually rounded out to the nickel, the blend or straight would retail per one-ounce drink for anywhere from 25¢ to 55¢ or higher, and the bond would retail for 40¢, 50¢, 60¢, 75¢ or higher.

Let us assume that a bar retails the blend or straight at 50¢ per one-ounce drink and the bond at 75¢. The gross profit on quarts, by the case and by the bottle, is as follows, compared with package store gross profits (spillage and other losses not calculated):

	Case		Bottle	
	Store	Bar	Store	Bar
Blend or Straight	$14.81	$142.01	$1.23	$11.83
Bond	21.85	213.85	1.82	17.82

When it comes to determining prices for mixed drinks—manhattans, martinis, old-fashioneds, etc.—the process becomes more involved. The cost of other alcoholic beverages (e.g., vermouth), non-alcoholic beverages (e.g., club soda, ginger ale), and other ingredients (e.g., fruit, sugar, ice), must be considered.

5. Price Classes

In comparing price classes, we will use New York fifth prices as a standard of comparison. A shift in federal taxes or in customs duties will change the prices shown here. However, the relationship between these prices will remain approximately the same.

Most distilled spirits sell from $3 to $8, with the great bulk of sales in the middle-price bracket of $4 to $4.50.

The table below provides a general idea of the price classes into which most of the largest-selling brands of distilled spirits fall.

Retail 5th Price	Whiskey	Gin	Cordials	Brandy	Rum	Vodka
$3-4	—	x	x	—	x	—
4.05	x	—	x	—	—	—
4.05-4.40	x	x	x	—	x	x
4.40-4.50	x	—	x	x	x	—
4.50-5	x	—	x	x	x	x
5-5.50	x	—	x	x	—	—
5.50-6	x	x	x	x	x	—
6-6.50	x	—	x	x	x	—
6.50-7	x	—	x	x	—	—
7-8	x	—	x	x	—	—

WHISKEY. The most important price classes for whiskey by types are indicated below:

Retail 5th Price	Spirit Blends	Blends of Straights	Straights	Bonds	Canadian	Scotch	Irish
$3-4	—	—	—	—	—	—	—
4.04	x	—	x	—	—	—	—
4.05-4.40	x	—	—	—	—	—	—
4.40-4.50	x	x	x	x	—	—	—
4.50-5	x	—	x	x	—	—	—
5-5.50	x	x	—	—	—	—	—
5.50-6	—	x	x	x	x	x	x
6-6.50	—	—	x	x	x	x	x
6.50-7	—	x	x	x	x	x	x
7-8	—	—	—	—	—	x	x

Few brands are sold below the $4 mark. Whiskey is sold in greatest volume in the $4.05 and $4.40 to $4.50 price ranges. As referred to by the trade, these are the "B" and "A" price classes, respectively. Most "B" whiskies are spirit blends, with straights also showing volume. Among "A" whiskies, both spirit blends and straights sell heavily, with blends outselling the straights. Some volume is attained by blends of straights in this class, and by low-priced bonds. Slightly above this range, other low-priced bonds account for additional volume. In the "A-plus" or "AA" class, blends at approximately $4.85 and $5.15 are significant, as are middle-priced straights and blends of straights. In the $5.50 to $6 range, lower-priced Canadian, Scotch and Irish whiskies, medium-priced bonds and higher-priced straights show volume. Medium-priced Scotch and Irish whiskies, top-priced Canadian whiskies and some high-priced straights cost between $6 and $6.50. Most premium bonds run about $6.59. Top-priced Scotch and Irish whiskies retail between $7 and $8.

GIN. Most gins range in price from $3.50 to $4. Gilbey's, at $3.99, dominates this category. Gordon's at $4.05, Seagram's Ancient Bottle at $4.20, and Booth's House of Lords (imported) at $5.52 represent volume in other price classes.

CORDIALS. These cut across all price classes. Some domestic brands fall below the $3 mark. Some imported brands sell above the $7, $8 and $9 marks.

BRANDY. Most important domestic brandies fall into a price range of $4.50 to $4.80. Popular prices for Cognac range from about $6.50 to a little over $7. Spanish brandies run somewhat lower.

RUM. Most American and Virgin Islands rums are priced between $3.30 and $4.50. Most Puerto Rican rums are priced between $4.20 and $4.50. Bacardi and Havana Club are the important Cuban rums. Bacardi White and Gold Labels are priced around the $6 mark. Havana Club White and Gold Labels are priced under $5. The important Jamaica rums are priced in the $5.50 to $6 range.

VODKA. Most vodkas are bottled at 80 proof and 100 proof. The former retail between $4 and $4.20, the latter between $4.75 and $5.

PREPARED COCKTAILS. The most important producers, Heublein, retail an extensive line of prepared cocktails between approximately $4.24 and $4.49. Some other producers retail in this price class, but there is also a sizable volume between $2 and $4.

The following list shows some of the important brands on the market today, together with their prices. This is not a complete list, nor does it include all brands retailing at each price and in each price class (prices shown for specific brands, in this and other chapters, may change to some extent within their particular price classes, and in some instances may be switched to other price classes).

$2-$3

$2.29	Old Mr. Boston Manhattan (prepared cocktail)

$3-$4

$3.18	Balzac Creme de Cacao (cordial)
3.32	Old St. Croix, Ron Zorro (Virgin Islands rums)
3.78	Bellow's Cruzan (Virgin Islands rum)
3.87	Hiram Walker's Manhattan (prepared cocktail)
3.95	Brugal (Puerto Rican rum)
3.99	Gilbey's (gin); Old Mr. Boston (flavored gins)

$4-$4.50

$4.05	Imperial, Corby's, PM, Cream of Kentucky, Paul Jones, Carstairs (spirit blends); PM, Ten High, Old Quaker (straights); Gordon's (gin)
4.15	Old Newburyport (American rum)
4.16	Smirnoff (80 proof vodka)
4.20	Seagram's (golden gin)
4.23	Royal Banquet (Scotch type whiskey)
4.24	Arrow (flavored gins), Heublein's Manhattan (prepared cocktail)
4.25	Fleischmann's Preferred, Park & Tilford Reserve (spirit blends); Pilgrim (straight New England rum)
4.29	Carioca (Puerto Rican rum)
4.37	De Kuyper Blackberry (cordial)
4.42	Old Classic (blend of straights); Old Sunny Brook (spirit blend)
4.44	Bacardi (Puerto Rican rum)
4.49	Christopher Columbus (Puerto Rican rum)

$4.50-$5

$4.50	Seagram's 7 Crown, Calvert Reserve, Schenley Reserve (spirit blends); Old Hickory, Old Sunny Brook (straights); Haller's County Fair (bond)
4.51	Aristocrat (brandy)
4.52	Old Stagg (straight)
4.55	Kentucky Bred (straight)
4.59	J. W. Dant (bond); Hartley (American brandy)
4.64	Coronet (brandy)
4.65	Glenmore (straight)
4.68	Havana Club White Label (Cuban rum)
4.74	Laird's (applejack)
4.78	Christian Brothers (brandy)
4.81	Arrow (fruit flavored brandies)
4.84	De Kuyper (fruit flavored brandies)
4.85	Four Roses, Melrose (spirit blends)
4.89	Early Times, Charter Oak (straights); Smirnoff (100 proof vodka)
4.95	Old Crow, Ancient Age (straights)
4.98	Havana Club Gold Label (Cuban rum)
4.99	Old Overholt, Mt. Vernon (bonds)

$5-$5.50

$5.10	Lord Calvert (spirit blend)
5.15	Sir John Schenley (spirit blend)
5.25	Park & Tilford Private Stock (blend of straights)

$5.50-$6

$5.50 Park & Tilford (bond)
5.52 Booth's House of Lords (gin)
5.53 Walker's de Luxe (straight)
5.59 Old Taylor (straight)
5.62 King William IV (Scotch)
5.79 Old Fitzgerald (bond); Whiteley's (Scotch)
5.86 John Jameson (7-year Irish)
5.88 Myers's (Jamaica rum)
5.92 James E. Pepper, Pebbleford (bonds); MacNaughton's, Wiser's (Canadian); Bacardi White Label (Cuban rum)
5.99 Old Crow, Yellowstone (bonds); Harwood's (Canadian)

$6-$6.50

$6.01 Power's (Irish)
6.04 (20 oz.) Strega (Italian liqueur)
6.05 Bacardi Gold Label (Cuban rum)
6.09 Black & White (Scotch)
6.10 Vat 69 (Scotch)
6.12 White Horse (Scotch)
6.13 Dewar's White Label, Gilbey's Spey Royal (Scotches)
6.15 Seagram's VO, Dominion Ten (Canadians); Martin's VVO (Scotch)
6.17 Canadian Club (Canadian)
6.19 Haig & Haig 5-Star (Scotch)
6.20 Old Charter (straight)
6.21 Johnny Walker Red Label (Scotch)
6.23 Teacher's (Scotch)
6.26 Cutty Sark (Scotch)
6.27 Ballantine's (Scotch)
6.39 Paddy's (Irish); Southern Comfort (specialty)
6.40 Kentucky Tavern (bond)
6.42 Pedro Domecq (Spanish brandy)

$6.50-$7

$6.59 Old Grand-Dad, Old Taylor, I. W. Harper, Old Forester (bonds)
6.79 House of Lords (Scotch)
6.80 Otard (cognac)
6.96 Bisquit (cognac)
6.99 Monnet (cognac)

$7-$7.50

$7.01 Martell 3-Star, Remy Martin 3-Star (cognacs)
7.02 John Jameson (12-year Irish)
7.09 Courvoisier 3-Star (cognac)
7.15 Hennessy 3-Star (cognac)
7.16 Old Bushmill's (9-year Irish)
7.22 Cusenier Anisette (cordial)
7.24 Amer Picon (specialty)
7.42 Johnny Walker Black Label (Scotch)
7.43 Dewar's Victoria Vat (Scotch)
7.45 Pernod (specialty)

$7.50–$8

$7.59 Haig & Haig Pinch (Scotch)
7.79 King's Ransom (Scotch)
7.86 Chivas Regal (Scotch)

$8–$9

$8.23 Chartreuse Yellow (cordial)
8.31 (24 oz.) Cherry Heering (cordial)
8.74 Grand Marnier (cordial)
8.99 (23 oz.) Benedictine, B.B. (cordials)

$9–$10

$9.20 (23 oz.) Drambuie (Scotch liqueur)
9.32 Chartreuse Green (cordial)

CHAPTER NINE

Sales and Sales Patterns

We are ready now to examine the major sales patterns which obtain for distilled spirits in this country. First, some general observations:

1. Four distilling organizations dominate national liquor sales volume.

2. Whiskey is far and away the top-selling class of spirits, selling about nine times as much as gin, its nearest competitor.

3. Whiskey and gin together account for more than 90% of the sale of all spirits.

4. Domestic whiskey alone accounts for about 70% of total sales.

5. Among domestic whiskies, about two-thirds of the volume is in spirit blends, with straights in second place.

6. Imported whiskey accounts for somewhat over 10% of total distilled spirits sales, outselling every class of domestic and imported spirits except domestic whiskey.

7. Most imported whiskey is Scotch and Canadian, with Irish whiskey an insignificant third in sales.

8. All other imported spirits combined, i.e., imported gin, cordials, brandy and rum, account for only about 2% of total distilled spirits sales.

9. More spirits are sold in December than in any other month, with the exception of gin and vodka. These liquors achieve largest single-month sales during the summer.

10. More spirits are sold in the fifth size than in any other size. In terms of gallonage, about one-half of total volume is in fifths. Pints are next in importance, accounting for about one-fourth of total gallonage. Quarts and half-pints make up the bulk of the remaining volume, with more spirits sold in half-pints than in quarts.

11. Off-premise retail outlets sell about twice the quantity of

spirits sold by on-premise outlets (despite the fact that there are about five on-premise outlets to every three off-premise outlets).

12. Total gallonage sales of distilled spirits vary from year to year. In recent years, annual gallonage has not fluctuated greatly, and has been in close proximity to the 200-million gallon mark. This is roughly the equivalent of 75 million cases.

We will now discuss sales and sales patterns in detail. First, we will become acquainted with major producers and importers, together with their leading brands. Next we will examine the sales picture for distilled spirits as a whole. Thereafter we will discuss and compare the sales of important classes, types and brands of spirits.

Sales and sales relationship are expressed throughout in terms of percentages, lists of leading states and brands, etc. These percentages and lists are based on case and gallonage sales which are current at the time this chapter is written, and will necessarily change as case and gallonage statistics change. However they cannot be expected to change so quickly, or to such a degree, as to affect drastically, in the years just ahead, the general sales picture which they are intended to represent. For example, let us examine the sales picture of:

	% Sales All Whiskies
Spirit blends	55.9
*Straights	21.5
*Bonds	8.4
Scotches	7.2
Canadians	5.6
Blends of straights	1.2
Other whiskies	0.2
	100.0

Although the percentages in this table will vary, major sales relationships which they disclose can be expected to obtain for some time. Thus, the following eventualities are probable in the highest degree:

Spirit blends will continue for years to outsell every other type of whiskey; straight whiskies will indefinitely outsell all types of whiskey other than spirit blends; other classifications will not overtake blends

* In all tables, for purposes of simplification, the words "straight" and "bond" (or "bonded") are used (as they are used throughout this volume in accordance with general practice) as abbreviated forms for "unbonded straight whiskey" and "bottled in bond straight whiskey," respectively.

or straights, and if any passes the 10% mark, it will not do so by any significant amount.

Minor sales relationships can be expected to change, of course. For example, bonds may gain or lose with respect to straights; Canadian whiskies may overtake or fall further behind Scotch whiskies; blends of straights may rise or fall slightly.

In a nutshell, the primary value of the percentage figures and the lists of sales leaders which appear in the following pages, and the primary purpose for which they are intended, are to indicate general sales relationships and to provide a basis for the study of future sales relationships. An understanding of such relationships, of course, is of basic importance to the liquor marketing and advertising man.

1. Major Producers and Importers

The "Big Four" in the liquor industry today, as at the time of repeal, are Seagram, National, Schenley and Walker, each of which operates as a distiller, rectifier and importer. In terms of annual dollar sales volume, Seagram, the leader, has averaged between $700 and $800 million. National, in second place, has averaged between $400 and $500 million. Schenley, in third place, has also averaged between $400 and $500 million. Hiram Walker has averaged between $300 and $400 million. Advertising expenditures per company are estimated as ranging from upwards of $5 million to approximately $25 million annually.

As might be expected, the bulk of business of each of these organizations is in the field of domestic whiskies. Seagram's, with its commanding lead, has achieved its position primarily with spirit blends, and has not entered the straight whiskey field. National, which built its reputation on Kentucky straights and bonds, today markets straights, bonds and blends, both Kentuckies and northerns. Schenley also markets Kentucky and northern straights, bonds and blends. Hiram Walker's primary brands are non-Kentucky straights and blends.

Leading brands marketed by the "Big Four":

DISTILLERS CORP.-SEAGRAMS, LTD.: Calvert Reserve, Carstairs, Four Roses, Gallagher & Burton's, Hunter, Kessler, Lord Calvert, Paul Jones, Seagram's 7 Crown, Wilson (domestic whiskies); Seagram's VO (Canadian whiskey); Chivas Regal, White Horse (Scotch whiskies); Seagram's Ancient Bottle, Calvert's Gin (domestic gins); Cusenier (imported cordials); Christopher Columbus Puerto Rican Rum.

NATIONAL DISTILLERS PRODUCTS CORPORATION: Bellows Partners Choice, Bellows Club Bourbon, Bond & Lillard, Bourbon de Luxe, Century Club, Hill & Hill, Mount Vernon, Old Crow, Old Dover, Old Grand-Dad, Old Hermitage, Old Log Cabin, Old Overholt, Old Sunny Brook, Old Taylor, PM (domestic whiskies); Dominion Ten (Canadian whiskey); King George IV (Scotch whisky); Gilbey's Gin (domestic); de Kuyper Cordials (domestic); Monnet Cognac; Merito Puerto Rican Rum; de Kuyper Vodka (domestic).

SCHENLEY INDUSTRIES, INC.: Ancient Age, Belmont, Cascade, Cream of Kentucky, J. W. Dant, Echo Springs, Gibson, Golden Wedding, I. W. Harper, Melrose, Old Charter, Old Quaker, Old Stagg, Park & Tilford brands (Bottled in Bond, Kentucky Bred, Private Stock, Reserve), Pebbleford, James E. Pepper, Schenley Reserve, Sir John Schenley, Three Feathers, Wilken Family (domestic whiskies); MacNaughton's (Canadian whiskey); Dewar's (Scotch whisky); Du Bouchett (domestic cordials); Marie Brizard (imported cordials); Coronet (domestic brandy); Otard Cognac; Carioca Puerto Rican Rum; Samovar Vodka (domestic).

HIRAM WALKER-GOODERHAM & WORTS, LTD.: Corby's Reserve, G. & W, Imperial, Ten High, Senator Corby, Walker's de Luxe (domestic whiskies); Canadian Club (Canadian whiskey); Old Smuggler (Scotch whisky); John Jameson (Irish whiskey); Hiram Walker's Gin (domestic); Drambuie Liqueur (imported); Hiram Walker's Cordials (domestic); Courvoisier Cognac; Hiram Walker's Vodka (domestic).

Top competitors of the "Big Four" are Publicker, Brown-Forman, Glenmore, Standard Brands, Renfield and Heublein.
Leading brands of each:

BROWN-FORMAN DISTILLERS CORP.: Early Times, King, Old Forester (domestic whiskies).

GLENMORE DISTILLERIES CO., INC.: Glenmore, Kentucky Tavern, Old Thompson, Yellowstone (domestic whiskies); House of Lords, King's Ransom (Scotch whiskies).

G. F. HEUBLEIN & BRO., INC.: Smirnoff Vodka; Heublein's Club Cocktails.

PUBLICKER INDUSTRIES, INC.: Charter Oak, Haller's County Fair, Kinsey, Old Classic, Old Hickory, Philadelphia, Planter's Club, Rittenhouse (domestic whiskies); Dixie Belle Gin (domestic).

RENFIELD IMPORTERS, LTD.: Old Discovery (domestic whiskey); Haig & Haig, King William IV (Scotch whiskies); Gordon's Gin (domestic); Cointreau Liqueurs (domestic); Remy Martin Cognac.

STANDARD BRANDS, INC.: Fleischmann Preferred (domestic whiskey); Black & White (Scotch whisky); Fleischmann's Gin (domestic).

Next in sales, marketing and advertising importance among producers, importers and other vendors, along with leading brands of each:

AMERICAN DISTILLING CO., INC.: Bourbon Supreme, Guckenheimer, Old American, Stillbrook (domestic whiskies).

ARROW LIQUEURS CORP.: Arrow Cordials (domestic); Arrow Vodka (domestic).

AUSTIN, NICHOLS & CO., INC.: Grant's (Scotch whisky); Mouquin Cordials (domestic).

BACARDI IMPORTS, INC.: Bacardi Rum; Gilbey's Spey Royal (Scotch whisky).

JAMES B. BEAM DISTILLING CO.: Jim Beam (domestic whiskey).

CANADA DRY GINGER ALE, INC.: Johnny Walker (Scotch whisky).

FROMM & SICHEL, INC.: Christian Brothers Brandy (domestic).

MCKESSON & ROBBINS, INC.: Chapin & Gore (domestic whiskey); Highland Queen, Martin's VVO (Scotch whiskies).

SCHIEFFELIN & CO.: Teacher's (Scotch whisky); Hennessy Cognac; Don Q Puerto Rican Rum.

SOUTHERN COMFORT CORP.: Southern Comfort (domestic specialty liqueur).

STITZEL-WELLER DISTILLERY, INC.: Cabin Still, Old Fitzgerald (domestic whiskies).

JULIUS WILE SONS & CO., INC.: Peter Dawson (Scotch whisky); Benedictine, B & B (imported liqueurs).

Among remaining important producers, importers and other vendors are Angostura-Wupperman Corporation (Angostura Bitters); Berke Bros. Distilleries, Inc. (Old Mr. Boston products); R.U. Delapenha Co., Inc. (Myers's Jamaica rum); H. Harvey & Co. (Harwood's Canadian whiskey); Hudson's Bay Co. (Hudson's Bay Canadian and

Scotch whiskies); Medley Distilling Co., Inc. (Medley whiskies); Twenty-One Brands, Inc. (Club Special, Ballantine's Scotch); Waterfill & Frazier Distillery Co. (Waterfill & Frazier whiskey).

2. Sales of Distilled Spirits

We will observe sales of distilled spirits from the viewpoints of open states and monopoly states, individual states, domestic and imported spirits, periods of the year, container sizes, retail outlets.

OPEN AND MONOPOLY STATES. Open states account for approximately 70%, and monopoly states 30%, of total sales of distilled spirits.

INDIVIDUAL STATES. The wet states are listed on page 118 in the order of sales volume.

DOMESTIC AND IMPORTED SPIRITS. Domestic spirits account for about 87% of total sales; imported spirits, 13%.

MONTHLY, QUARTERLY AND SEMI-ANNUAL SALES.* Sales for all distilled spirits usually run from 7% to 8% of the year's total during each of the first nine months of the year, with slight peaks in May and August. In October and November sales are approximately 9%, and in December turn up sharply to about 14%. The following is a percentage breakdown for a typical year:

January	7.0%	July	7.2%
February	7.4%	August	8.4%
March	7.4%	September	7.8%
April	7.4%	October	8.9%
May	8.2%	November	9.2%
June	7.0%	December	14.1%

A rough percentage by quarters breaks down as follows:

1st quarter	22%
2nd "	23%
3rd "	23%
4th "	32%

Semi-annually:

1st half	45%
2nd "	55%

* See also chart on page 119.

	% Total Sales	Rank in Wet Population
1. New York	12.0	1
2. California	10.5	2
3. Illinois	6.6	4
4. Ohio (M)	5.7	5
5. Pennsylvania (M)	5.2	3
6. Michigan (M)	4.2	6
7. New Jersey	4.2	7
8. Texas	3.9	9
9. Massachusetts	3.4	8
10. Florida	3.1	17
11. Virginia (M)	3.0	13
12. Missouri	2.6	10
13. Connecticut	2.2	21
14. District of Columbia	2.2	33
15. Wisconsin	2.1	12
16. Louisiana	2.1	18
17. North Carolina (M)	2.0	23
18. Minnesota	1.9	14
19. Maryland	1.9	19
20. Georgia	1.7	28
21. Indiana	1.6	11
22. Washington (M)	1.5	16
23. Kentucky	1.5	26
24. Tennessee	1.3	30
25. Kansas	1.0	32
26. Iowa (M)	1.1	15
27. Oregon (M)	1.1	25
28. West Virginia (M)	1.0	22
29. Alabama (M)	1.0	24
30. South Carolina	1.0	20
31. Colorado	0.9	29
32. Nebraska	0.8	27
33. Arkansas	0.6	31
34. Maine (M)	0.6	37
35. New Hampshire (M)	0.5	43
36. Arizona	0.5	35
37. Montana (M)	0.5	41
38. Rhode Island	0.4	34
39. Delaware	0.4	44
40. South Dakota	0.3	38
41. North Dakota	0.3	40
42. New Mexico	0.3	39
43. Nevada	0.3	47
44. Idaho (M)	0.3	42
45. Utah (M)	0.3	36
46. Vermont (M)	0.2	45
47. Wyoming (M)	0.2	46
	100.0	

(M)=Monopoly state

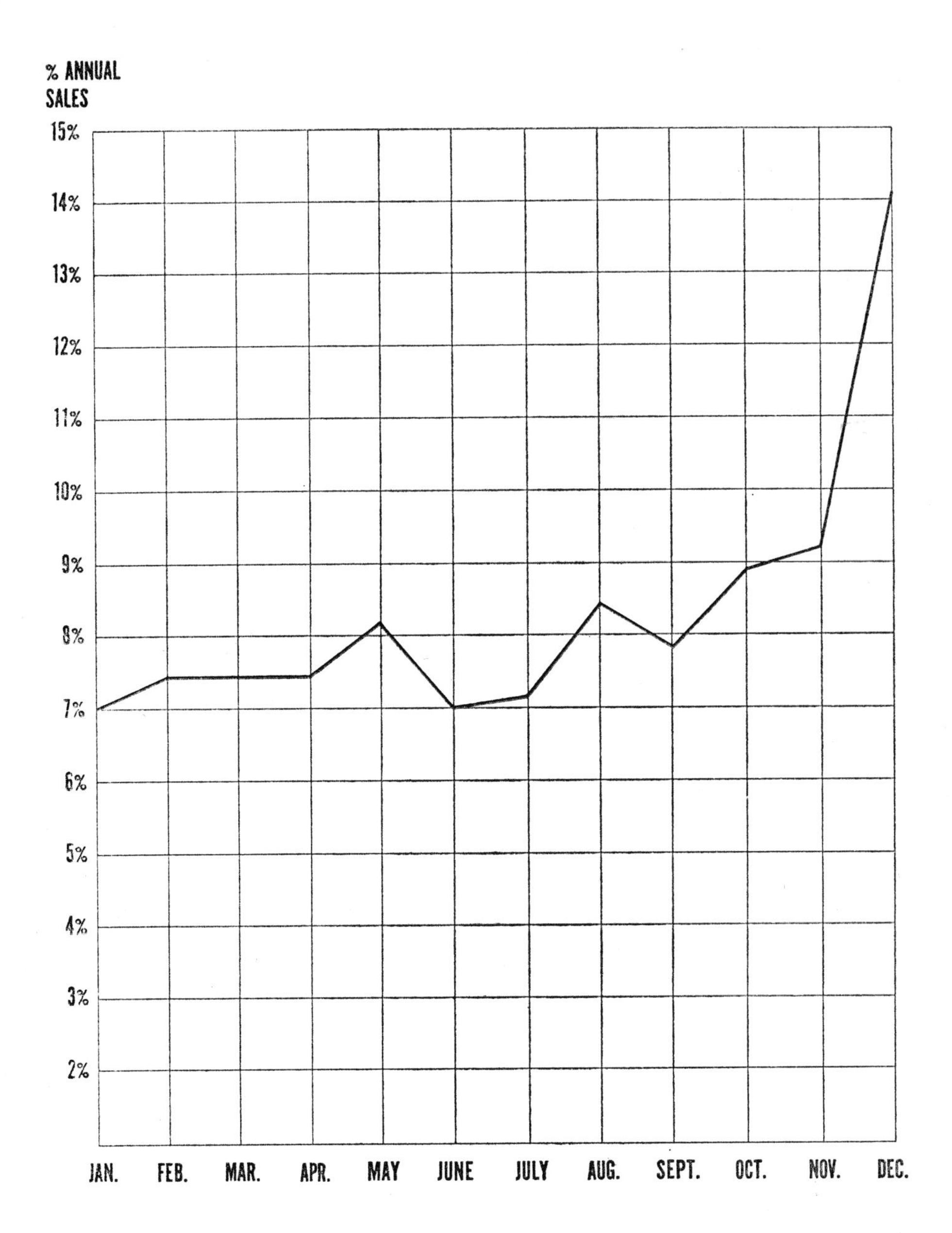

SALES OF DISTILLED SPIRITS BY MONTHS

SALES BY SIZES. Sales of distilled spirits by sizes are in approximately these proportions:

	By Number of Bottles	By Number of Wine Gallons
Less than ½ pint	3.7%	0.4%
½ pint	31.8%	15.1%
⅘ pint	1.2%	0.9%
1 pint	24.8%	23.2%
⅘ quart	32.1%	48.4%
Quart	6.2%	11.6%
Other sizes (¾ pt., ¾ qt., ½ gal., 1 gal.)	0.2%	0.4%
	100.0%	100.0%

SALES BY RETAIL OUTLETS. Off-premise outlets sell approximately 65% of all distilled spirits; on-premise outlets, 35%. The average off-premise outlet outsells the average on-premise outlet by more than 3 to 1.

3. Comparative Sales of Classes of Spirit

Whiskey and gin account for more than 90% of all sales of distilled spirits. Cordials rank third, followed by brandy, rum and vodka. Approximate percentage of sales for each class of spirits:

Whiskey	82.3%
Gin	8.9%
*Cordials	3.4%
Brandy	2.0%
Rum	1.5%
Vodka	1.4%
**Other spirits	0.5%
	100.0%

OPEN AND MONOPOLY STATES. The ratio of sales in open and monopoly states is approximately as follows:

	Open States	Monopoly States
Whiskey	70%	30%
Gin	76%	24%
Cordials	81%	19%
Brandy	85%	15%
Rum	80%	20%
Vodka	85%	15%

* The term "cordials" throughout this chapter will include liqueurs, flavored brandies, flavored gins and specialties of the cordial type.

** Under this designation are included prepared cocktails, bitters, and miscellaneous spirits, e.g., tequila, akvavit.

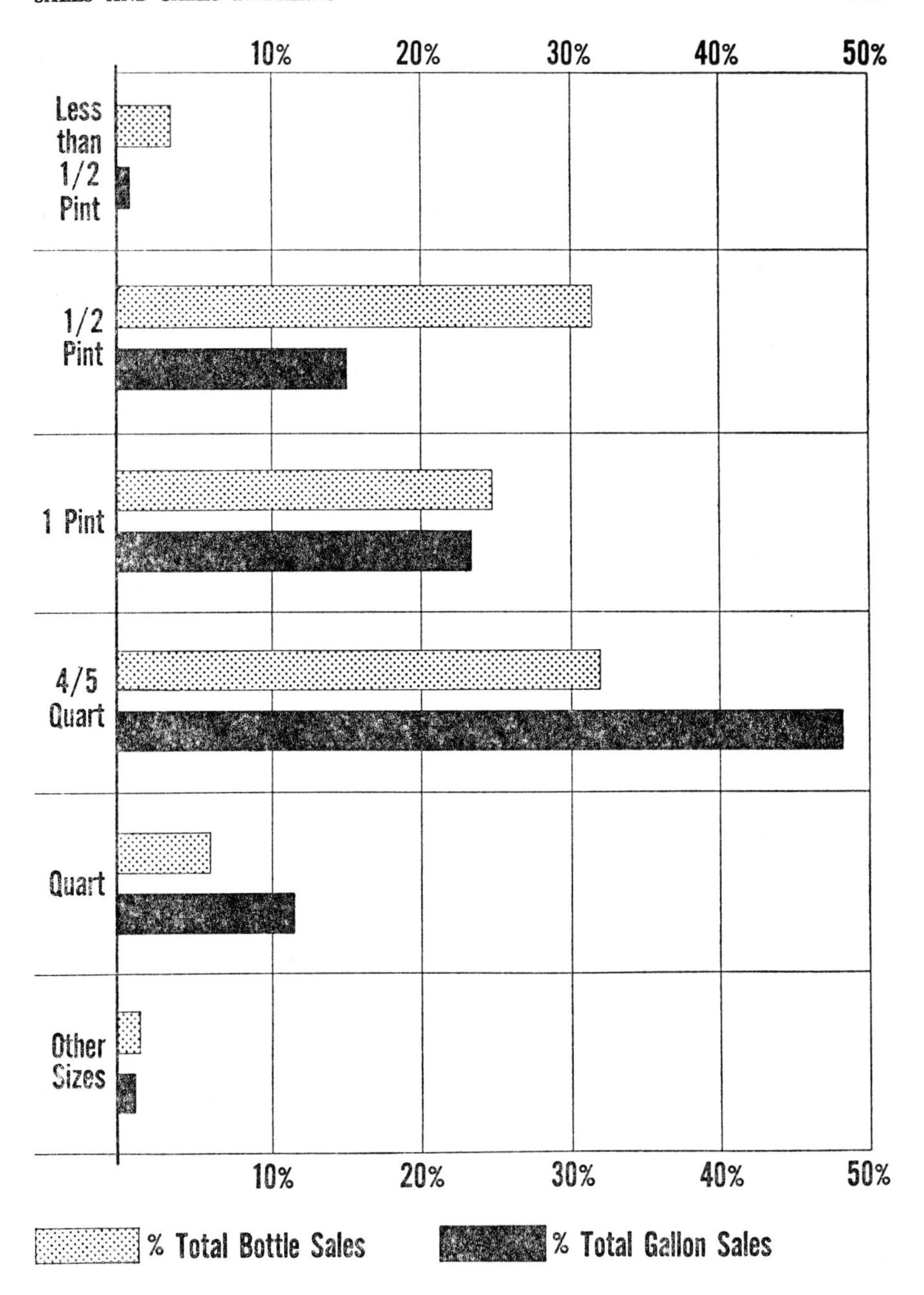

SALES OF DISTILLED SPIRITS BY SIZES

INDIVIDUAL STATES. In the following table, numerals indicate the sales rank in each state of the class of spirits specified. Relative rank may change from time to time, especially with respect to cordials, brandy, rum and vodka, but most rankings may be expected to remain stable:

	Whiskey	Gin	Cordials	Brandy	Rum	Vodka
Alabama	1	2	3	6	4	5
Arizona	1	2	4	6	5	3
Arkansas	1	2	3	6	4	5
California	1	2	4	5	6	3
Colorado	1	2	4	6	5	3
Connecticut	1	2	3	4	5	6
Delaware	1	2	3	5	4	6
D.C.	1	2	3	4	5	6
Florida	1	2	4	5	3	6
Georgia	1	2	3	6	5	4
Idaho	1	3	4	6	5	2
Illinois	1	2	3	4	6	5
Indiana	1	2	3	4	5	6
Iowa	1	2	3	4	5	6
Kansas	1	2	3	6	5	4
Kentucky	1	2	4	3	5	6
Louisiana	1	2	3	6	4	5
Maine	1	2	5	4	3	6
Maryland	1	2	3	4	5	6
Massachusetts	1	2	3	4	5	6
Michigan	1	2	3	4	5	6
Minnesota	1	2	4	3	5	*
Missouri	1	2	3	6	4	5
Montana	1	2	3	5	6	4
Nebraska	1	2	3	4	6	5
Nevada	1	2	4	6	5	3
New Hampshire	1	2	5	4	3	6
New Jersey	1	2	3	5	4	6
New Mexico	1	2	4	6	5	3
New York	1	2	3	4	5	6
North Carolina	1	2	3	4	5	6
North Dakota	1	3	2	4	6	5
Ohio	1	2	3	5	4	6
Oregon	1	2	4	6	5	3
Pennsylvania	1	2	3	4	5	6
Rhode Island	1	2	3	4	5	6
South Carolina	1	2	3	6	5	4
South Dakota	1	2	3	4	6	5
Tennessee	1	2	3	6	5	4
Texas	1	2	3	6	4	5
Utah	1	2	4	5	6	3
Vermont	1	2	5	4	3	6
Virginia	1	2	3	5	4	6
Washington	1	2	5	6	4	3
West Virginia	1	2	3	4	5	6
Wisconsin	1	3	4	2	6	5
Wyoming	1	2	3	5	6	4

*Vodka is not marketed in Minnesota.

The table indicates several facts regarding the relative popularity in individual states and regions of the various classes of spirits.

Whiskey: Ranks first in all states.

Gin: Ranks second in all but a few states.

Cordials: In third place in most states. Weakest showing compared to other classes of spirits is in western states and New England.

Brandy: Ranks from second place in one state (Wisconsin) to sixth place in sixteen states.

Rum: Does not rank above third in any state. In fifth place in about one-half the states.

Vodka: Ranks third after whiskey and gin in many western states. In one western state, Idaho, it ranks second.

In terms of total sales, the pattern changes, as indicated by the following table, which lists the ten leading states, in approximate order of sales volume, for each class of spirits:

All Spirits	Whiskey	Gin	Cordials	Brandy	Rum	Vodka
N.Y.	N.Y.	N.Y.	N.Y.	N.Y.	N.Y.	Calif.
Calif.	Calif.	Ill.	Ill.	Wis.	Calif.	Ill.
Ill.	Ill.	Calif.	Calif.	Calif.	Ill.	N.Y.
Ohio	Ohio	Ohio	N.J.	Ill.	N.J.	Wash.
Pa.	Pa.	N.J.	Mich.	N.J.	Mass.	N.J.
Mich.	Mich.	Mich.	Mass.	Mass.	Fla.	Ore.
N.J.	N.J.	Pa.	Pa.	Minn.	Conn.	Tex.
Tex.	Tex.	Fla.	Wis.	Conn.	Pa.	Fla.
Mass.	Mass.	Tex.	Conn.	Mich.	Ohio	Mass.
Fla.	Va.	Mo.	Md.	Pa.	Me.	Ariz.

DOMESTIC AND IMPORTED SPIRITS. The following is a breakdown of sales of domestic and imported spirits:

	Domestic	Imported
Whiskey	87%	13%
Gin	99%	1%
Cordials	96%	4%
Brandy	75%	25%
Rum	15%	85%*
Vodka	100%	--
All spirits	87%	13%

* Includes Puerto Rican and Virgin Island rums.

In order of sales volume, domestic and imported spirits rank as follows:

	% Sales All Spirits
Domestic whiskey	71.7
Imported whiskey	10.6
Domestic gin	8.8
Domestic cordials	3.3
Domestic brandy	1.5
Domestic vodka	1.4
Imported rum	1.3
Imported brandy	0.5
Domestic rum	0.2
Imported gin	0.1
Imported cordials	0.1
Other spirits	0.5
	100.0

Relative sales of domestic and imported spirits may also be regarded from this viewpoint:

	Domestic	Imported	Total
Whiskey	71.7%	10.6%	82.3%
Gin	8.8%	0.1%	8.9%
Cordials	3.3%	0.1%	3.4%
Brandy	1.5%	0.5%	2.0%
Rum	0.2%	1.3%	1.5%
Vodka	1.4%	--	1.4%
Other spirits	0.4%	0.1%	0.5%
	87.3%	12.7%	100.0%

Among the sales relationships indicated by the tables above are the following:

With the exception of rum, each class of domestic spirits outsells each class of imported spirits, with sales of gin and vodka almost exclusively in the domestic category.

While imported rum outsells, by 2 to 1, imported gin, cordials and brandy combined, it is itself outsold by imported whiskey by approximately 8 to 1.

Imported whiskey outsells all other imported spirits combined by approximately 5 to 1, but is itself outsold by domestic whiskey by approximately 7 to 1.

MONTHLY, QUARTERLY AND SEMI-ANNUAL SALES. The following indicates the approximate monthly percentage of sales for each class of spirits:

	Whiskey	Gin	Cordials	Brandy	Rum	Vodka
January	7.2%	5.4%	7.6%	7.6%	6.5%	7%
February	7.6	5.5	7.1	7.2	6.0	7
March	7.6	5.6	6.9	7.2	6.0	7
April	7.6	6.3	7.1	7.2	7.0	7
May	8.3	7.9	6.8	7.4	7.0	8
June	6.8	10.2	6.0	5.8	8.0	10
July	6.5	13.4	6.0	5.9	9.2	11
August	8.0	11.5	7.6	5.9	8.2	11
September	7.5	9.7	7.7	6.9	7.2	8
October	9.1	7.8	9.1	8.7	6.7	7
November	9.5	7.3	9.9	9.9	7.7	8
December	14.3	9.4	18.2	20.3	20.5	9

Quarterly:	Whiskey	Gin	Cordials	Brandy	Rum	Vodka
1st Quarter	22%	17%	22%	22%	18%	21%
2nd "	23	24	20	20	22	25
3rd "	22	35	21	19	25	30
4th "	33	24	37	39	35	24
Semi-annually:						
1st half	45%	41%	42%	42%	40%	46%
2nd "	55	59	58	58	60	54

4. Whiskey Sales

For purposes of convenient reference, major sales statistics concerning whiskey as a class of spirits are repeated:

SALES OF WHISKEY AS A CLASS OF SPIRITS

a. *National market.* Whiskey ranks first in national sales, and accounts for approximately 82% of total distilled spirits sales.

b. *Open and monopoly states.* 70% of whiskey is sold in open states, 30% in monopoly states.

c. *Individual states.* Whiskey ranks first in all states. The ten leading whiskey states are New York, California, Illinois, Ohio, Pennsylvania, Michigan, New Jersey, Texas, Massachusetts and Virginia. These states account for approximately 60% of total whiskey volume.

d. *Domestic and imported whiskies*

	% Sales All Whiskies	% Sales All Spirits
Domestic	87.1	71.7
Imported	12.9	10.6
	100.0	82.3

e. *Monthly, quarterly and semi-annual sales*

January	7.2%	July	6.5%
February	7.6%	August	8.0%
March	7.6%	September	7.5%
April	7.6%	October	9.1%
May	8.3%	November	9.5%
June	6.8%	December	14.3%

Quarterly:

1st quarter	— 22%
2nd "	— 23%
3rd "	— 22%
4th "	— 33%

Semi-annually:

1st half	— 45%
2nd "	— 55%

It will be observed that, except for a slight summer valley, sales maintain a fairly steady monthly level before peaking up sharply during the last quarter of the year.

SALES OF WHISKEY BY TYPES AND BRANDS

a. *National market.* The following, in the order of sales volume, are the major types of whiskey on the market today:

	% Sales All Whiskies	% Sales All Spirits
Spirit blends	55.9%	46.0%
Straights	21.5%	17.7%
Bonds	8.4%	6.9%
Scotches	7.2%	5.9%
Canadians	5.6%	4.6%
Blends of straights	1.2%	1.0%
Other whiskies (Irish, corn, Scotch type, etc.)	0.2%	0.2%
	100.0%	82.3%

The following is a breakdown of sales of domestic whiskies:

	% Sales Domestic Whiskies
Spirit blends	64.1%
Straights	24.7%
Bonds	9.6%
Blends of straights	1.4%
Other domestic whiskies	0.2%
	100.0%

The following is a breakdown of sales of imported whiskies:

	% Sales Imported Whiskies
Scotch	56.0%
Canadian	43.6%
Irish	0.4%
	100.0%

Among straight whiskies, approximately 90% is bourbon. Among bonded whiskies, approximately 98% is bourbon. Hence it may be observed that the largest selling whiskies on the market today are spirit blends, straight bourbons, bonded bourbons, Scotch and Canadian. Placing other types in the "other whiskies" column, we arrive at the following:

	% Sales All Whiskies	% Sales All Spirits
Spirit blends	55.9%	46.0%
Straight bourbons	19.3%	15.9%
Bonded bourbons	8.2%	6.8%
Scotch whiskies	7.2%	5.9%
Canadian whiskies	5.6%	4.6%
Other whiskies	3.8%	3.1%
	100.0%	82.3%

1. *Spirit blends.* This type of whiskey outsells all other whiskies, and, in fact, all other types of spirits. In the whiskey category, spirit blends sell more than double the quantity of the runner up, straight whiskey. Blends have not always held the lead, however. While more blended whiskey than straight whiskey was marketed prior to Prohibition, straight whiskey took the lead after Repeal, outselling blends by approximately 50%. Just before World War II, straights increased their lead, outselling blends by about two to one. During the war, when it became necessary to stretch available whiskey supplies, many straights were converted into blends. As a result, before the war was over, blends regained their lead. In the late 1940's, while straights which were produced after the war were still aging, and while marketable straights continued to diminish, blends kept increasing their lead. By 1950, blends were outselling straights by about eight to one. As straights distilled in post-war years began reaching the market, the blend lead was gradually whittled down. Blends have continued to

lose volume, while straights have continued to gain volume. Moreover, blends have been declining at a more rapid rate than straights have been accelerating (thus indicating a trend not only to straights but to other spirits). It is a definite possibility, if not a probability, that straights will eventually outsell blends.

Most spirit blends are labeled and marketed as Kentucky Blended Whiskey or simply as Blended Whiskey. Under the latter designation, some brands contain Kentucky whiskey, others do not. Brands labeled "Blended Whiskey" dominate the spirits blend market, enjoying their greatest popularity in the area north of the Mason Dixon line and east of the Alleghenies. Brands labeled "Kentucky Blended Whiskey" reveal a different sales pattern, with greater relative strength in other parts of the country. In this sense, they follow the sales pattern of straight whiskies in general and Kentucky straights in particular.

Variations in sales patterns may be noted with respect to price. It will be recalled that volume sales of spirit blends are in the A and B price classes (approximately $4.50 and $4.05, respectively, for New York fifths). A blends outsell B blends throughout the country (before the war, the opposite was true). B blends are most popular in the primary blend territory in the East. In the remainder of the country, A's outsell B's conclusively.

Among A blends, the market is dominated by brands labeled "Blended Whiskey." Belonging to this category are the largest selling whiskey brands (also the largest selling brands among all classes of spirits): Seagram's 7 Crown, Calvert Reserve and Schenley Reserve. Seagram's 7 Crown is a sales phenomenon. This brand alone accounts for about 15% of the sale of all whiskies, and more than 10% of the sale of all spirits. It outsells its nearest competitor, Calvert Reserve (also a Seagram brand) by two to three times. Only a dozen or so whiskies manage to sell over a million cases annually. Seagram's 7 Crown has been selling in the eight million range.

Next in sales volume to A blends labeled "Blended Whiskey" are B blends labeled "Blended Whiskey." The leaders in this classification are Imperial (Hiram Walker), Corby's Reserve (Hiram Walker), PM (National Distillers), Carstairs (Seagram), Paul Jones (Seagram), Old Thompson (Glenmore).

The top-selling Kentucky Blended Whiskey in the A range (also sold as a Kentucky straight) is Old Sunny Brook (National Distillers). Other leading Kentucky A blends include Hill & Hill and Bourbon de Luxe (both National, both also sold as Kentucky straights).

Among Kentucky B blends, Cream of Kentucky (Schenley) is the leader.

Between the A and B range, Fleischmann's Preferred (Standard Brands, blended whiskey, $4.25) ranks among national sales leaders.

Among higher priced blends, only one brand, Four Roses (Seagram, blended whiskey, $4.85) has a place among national brand leaders. The leading top-priced blend is Lord Calvert (Seagram, blended whiskey, $5.10).

2. *Straight whiskies.* We have observed that, among straight whiskies, only straight bourbon sells in substantial volume. There is comparatively little call for rye. This situation differs from pre-war days, when rye won great popularity in what was then judged to be the traditional and perennial rye-drinking East.

Straight bourbons amass their greatest relative sales throughout most of the country south of the Mason Dixon line and west of the Alleghenies. Within this region, many states sell more bourbon than blends.

Of the two varieties of straight bourbon, Kentucky and northern, the former dominates the bourbon market.

Price-wise, most straight bourbon is sold at the same price as A blends. But whereas B blends account for tremendous volume, B straights account for a good deal less volume, and fail to place any brands among national sales leaders.

Among leading brands of straights in the A price range are the following:

Kentucky bourbons—Old Stagg (Schenley), Echo Springs (Schenley), Old Sunny Brook (National).

Northern bourbons—Old Hickory (Publicker), Old American (American), Century Club (National).

Among straights in the B range, northerns lead: PM (National), Old Quaker (Schenley). Among Kentucky B straights, Olde Bourbon (Schenley) represents some volume.

The nation's largest selling brands of straight bourbon retail above the A price but below $5: Old Crow (National, Kentucky, $4.95) and Early Times (Brown-Forman, Kentucky, $4.89). The largest selling brands of blends, it will be recalled, are in the A and B categories.

While age has a strong appeal to many bourbon buyers, the largest selling bourbon, Old Crow, and the runner-up, Early Times, both attained leadership with four-year whiskey while lower price straights were marketing and advertising five-, six- and seven-year whiskey.

In taking the lead among straight bourbons, Old Crow created a sensation in the liquor industry. Until well into 1953, the brand was marketed as a bonded whiskey. During that year, the present 86 proof straight was introduced as a companion whiskey to the bond. Aided by one of the most powerful marketing and advertising campaigns ever launched for any brand of spirits, Old Crow 86 proof rose in approximately eight months to a place among top-selling brands of the nation.

Above the $5 mark, Walker's de Luxe (Hiram Walker, northern, $5.53) and Old Taylor (National, Kentucky, $5.59) are important volume brands.

3. *Bonded whiskies.* We have observed that, in the bottled in bond classification, bonded bourbon is the overwhelming favorite. Old Overholt (National, Pennsylvania, $4.99) dominates the small bonded rye field.

Along with free bottled straights, bonded whiskies became less and less available during the war years, and did not return to the market in increasing volume until four years after the war. Today, like the straights, they are in full supply and are advancing in sales.

Both Kentucky and northern bonded bourbons are marketed. Kentucky bonds dominate.

Low-priced bonded bourbons, selling at or somewhat above the A price, chalk up substantial volume, with J. W. Dant (Schenley, Kentucky) the largest selling of all bonded whiskies. This brand skyrocketed to leadership when first introduced in recent years, primarily because it was the first bonded whiskey to be promoted in the A price range. Today it ranks among top-selling brands. County Fair (Publicker, northern) also sells substantially in the low price category.

The bulk of bonded bourbon business, however, is done by higher-priced and premium brands. The nation's largest selling premium bond is Old Grand-Dad (National, Kentucky, $6.59). Other famous brands, all at $6.59, account for sizable volume: Old Taylor (National, Kentucky), I. W. Harper (Schenley, Kentucky), Old Forester (Brown-Forman, Kentucky). Below $6.59, but still above $6, Kentucky Tavern (Glenmore) sells in volume. In the $5.50 to $6 range, leaders include Old Crow (National, Kentucky), Yellowstone (Glenmore, Kentucky), Old Fitzgerald (Stitzel-Weller, Kentucky).

The market for low-priced bourbon bonds generally follows that for straight bourbons. The market for higher-priced bonds differs. In addition to the dyed-in-the-wool bond drinker, who likes his bourbon at 100 proof, there is the bond buyer in large metropolitan centers who calls for higher-priced bonded bourbon for reasons of sophistication, or because it represents prestige whiskey. This point may be illustrated by comparing the ten leading straight bourbon states with the ten leading bond states. Four states appear in the bond column which do not appear in the straight column: Kentucky, New York, Pennsylvania, and Indiana. We know that Kentucky consumes more bonded bourbon than any other state (primarily because it is the home state for Kentucky bourbon). The other three states tell a different story. New York, Pennsylvania, and Indiana may hardly be considered as prime bourbon territory, yet bonded bourbon consumption in these markets is relatively high.

4. *Blends of straights.* Although blends of straights outsell straight ryes, this class of spirits is not particularly popular, and holds only a small segment of the market. Old Classic (Publicker) in the A price range, and Park & Tilford Private Stock (Schenley) at $5.25, are leading brands.

5. *Scotch.* This type of whisky was little known in this country before Prohibition. During Prohibition, however, Scotch was imported, found to be trustworthy whisky, and gained a foothold which it has maintained and consolidated. During the war and in the years immediately following it, Scotch distillers found their inventories diminishing steadily. As against 150 million imperial gallons of Scotch on hand in 1939, for example, approximately 100 million were on hand in 1949. The period of acute shortage has since passed, and while shortages still exist, the supply situation is gradually returning to normal. The market for Scotch in this country is active and growing.

Price-wise, Scotch was sold at a higher price than premium bonds before the war. Today volume Scotches are priced below premium bonds (approximately $6.15 vs. $6.59).

In the volume price range, the following brands are leaders: Black & White (Standard Brands), White Horse (Seagram), Dewar's White Label (Schenley), Teacher's (Schieffelin), Ballantine's ('21' Brands), Haig & Haig 5-Star (Renfield), Johnnie Walker Red Label (Canada Dry). Among the lower priced, so-called B or secondary Scotches ($5.60-$5.80), King William IV (Renfield) represents volume. Premium Scotches (between $7 and $8) include Chivas Regal (Seagram), Johnnie Walker Black Label, Haig & Haig Pinch Bottle, King's Ransom (Glenmore). Chivas Regal is another example of a whisky which quickly rose from obscurity to sales leadership in recent years. It ranks today as a top selling premium Scotch.

To an even greater extent than high-priced bonds, the market for Scotch is concentrated in large metropolitan centers, e.g., New York, Boston, Chicago, Washington, D.C., Detroit, Los Angeles, San Francisco. Aside from drinkers who genuinely prefer the lightness and smoky taste of Scotch, there is a large group who buy for reasons of sophistication and prestige, as in the case of high-priced bonds. The following states are among the nation's ten top Scotch states; none are among the top ten bond states: California, New Jersey, Massachusetts, Michigan, Florida, District of Columbia.

6. *Canadian whiskies.* Canadian whiskey has always been popular in this country, and along with bonds and Scotch, dominates the higher-priced whiskey market. Volume sales are in the top Canadian price class (approximately $6.15). During the war, Canadian Club, the leader at the time, lost volume as a result of shortages and Seagram's VO moved in to take, and retain, top sales position. The market today is dominated almost completely by these two brands. Among other Canadian whiskies, better known brands are Dominion Ten (National), which retails in the same price class as Canadian Club and VO; MacNaughton's (Schenley, $5.92); Wiser's De Luxe (Standard Brands, $5.92); Harwood's (Harvey, $5.99).

The market for Canadian corresponds roughly to that for Scotch, with sales concentrated in large metropolitan centers. Inasmuch as Canadian is a light, mild blend, it is a favorite with those who want finer, higher-priced whiskey and who dislike the smoky taste of Scotch or the bourbon flavor and high proof of bonds.

Canadian whiskies have shown marked sales vitality. Seagram's VO and Canadian Club rank among the nation's leading whiskey brands, outselling all bonds and Scotches, and some leading blends and straights.

The sales performance of VO and Canadian Club is especially noteworthy when it is considered that these brands, each retailing at $6.15, are priced from $1.20 to $2.10 higher than top-selling non-Canadian brands, such as Seagram's 7 Crown, Calvert Reserve, Schenley Reserve, Imperial, Corby's, Old Crow, Early Times, Old Sunny Brook, and PM.

7. *Irish whiskies.* Although Irish is a fine whiskey, with some similarity to domestic blends, seven years or older and available at $6 or less, it has never won any great popularity in this country. John Jameson (Hiram Walker, $5.86) and Old Bushmill's (Quality Importers, $7.16) are leading brands.

* * * * *

The nation's top selling whiskies, in approximate order of sales, are as follows:

Seagram's 7 Crown	Blend	Seagram
Calvert Reserve	Blend	Seagram
Schenley Reserve	Blend	Schenley
Imperial	Blend	Walker
Corby's	Blend	Walker
Old Crow	Bond and Straight	National
Seagram's VO	Canadian	Seagram
Canadian Club	Canadian	Walker
Old Sunny Brook	Blend and Straight	National
Early Times	Straight	Brown-Forman
PM	Blend and Straight	National
Carstairs	Blend	Seagram
Four Roses	Blend	Seagram
Old Stagg	Straight	Schenley
Paul Jones	Blend	Seagram
Fleischmann's	Blend	Standard Brands
J. W. Dant	Bond	Schenley
Jim Beam	Straight	Beam
Echo Springs	Straight	Schenley
Ancient Age	Straight	Schenley

The following are some points of interest in connection with the table above:

Eleven of the twenty brands are marketed as spirit blends.

The top five brands are spirit blends. Of these five, the top three are A blends; the remaining two are B blends.

Nine of the twenty brands are marketed as straight bourbons, bonded and unbonded.

Two brands are Canadian whiskies.

Scotch whisky is not represented.

Six brands are Seagram brands, five are Schenley, three are National, three are Hiram Walker. Brown-Forman, Standard Brands and Beam each place one brand.

Prices range from $4.05 (B blends) to $6.15 (Canadian whiskies).

b. *Open and monopoly states.* Sales ratios in open and monopoly states are approximately as follows:

	Open states	Monopoly states
Spirit blends	67%	33%
Straight bourbons	75%	25%
Bonded bourbons	75%	25%
Scotches	84%	16%
Canadians	75%	25%

c. *Individual states.* Listed below are the ten leading states, in approximate order of sales volume, for each major whiskey type:

	Spirit Blends	Straight Bourbons	Bonded Bourbons	Scotch	Canadian
1.	New York	California	Kentucky	New York	New York
2.	Pennsylvania	Illinois	Ohio	California	Illinois
3.	California	Texas	Texas	Illinois	California
4.	Ohio	Missouri	New York	New Jersey	Michigan
5.	Michigan	Ohio	Illinois	Texas	Ohio
6.	Illinois	Virginia	Missouri	Massachusetts	New Jersey
7.	New Jersey	Louisiana	Pennsylvania	Michigan	Florida
8.	Massachusetts	Tennessee	Indiana	Florida	Massachusetts
9.	Virginia	Georgia	Louisiana	D.C.	Pennsylvania
10.	Florida	Kansas	Virginia	Ohio	Texas

Note how eastern, north central and southeastern states monopolize the picture with respect to spirit blends. California is the one notable exception. In the case of straight bourbon, the swing is sharply to the midwest, south and west. In the case of bonded bourbon, Scotch and Canadian, with primary markets in large metropolitan areas, observe the predominance of states with high-population cities in most sections of the country.

Although spirit blends outsell all other types of whiskies combined, this type does not lead in all states. Bonded whiskey outsells any other type in Kentucky, with straights also ahead of blends. In the following states, straight bourbon occupies the top volume spot: Alabama, Arkansas, Kansas, Louisiana, Missouri, Nebraska, New Mexico, Tennessee, Texas, Utah.

In some states, in addition to Kentucky, bonds outsell straights: Delaware, Indiana, New Jersey, New York, Pennsylvania, Vermont. In all of these states, blends lead.

In some states, Scotch places second to blends: Connecticut, Massachusetts, New Jersey, New York, Rhode Island, Vermont.

In two states, Delaware and Michigan, Canadian whiskey places second to blends.

It is of interest to note the percentage of total national sales for the leading state in each classification:

Classification	State	State % of National Sales
Spirit blends	New York	14%
Straights	California	15%
Bonds	Kentucky	10%
Scotches	New York	25%
Canadians	New York	15%

d. *Monthly, quarterly and semi-annual sales*

	Spirit Blends	Straights	Bonds	Scotches	Canadians
January	7.6%	6.8%	5.8%	5.4%	5.6%
February	7.9%	7.5%	6.7%	6.5%	6.7%
March	7.8%	7.6%	6.4%	6.7%	6.5%
April	7.7%	7.7%	6.4%	7.0%	6.6%
May	8.3%	8.2%	7.3%	8.2%	8.0%
June	6.9%	6.9%	5.6%	7.3%	6.6%
July	6.7%	6.8%	5.6%	6.8%	6.1%
August	8.0%	8.0%	7.6%	8.3%	8.0%
September	7.5%	7.6%	7.4%	7.5%	7.5%
October	9.1%	9.1%	9.4%	9.5%	9.7%
November	9.3%	9.8%	11.0%	9.5%	10.6%
December	13.2%	14.0%	20.8%	17.3%	18.1%
	100.0%	100.0%	100.0%	100.0%	100.0%
Quarterly:					
1st quarter	23%	22%	19%	19%	19%
2nd "	23%	23%	19%	22%	21%
3rd "	22%	22%	21%	23%	22%
4th "	32%	33%	41%	36%	38%
Semi-annually:					
1st half	46%	45%	38%	41%	40%
2nd "	54%	55%	62%	59%	60%

It will be noted that blends and straights follow a similar sales pattern from month to month. This sales pattern differs from that for bonds, Scotches and Canadians. These whiskies sell proportionately in heavier quantity in the closing months of the year. This is explained, of course, by the fact that, as higher-priced spirits, they are in relatively greater demand than other types of whiskey during the holiday season.

In the top-volume month of December, as well as in the fourth quarter and the second six months of the year, bonds sell in larger volume, percentage-wise, than other whiskies.

It is of interest to observe how closely percentages for the third quarter approximate each other for all types.

5. Gin Sales

Prohibition "bathtub" gin familiarized the American public with gin to the point where legally produced gin had a market ready and waiting at the time of repeal. As a result, gin rose to immediate popularity and entrenched itself as a favorite second only to whiskey.

During the war, gin, like other domestic spirits, suffered saleswise because of shortages. Following the war, however, gin took little time to establish itself on a volume basis. An important reason for its quick recovery is the fact that gin, unlike whiskey, need not be aged and is marketable directly after distillation.

Domestic distilled (London) dry gin completely dominates the market. Statistics for gin as a class of spirits apply in general to this type of gin.

SALES OF GIN AS A CLASS OF SPIRITS

a. *National market.* Gin ranks second to whiskey in national sales and accounts for approximately 9% of total distilled spirits sales. With the exception of spirit blends and straight bourbons, gin outsells all types of whiskies:

	% Sales All Spirits
Spirit blends	46.0%
Straight bourbons	15.9%
Gin	8.9%
Bonded bourbons	6.8%
Scotches	5.9%
Canadians	4.6%
Other whiskies	3.1%
	91.2%

b. *Open and monopoly states.* Approximately 76% of gin sales are in open states, 24% in monopoly states.

c. *Individual states.* Gin ranks second to whiskey in all but a few states. The ten leading gin states are New York, Illinois, California, Ohio, New Jersey, Michigan, Pennsylvania, Florida, Texas and Missouri. These states account for approximately 55% of total gin volume. Eight of the ten top gin states are among the ten top whiskey states.

d. *Domestic and imported gin*

	% Sales All Gins	% Sales All Spirits
Domestic	99%	8.8%
Imported	1%	0.1%
	100%	8.9%

e. *Monthly, quarterly and semi-annual sales*

January	— 5.4%	July	— 13.4%
February	— 5.5%	August	— 11.5%
March	— 5.6%	September	— 9.7%
April	— 6.3%	October	— 7.8%
May	— 7.9%	November	— 7.3%
June	— 10.2%	December	— 9.4%

Quarterly:	
1st quarter	— 17%
2nd "	— 24%
3rd "	— 35%
4th "	— 24%
Semi-annually:	
1st half	— 41%
2nd "	— 59%

It will be noted that gin sales peak up sharply in summer months, fall off somewhat before rising to a secondary peak in December, then drop down until the onset of warm weather.

GIN SALES BY BRANDS. The largest selling brands of gin today are Gordon's (Renfield, $4.05), Gilbey's (National, $3.99) and Seagram's Ancient Bottle ($4.20). At and below the Gilbey price, many producers market distilled dry gins, most of which are bottled at 90 proof, which is also the proof of Gilbey's and of Seagram's Ancient Bottle. Gordon's is marketed at 94.4 proof.

Ancient Bottle, which ranks in third place nationally after Gordon's and Gilbey's, is unlike most other gins in that it has a pale golden color. Golden gin was unknown to the American public when Seagram pioneered it some years ago. Since the introduction of Ancient Bottle, other brands of golden gin have made their appearance.

Imported gins, primarily from England and Holland, are not factors on the American market. Among English gins, Booth's House of Lords, Burrough's Beefeater and Coates Plymouth enjoy some volume. These brands retail at approximately $5.50 to $5.55.

6. Cordial Sales

Flavored brandies, flavored gins, and specialties of the cordial type will be included under the heading of cordials in the discussion which follows.

Volume-wise, cordials were not affected adversely by the war. In fact, volume increased during this period. Domestic producers found it possible to obtain spirits distilled from fruit and molasses as a base for their products, and so were able to maintain production. As a result, cordials moved in to help fill the sales gap created by shortages of whiskey and gin. Many new brands supplemented increased supplies of established brands. After the war, when whiskey and gin returned in quantity, most war-born brands of cordials were forced out, and established brands suffered reverses. As a result, cordials as a class of spirits fell back quickly to pre-war sales levels. However, they began advancing steadily almost immediately after their post-war setback, and have now gone so far as to double pre-war volume.

Cordials, especially imported cordials, are sold primarily in large metropolitan centers. Sales are concentrated in northeastern and north central states. California, a good cordial state, is the one important exception.

The consumer market for cordials differs from markets for other classes of spirits. Generally speaking, cordial drinkers are of a higher average age, are in higher income brackets, and number a larger percentage of women drinkers.

SALES OF CORDIALS AS A CLASS OF SPIRITS

a. *National market.* Cordials rank third among all classes of distilled spirits, and account for approximately 3½% of total distilled spirits sales.

b. *Open and monopoly states.* Approximately 81% of cordials are sold in open states, 19% in monopoly states.

c. *Individual states.* Cordials rank third in about 30 states. In the remainder they rank second, fourth or fifth. The ten leading cordials states are New York, Illinois, California, New Jersey, Michigan, Massachusetts, Pennsylvania, Wisconsin, Connecticut, Maryland. These states account for approximately 70% of total cordials volume. New York alone accounts for about 20% of total volume.

d. *Domestic and imported cordials*

	% Sales All Cordials	% Sales All Spirits
Domestic	96%	3.3%
Imported	4%	0.1%
	100%	3.4%

e. *Monthly, quarterly and semi-annual sales*

January	— 7.6%	July	— 6.0%
February	— 7.1%	August	— 7.6%
March	— 6.9%	September	— 7.7%
April	— 7.1%	October	— 9.1%
May	— 6.8%	November	— 9.9%
June	— 6.0%	December	— 18.2%

Quarterly:

1st quarter	— 22%
2nd "	— 20%
3rd "	— 21%
4th "	— 37%

Semi-annually:

1st half	— 42%
2nd "	— 58%

Cordials sell at a fairly even monthly rate, fall off in the summer months, rise gradually in September, October and November, then leap sharply upward in December.

SALES OF CORDIALS BY TYPES AND BRANDS. We will treat domestic and imported cordials separately, inasmuch as leading brands of imported cordials do not all fit readily into major classifications.

a. *Domestic cordials.* The following is an estimated breakdown of sales of domestic cordials, cordial specialties, flavored brandies and flavored gins:

	% Sales All Cordials	% Sales All Spirits
Cordials and cordial specialties	63%	2.1%
Flavored brandies	29%	0.9%
Flavored gins	8%	0.3%
	100%	3.3%

Among cordials and cordial specialties, varieties which sell in heaviest volume are blackberry, crême de menthe, sloe gin, crême de cacao and rock and rye.

Among flavored brandies, blackberry and apricot lead, followed by ginger, peach and cherry.

Among flavored gins, mint has the lead, with orange in second place, and lemon in third place.

The top-selling lines of domestic cordials are Arrow, Hiram Walker, Old Mr. Boston (Berke), de Kuyper (National) and Du Bouchett (Schenley). Other well known lines include Bols, Cointreau, Garnier,

Heublein, Jacquin, Leroux, Mouquin, Nuyens, Peter Hagen. Special mention must be made of Southern Comfort ($6.39), a specialty liqueur which accounts for important volume.

Domestic cordials are retailed in a wide range of prices. An idea of prices for volume brands may be gathered from the following prices of some of the varieties of two leading producers.

	Arrow	Hiram Walker
Anisette	$4.16	$3.79
Fruit cordials (apricot, blackberry, cherry, peach)	4.10	4.48
Creme de cacao	4.55	3.90
Creme de menthe	4.25	3.88
Rock & rye	4.40	4.33
Sloe gin	--	4.11
Peppermint schnapps	4.12	3.76
Triple sec	5.01	4.85
Flavored brandies (apricot, blackberry, cherry, peach)	4.81	4.73
Flavored gins (mint, orange, lemon)	4.24	--

b. *Imported cordials.* Nearly 50% of all imported cordials come from France. The second largest shipper, Denmark, accounts for approximately 15%.

Best known and largest selling brands, all in upper or premium price brackets, are Benedictine (23 oz., $8.99); B & B (23 oz., $8.99); Cherry Heering (24 oz., $8.31); Drambuie (23 oz., $9.20); Chartreuse (green, $9.32; yellow, $8.23); Strega (20 oz., $6.04); Grand Marnier ($8.74); Vielle Cure ($7.09); Cordial Medoc ($8.40); Amer Picon ($7.24); Pernod (100 proof, $7.45; 90 proof, $6.40).

The following are among the leading lines of imported cordials; some, it will be noted, are also produced domestically: Bischoff, Bols, Cusenier, Dolfi, Garnier, Kord, Marie Brizard, Zwack.

7. Brandy Sales

Brandy increased its sales during the war just as cordials did. Domestic supplies were supplemented by shipments from foreign countries (chiefly Spain and Portugal). Also, most wartime brands disappeared when whiskey and gin returned in quantity. Brandy as a class of spirits slumped in sales after the war, but at present the market is somewhat above pre-war levels and expanding slowly.

Brandy sales are concentrated in northeastern and north central states, with California, a good brandy state, providing the lone exception to this area of concentrated volume.

Among domestic and imported brandies, grape and apple brandies are the only commercially important types. Grape brandies outsell apple brandies by about twenty to one. Among imported brandies only grape brandy, principally Cognac, is important.

SALES OF BRANDY AS A CLASS OF SPIRITS

a. *National market.* Brandy ranks fourth among all classes of spirits, and accounts for approximately 2% of total distilled spirits sales.

b. *Open and monopoly states.* Approximately 85% of all brandy is sold in open states, and 15% in monopoly states.

c. *Individual states.* Brandy ranks fourth in about twenty states. In other states it ranks second, third, fifth and sixth. The ten leading brandy states are New York, Wisconsin, California, Illinois, New Jersey, Massachusetts, Minnesota, Connecticut, Michigan, Pennsylvania. These states account for approximately 70% of total brandy volume. New York accounts for about 18% of total volume, and Wisconsin for about 17%.

d. *Domestic and imported brandies*

	% Sales All Brandies	% Sales All Spirits
Domestic	75%	1.5%
Imported	25%	0.5%
	100%	2.0%

e. *Monthly, quarterly and semi-annual sales*

Month	%	Month	%
January	7.6%	July	5.9%
February	7.2%	August	5.9%
March	7.2%	September	6.9%
April	7.2%	October	8.7%
May	7.4%	November	9.9%
June	5.8%	December	20.3%

Quarterly:

1st quarter	22%
2nd "	20%
3rd "	19%
4th "	39%

Semi-annually:

1st half	42%
2nd "	58%

Brandy sales maintain a fairly steady monthly pace until June, dip down during the summer months, rebound in October and November, then skyrocket in December. Percentage-wise, brandy sells more heavily in the last quarter of the year than any other class of spirits.

SALES OF BRANDY BY TYPES AND BRANDS. Approximately 90% of all domestic brandy is grape brandy, most of it produced in California. Apple brandy (applejack) accounts for most of the remainder, with a small sale of slivovitz, kirschwasser and other types.

The popular market for domestic brandies starts at the A blend price and runs to about 30¢ higher. Coronet (Schenley, $4.64) and Christian Brothers (Fromm & Sichel, $4.78) are the leaders among grape brandies. Other brands include Aristocrat ($4.51), Lejon ($4.79). Among apple brandies, Laird's ($4.74) dominates the market.

Approximately 80% of all imported brandies, most of it Cognac, comes from France. Hennessy (Schieffelin, $7.15) far outsells its competition. Other important cognacs include Bisquit ($6.96), Courvoisier ($7.09), Hine ($6.69), Martell ($7.01), Monnet ($6.99), Otard ($6.80), Remy Martin ($7.01). Prices are for popular labels; other varieties under some of these brand names retail up to and over $30.

Pedro Domecq (Fundador, $6.42; Three Vines, $5.42) and Duff Gordon ($5.56) are among the leaders in Spanish brandies.

8. Rum Sales

At one time in our history the largest seller among all spirits, rum now occupies, with vodka, the lower rungs on the sales ladder. Directly after Repeal, American and Cuban rums supplied the bulk of the market. Some five years later, Puerto Rico, which had been building its rum industry, emerged as the most important supplier.

During the war, as whiskey and gin shortages developed, Caribbean and other rums were imported in tremendous quantities and flooded the country. Unfortunately, a good deal of this rum was poor in quality. As the end of the war brought back increased supplies of whiskey and gin, rum backed up on the retailer and consumer levels. Since that time, rum has been attempting to regain its reputation, and has been staging a prolonged and moderately successful comeback.

In addition to rums which are produced in the continental United States, the most important rums from a sales viewpoint are those produced in Puerto Rico, the Virgin Islands, Jamaica and Cuba. Puerto Rican rum dominates the market. Part of the sales success of Puerto

Rican rum, together with that of Virgin Islands rum, may be attributed to the fact that these rums are duty-free.

Except for California and Florida, the market for rum is highly concentrated in northeastern states, with significant sales volume absent west of Illinois.

SALES OF RUM AS A CLASS OF SPIRITS

a. *National market.* As this is written, latest available statistics reveal that rum outsells vodka by a slight margin. However, it is to be expected that vodka will very shortly overtake and pass rum to take fifth place among all classes of distilled spirits. At present rum and vodka each account for approximately 1½% of national sales.

b. *Open and monopoly states.* Approximately 80% of rum is sold in open states, 20% in monopoly states.

c. *Individual states.* Rum ranks fifth in about 25 states, occupying third, fourth and sixth place in other states. The ten leading rum states are New York, California, Illinois, New Jersey, Massachusetts, Florida, Connecticut, Pennsylvania, Ohio, Maine. These states account for approximately 72% of total rum volume.

d. *Domestic and imported rums*

	% Sales All Rums	% Sales All Spirits
Domestic*	15%	0.2%
Imported**	85%	1.3%
	100%	1.5%

e. *Monthly, quarterly and semi-annual sales*

January	— 6.5%	July	— 9.2%
February	— 6.0%	August	— 8.2%
March	— 6.0%	September	— 7.2%
April	— 7.0%	October	— 6.7%
May	— 7.0%	November	— 7.7%
June	— 8.0%	December	— 20.5%

Quarterly:

1st quarter	— 18%
2nd "	— 22%
3rd "	— 25%
4th "	— 35%

Semi-annually:

1st half	— 40%
2nd "	— 60%

* Rums produced in the continental United States.

** Includes Puerto Rican and Virgin Islands rums.

Rum sales rise in the summer months, but not as sharply as gin. After leveling off in September, October and November, sales leap up sharply in December at about the same rate as brandy.

SALES OF RUM BY TYPES, VARIETIES AND BRANDS. Puerto Rican rum accounts for approximately two-thirds of total rum sales. Volume may be estimated as follows:

	% Sales All Rums	% Sales All Spirits
Puerto Rican rum	65%	0.97%
American rum	15%	0.22%
Virgin Islands rum	12%	0.18%
Jamaica rum	4%	0.06%
Cuban rum	3%	0.05%
Other rums (Barbados, French West Indies, etc.)	1%	0.02%
	100%	1.50%

With the exception of New England and Jamaica rums, most rums are sold as Gold Label, Silver Label or both. Silver Label volume is approximately twice that of Gold Label.

Bacardi, which is produced both in Puerto Rico and Cuba, dominates the market. The Puerto Rican variety ($4.44) leads the field by far.

Next to Bacardi among Puerto Rican rums, sales leaders include Carioca ($4.29), Ronrico ($4.29); Merito ($4.22), Don Q ($4.32), Riondo ($4.29), Christopher Columbus ($4.49).

Well known American rums include Siboney ($3.66), Libre ($3.54), Old Newburyport ($4.15).

Among Virgin Islands rums, sales leaders include Old St. Croix ($3.32), Cruzan ($3.78), Ron Virgin ($4.31), Government House ($3.29).

Among Jamaica rums, Myers's Planters' Punch ($5.88) dominates a small field, which includes, in the $5.50 to $6 range, Lemon Hart, Wray's Dagger Punch, Red Heart, Hudson's Bay. Some Jamaica rums are bottled at 151 proof and retail up to approximately $8.35.

Among Cuban rums, Bacardi (Gold, $6.05; White, $5.92) leads. Havana Club (Gold, $4.98; White, $4.68) shows some volume.

9. Vodka Sales

As we have already observed, vodka is a post-war sales phenomenon. Coming from seemingly nowhere, it has established itself, since 1950, as a major class of spirits and seems destined to permanently outrank rum, with some possibility that it may eventually overtake and outrank brandy.

Only domestically produced vodka is commercially important. The product is bottled at 80 proof and at 100 proof, with many distillers marketing both. Eighty proof vodka is the popular-priced volume item.

The geographical sales pattern for vodka differs from that of other spirits. One state, California, alone consumes close to 50% of all vodka. It was in this state that vodka began its swift rise to popularity. Two other western states, Washington and Oregon, are among the top ten vodka states. Remaining principal volume is accounted for by the southwest (Arizona and Texas), the northeast and north central area (New York, New Jersey, Massachusetts and Illinois), and one southern state (Florida).

Since vodka sales patterns are still in the formative stage, it is probable that markets will shift in importance, geographically, within a relatively short time. For the same reason it is also probable that sales relationships as represented by percentages given below will also soon change. The reader who has a special interest in vodka marketing and advertising is advised to consult latest available statistics in order to arrive at a completely reliable picture of vodka sales patterns.

Sales of vodka as a class of spirits

a. *National market.* At present, vodka accounts for approximately 1½% of total distilled spirits sales.

b. *Open and monopoly states.* At present, about 85% of sales are in open states, 15% in monopoly states. It is to be expected that monopoly states will eventually command a larger percentage.

c. *Individual states.* Vodka ranks second, third, fourth or fifth in approximately one-half the states. In the remaining half, it ranks sixth. The ten leading vodka states are at present California, Illinois, New York, Washington, New Jersey, Oregon, Texas, Florida, Massachusetts, Arizona. These states account for approximately 75% of total vodka volume. California is currently outselling its closest rival, Illinois, by about six to one.

d. *Monthly, quarterly and semi-annual sales.* Since vodka sales are accelerating, statistics concerning past performance are unreliable in arriving at monthly, quarterly and semi-annual sales percentages. The following is based on an estimate for such time as sales of the product stabilize:

January	— 7%	July	— 11%
February	— 7%	August	— 11%
March	— 7%	September	— 8%
April	— 7%	October	— 7%
May	— 8%	November	— 8%
June	— 10%	December	— 9%

Quarterly:

1st quarter	— 21%
2nd "	— 25%
3rd "	— 30%
4th "	— 24%

Semi-annually:

1st half	— 46%
2nd "	— 54%

It is to be expected that vodka will sell at a fairly level rate until the onset of warm weather, at which time sales should peak up, then fall off before rising to a secondary peak in the last quarter of the year. Thus, the vodka sales pattern throughout the year is likely to approximate that of gin.

SALES OF VODKA BY BRAND. The Heublein company, producers of Smirnoff Vodka, is to be credited with the feat of putting vodka on the sales map. Volume followed in the wake of Heublein's introduction, in California, of a drink called the Moscow Mule, the recipe for which calls for vodka.

Smirnoff Vodka, both at 80 proof ($4.16) and at 100 proof ($4.89), accounts for probably 40% or more of the sales of all vodka. Smirnoff prices represent the general price levels for competitive vodkas, which include Arrow, Crown Russe, de Kuyper, Hiram Walker, Leroux, Old Mr. Boston, Relska, Rimski, Samovar.

CHAPTER TEN

The Consumer

For the most part, we have thus far spoken of the consumer only in impersonal terms as a "market" for distilled spirits. We have, in addition, noted the activity of this market from the viewpoint of sales and sales patterns. Now we will become acquainted with the consumer on a personal level.

For what purposes does he buy liquors? What are the factors which influence him to buy as he does? Where and how does he drink the liquors he buys?

1. Consumer Buying

PURPOSES FOR WHICH DISTILLED SPIRITS ARE PURCHASED. Some consumers purchase liquors for sacramental, medicinal or cooking purposes. The bulk of consumer buying of spirits is, of course, for use as beverages:

a. *Personal consumption and enjoyment.* This reason underlies the purchase of most spirits.

b. *Entertainment.* Liquors are purchased for entertainment purposes, both social and business. As to the latter, expense-account buying represents sizable volume.

c. *Gifts.* Purchase of spirits for birthdays, anniversaries, holidays and other occasions is substantial. Liquors are popular both as personal gifts and as business gifts.

FACTORS INFLUENCING CONSUMER PURCHASE AND CONSUMPTION OF DISTILLED SPIRITS

a. *Availability.* As we have observed, some areas of the country are wet, others are dry. In addition, within wet areas, retail outlets are plentiful in some locales, but relatively scarce in others. In some markets, local law limits the number of retail outlets.

b. *Types of retail outlets*

1. *Off-premise outlets.* In open states, retailer salesmanship, point-of-sale material, and methods of merchandise display serve to influence the consumer in his choice of classes, types or brands of spirits. In monopoly states, which prohibit sales pressure on the consumer in state stores, either by personal salesmanship or otherwise, the consumer is not influenced in this manner.

2. *On-premise outlets.* We have noted that on-premise outlets are not permitted in some states. This fact obviously affects consumer buying and consumption habits in these states, as compared to states where on-premise outlets are in operation. In on-premise outlets in both open and monopoly states, the consumer is open to personal salesmanship on the part of the retailer.

In passing, it may be stated that comparatively few retailers, off-premise or on-premise, engage in effective personal salesmanship. The majority of retailers operate as order-takers rather than as promoters. Among those retailers who are promotion-minded may be found many outstanding business successes.

c. *Size.* Whether or not liquors in a given locality are available in small sizes, e.g., miniatures and half-pints, in addition to standard larger sizes, has an important bearing on buying and drinking habits. Larger sizes are "take-home" sizes. Miniatures, half-pints and pints are often purchased for consumption outside the home when not chosen strictly on the basis of low price.

d. *Sociological factors.* Buying and drinking habits are influenced by the attitude toward spirits which prevails in one's community or social circle. Liquors may be frowned upon, may be considered merely as acceptable, or may be welcomed as an expression of sophisticated living. A similar gamut of attitudes exists with respect to drinking by women.

Generally speaking, liquors are more acceptable in areas of higher population, and among higher income families.

e. *Product characteristics.* Taste, quality, alcoholic strength, body, and dryness vs. sweetness are the primary product characteristics which influence consumer buying and drinking. In the case of whiskies and brandies, age is also an important product characteristic which the consumer takes into account.

With respect to taste, sales statistics tell us that more people in this country prefer the flavor of whiskey to that of other spirits. Gin, with its juniper flavor, is next in popularity. Cordials, gin and rum have their loyal adherents, although fewer in number, with vodka winning a strong following presumably because of its lack of taste. Within each classification of spirits, consumer preferences based on taste also prevail. Among whiskey drinkers, for example, we have those who like the bourbon flavor of Kentucky whiskey, those who like the smoky taste of Scotch, those who like the comparatively neutral flavor of spirit blends and Canadian whiskies. And so on. In general, the average consumer prefers neutral flavored rather than strongly flavored spirits.

In the matter of quality, which also includes the concepts of mellowness and smoothness, consumer preferences are naturally in the direction of finer products.

In connection with alcoholic strength, light is thrown on consumer preferences by the fact that most spirits (the bulk of them whiskies) are marketed at 86 proof. Other products are marketed, as we have seen, at anywhere from 40 proof to 151 proof. The popular proof range is from 86 to 90.

Most consumers prefer light-bodied spirits. The popularity of spirit blends is evidence of this fact.

Product age, particularly with respect to whiskies and brandies, often influences consumer buying. Greater age is considered to be tantamount to finer quality, although, as we have learned, this is not always the case.

The American consumer has a sweet tooth for many products, but when it comes to spirits, his preference is for dry liquors. Cordials, which are definitely sweet in flavor, account for a small percentage of total consumer purchases.

To sum up, the average drinker in this country prefers liquors with the following qualities: dryness, light to neutral flavor, light body, fine quality, moderate proof.

f. *Price.* Price is of course a vital factor in consumer buying. As we have already observed, low-income buyers tend toward lower priced brands but purchase middle- and higher priced brands in small sizes or by the drink. Middle-income groups tend toward middle-priced brands but also in many cases purchase more expensive brands in small sizes or at on-premise outlets. Higher income groups naturally tend toward higher priced brands, except for such lower and middle-price brands as they may purchase in volume for entertaining purposes. All income groups trade up during the year-end holiday season.

Another factor in connection with price should be noted. Price is sometimes relatively more important, and type of spirits relatively less important, in the high price range. High price suggests prestige and superior quality, with the result, for example, that many whiskey buyers will indiscriminately purchase high-priced bonds, Scotches or Canadians, either for personal consumption or for entertaining or gifts.

g. *Season and climate.* Consumer buying and drinking are affected by weather and by climate. For example, gin, rum and vodka sales swing up sharply in the summer. During this period, increased purchases of these classes of spirits are largely for consumption in the form of iced drinks. In cold weather, there is some consumption of spirits in hot drinks. However, hot drinks in winter do not approach the popularity of cold drinks in summer.

Variations in consumer purchasing may also be noted in areas which differ as to climate.

h. *Holidays.* Purchase and consumption of spirits increases at Thanksgiving, Christmas, New Year's and at other holiday periods.

i. *Vacation and tourist areas.* Purchase and consumption of spirits is relatively large in these locales.

j. *Advertising, publicity and packaging.* Thus far we have spoken of consumer reaction to classes and types of spirits. As to brands of spirits, the great and powerful influences which steer the consumer to one brand as against another are the forces of advertising and point-of-sale promotion. Also influencing the consumer in his choice of brands (aside from retailer salesmanship) are brand publicity, word-of-mouth recommendations, suggestions or connotations contained in the brand name, and bottle, label and carton designs.

* * *

Before going on to a discussion of consumer use of spirits, it will be of interest to note a buying idiosyncrasy in connection with spirit blends. In the East, the name for blended whiskey is "rye" as far as the average consumer is concerned. At Eastern bars, for example, most customers who call for rye expect to be served a blend, and will be dissatisfied if the bartender pours a rye whiskey. Bartenders understand this situation and act accordingly. In other parts of the country, a similar situation exists. In these areas, however, the customer calls for bourbon when he wants a blend. If he wants to make certain of being served a straight bourbon, he will use the word "straight."

2. Consumer Use of Distilled Spirits

The consumer uses distilled spirits in one of the following ways: straight; mixed with water; on the rocks; mixed with shaved ice; mixed with other ingredients, e.g., club soda, ginger ale, cola, ginger beer, quinine water, fruit juices, vermouth, bitters, sugar, syrup, special mixers, and other distilled spirits.

STRAIGHT (also called "neat") drinks consist of the spirits only. A shot glass of whiskey is an example of a "straight" or "neat" drink. Sometimes a chaser, usually water, is taken immediately after a straight drink.

MIXED WITH WATER. The spirits may be mixed with water. Ice cubes and a twist of lemon peel may be added. Whiskey is often consumed in this fashion.

ON THE ROCKS. The "rocks" are ice cubes, which are placed in a short glass, usually an Old-Fashioned glass. The desired spirit is simply poured over the ice; sometimes a twist of lemon peel is added. Cocktails and other mixed drinks, in addition to unmixed spirits, are becoming increasingly popular "on the rocks."

MIXED WITH SHAVED ICE. The spirits are poured into a glass filled with shaved ice. The Scotch Mist and the crême de menthe frappé are examples of this type of drink.

MIXED WITH OTHER INGREDIENTS. Each of the following is an example of drinks consisting of distilled spirits mixed with other ingredients:

Cocktail	Punch
Collins	Rickey
Daisy	Sling
Egg nog	Smash
Fizz	Sour
Highball	Swizzle
Julep	Toddy

Of these mixed drinks, highballs, cocktails and collinses are most popular. Cocktails are used primarily as aperitifs.

Among highballs, whiskey highballs are most popular. Among

cocktails, the manhattan (made with whiskey) and the martini (made with gin) are top favorites. Among collins drinks, the Tom Collins (made with gin) receives the largest call.

The following mixers and other ingredients are in most frequent use:

a. *Carbonated water.* This goes under many names, viz., soda, club soda, sparkling water, charged water, seltzer. As its name implies, carbonated water consists of water charged with carbon dioxide gas. Good carbonated waters are highly effervescent and retain their effervescence for a considerable time after they are poured.

b. *Ginger ale.* A sweet carbonated beverage which derives its primary flavor from ginger, and which sometimes also contains cinnamon, clove and lemon flavorings. Ginger ale and club soda are the popular mixers for highballs.

c. *Cola.* Primarily used with rum in making the Cuba Libre.

d. *Collins mixer.* Because of the great popularity of the Tom Collins and collinses made with whiskey, rum and vodka, the collins mixer has developed for standard use.

e. *Citrus-flavored sodas.* Lemon soda, lemon sour, lime rickey and lemon-lime rickey. Used a great deal in making gin drinks.

f. *Ginger beer.* Primarily used with vodka in making the Moscow Mule.

g. *Quinine water.* Contains lime and lemon oils, citric acid, sugar and a small amount of quinine sulphate. Used primarily for Gin and Tonic. Quinine sulphate provides the "tonic" flavor.

h. *Mineral water.* Used as a substitute for tap water.

i. *Fruit juices.* Lemon and lime juices are used most often; orange juice is used in some mixed drinks.

j. *Fruits, etc.* Used for decorative and flavoring purposes, e.g., maraschino cherries, olives, pearl onions, orange slices, orange peel, lemon slices, lemon peel, lime slices, lime peel.

k. *Vermouth.* An aromatic aperitif wine. Primarily used in making the manhattan and martini cocktails. There are two types: dry (French) vermouth and sweet (Italian) vermouth.

l. *Sweeteners.* Granulated sugar, lump sugar, sugar syrup and Grenadine are the primary sweeteners. Grenadine is a red syrupy liquid whose primary flavor is pomegranate. Falernum, another flavoring syrup, is used principally in rum drinks.

m. *Bitters.* Aromatic bitters are used most frequently, although some recipes call for orange, lemon or lime bitters.

What about glassware? Glasses used for straight and mixed drinks, together with the size or range of sizes for each type of glass, are as follows:

Cocktail	2 oz. to 3½ oz.
Collins	10 oz. to 14 oz.
Cordial	¾ oz. to 1 oz.
Delmonico	5 oz. to 7 oz.
Goblet	8 oz. to 12 oz.
Highball	8 oz. to 10 oz.
Old-Fashioned	4 oz. to 6 oz.
Pony	1 oz.
Shot	1 oz. to 2½ oz.
Tumbler	8 oz. to 12 oz.

The following measures are in standard use:

1 pony	1 oz.
1 jigger	1½ oz.
1 teaspoonful	⅛ oz.
1 dash	⅙ teaspoonful

Mixed drinks made with fruit juices are usually shaken; others are stirred.

There is a striking variety of mixed drinks. Recipes for the more popular of these appear below.

When specific quantities of ingredients are given rather than proportions (for example, 1 jigger of whiskey is a specific quantity, but ⅓ whiskey indicates a proportion), then the size of the particular glass to be used is the smallest size, unless the size is specifically stated. Larger glasses will require ingredients in relatively larger quantities.

Whiskey Drinks

HIGHBALL. Ice cubes, 1 jigger whiskey. Fill highball glass with soda or ginger ale. Stir slightly.

ON THE ROCKS. Pour 1 jigger of whiskey on ice cubes in an Old-Fashioned glass. Add twist of lemon peel. Stir.

MANHATTAN. ⅔ whiskey, ⅓ sweet vermouth, dash of aromatic bitters. Stir in mixing glass filled with cracked ice. Strain into cocktail glass. Add maraschino cherry. For the dry manhattan cocktail, use dry vermouth; add a twist of lemon peel instead of cherry.

OLD-FASHIONED. 1 lump of sugar, 2 dashes of bitters, 1 teaspoonful of water or a splash of soda. Muddle until the sugar is dissolved. Add ice cubes and 1 jigger of whiskey. Decorate with a slice of lemon or orange. Stir well.

WHISKEY SOUR. 1 teaspoonful of sugar, juice of ½ lemon, 1 jigger of whiskey, 3 dashes of bitters. Shake well with ice. Strain into delmonico glass. Add maraschino cherry. Decorate with a slice of orange.

MINT JULEP. In a collins glass, muddle 1 teaspoonful of sugar with about a dozen leaves of fresh mint. Fill the glass with shaved ice. Add 1 or 2 jiggers of whiskey (bourbon is traditional for the mint julep). Stir until the glass frosts. Decorate with mint sprigs.

WHISKEY COLLINS. 1 jigger of whiskey, juice of ½ lemon, 1 teaspoonful of sugar in a collins glass. Add ice cubes and fill with soda. Stir. Add cherry. Decorate with slices of lemon and orange.

WARD 8. 1 jigger of whiskey, ½ ounce of Grenadine, ¾ ounce of lemon juice. Sugar as desired. Shake with ice and strain into 8-ounce glass. Add cherry. Decorate with a slice of orange. Fill glass with soda.

HOT TODDY. Place a spoon in an Old-Fashioned glass and add boiling water until about ⅔ full. Add a small piece of cinnamon, a slice of lemon garnished with cloves, 1 teaspoonful of sugar and a twist of lemon peel. Next add 1 jigger of whiskey. Stir slightly.

EGG NOG (9 *servings*). Beat yolks of 6 eggs with 2 tablespoonsful of sugar. Add 9 ounces of whiskey, 1 pint of milk, 3 ounces of brandy or rum, 1 pint of whipped cream. Next add beaten egg whites. Chill for 3 hours.

ROB ROY. This is a manhattan cocktail made with Scotch whisky.

SCOTCH MIST. Pour 1 jigger of Scotch into an Old-Fashioned glass containing shaved ice.

SCOTCH AND SODA. Ice cubes, 1 jigger of Scotch whisky. Fill highball glass with soda. Stir slightly.

Gin Drinks

DRY MARTINI. ⅔ gin, ⅓ dry vermouth. Stir in cracked ice and strain into a cocktail glass. Add olive. Dry martinis may also be made with a larger proportion of gin and a smaller proportion of vermouth.

MEDIUM MARTINI. ½ gin, ¼ dry vermouth, ¼ sweet vermouth. Stir in cracked ice and strain into a cocktail glass. Add olive.

SWEET MARTINI. ⅔ gin, ⅓ sweet vermouth, dash of orange bitters. Stir in cracked ice and strain into a cocktail glass.

Of the three types of martinis mentioned above, the dry martini is by far the most popular.

GIBSON. This is a dry martini in which a pearl onion (small pickled onion) is substituted for the olive.

TOM COLLINS. 1 jigger of gin, 1 teaspoonful of sugar, juice of 1 lemon. Shake with cracked ice. Pour unstrained into a collins glass. Add ice cubes and fill with soda. Stir. Decorate with slices of lemon and orange.

GIN AND TONIC. Pour 1 jigger of gin over ice cubes in an 8-ounce glass. Add slice of lime or lemon. Fill with quinine water.

GIN AND BITTERS. To 5 dashes of aromatic bitters in an Old-Fashioned glass add one ice cube and 1 jigger of gin. Stir.

BRONX. ½ dry gin, ¼ dry vermouth, ¼ sweet vermouth, juice of ½ orange. Shake with cracked ice. Strain into cocktail glass.

ORANGE BLOSSOM. 1 jigger of gin, 1 ounce of orange juice, 1 teaspoonful of sugar. Shake with cracked ice. Strain into cocktail glass.

GIN RICKEY. Juice of ½ lime in highball glass. Add squeezed lime shell, ice cubes, 1 jigger of gin, fill with soda.

GIN DAISY. 1 jigger of gin, 1 ounce of Grenadine, 1 ounce of lemon juice. Shake with cracked ice, pour unstrained into highball glass. Fill with soda. Decorate with fruit.

ALEXANDER. 1 ounce of gin, ¾ ounce of sweet cream, ¾ ounce of crême de cacao. Shake with cracked ice and strain into large cocktail glass.

GIN FIZZ. 1 jigger of gin, 1 ounce of lemon juice, 1 teaspoonful of sugar. Shake with cracked ice, strain into highball glass, fill with soda. Stir slightly.

GIN SLING. To cracked ice in highball glass add 3 dashes of aromatic bitters, 1 jigger of gin, a twist of lemon peel. Fill with soda. Stir slightly.

PINK LADY. ½ jigger of gin, ¼ ounce of apple brandy, ½ ounce of lemon juice, ½ ounce of Grenadine, white of one egg. Shake with cracked ice. Strain into cocktail glass.

FRENCH '75. 2 ounces of gin, juice of 1 lemon, 1 teaspoonful of sugar. Shake with cracked ice and pour into a highball glass. Fill with champagne. Stir slightly.

DUBONNET. ½ gin, ½ Dubonnet. Stir in ice. Strain into cocktail glass.

CLOVER CLUB. 1 jigger of gin, ½ ounce of lemon or lime juice, ½ teaspoonful of sugar, white of one egg, ½ ounce of Grenadine. Add ice. Shake well and strain into a large cocktail glass.

Cordial Drinks

Cordials are used primarily as after-dinner liqueurs and are served in ¾ ounce to 1 ounce cordial glasses. Among the recipes for mixed drinks:

CRÊME DE MENTHE FRAPPÉ. Fill and mound a cocktail glass with shaved ice. Add green (or white) crême de menthe. Serve with short straws.

SLOE GIN FIZZ. 2 ounces of sloe gin, juice of ½ lemon, 1 teaspoonful of sugar. Shake well with cracked ice. Strain into highball glass. Fill with soda. Decorate with slice of lemon.

ANGEL'S TIP. Fill a cordial glass ⅔ full with crême de cacao. Float sweet cream on the top.

Pousse Café. Liqueurs of differing weights and colors are floated one on top of the other in a pony glass. Choice of liqueurs depends upon the drinker or the bartender.

Alexander. See under "Gin Drinks."

Sidecar. See under "Brandy Drinks."

Stinger. See under "Brandy Drinks."

Brandy Drinks

Brandies are used straight as after-dinner drinks and are also used as ingredients in mixed drinks.

Brandy and Soda. 1 jigger of brandy in a highball glass. Add cracked ice or ice cubes. Fill with soda. Stir slightly.

Sidecar. ⅓ brandy, ⅓ cointreau, ⅓ lemon juice. Shake with ice. Strain into cocktail glass.

Stinger. 1¼ ounces of brandy, 1 ounce of white crême de menthe. Shake with cracked ice. Strain into cocktail glass.

French '75. The same recipe as noted under gin drinks, except that brandy is substituted for gin.

Brandy Alexander. Same recipe as for the Alexander, with brandy substituted for gin.

Among recipes for apple brandies are the following:

Jack Rose. 1 jigger of apple brandy, juice of ½ lemon, ½ ounce of Grenadine. Shake with cracked ice. Strain into cocktail glass.

Pink Lady. See under "Gin Drinks."

Star. ½ apple brandy, ½ dry vermouth, 2 dashes of aromatic bitters. Stir in ice. Strain into cocktail glass. Add a twist of lemon peel.

Rum Drinks

White Label rums are used in mixed drinks, e.g., the Daiquiri, where rum flavor is not intended to come through strongly. In tall drinks and in some cocktails, e.g., Rum and Soda and the Rum Manhattan, where pronounced rum flavor is important, Gold Label is used. Heavy-bodied rums, e.g., Jamaica and Demerara, are used primarily for drinks like the Planter's Punch.

DAIQUIRI. 1 jigger of White Label, juice of ½ lime, 1 teaspoonful of sugar. Shake with cracked ice. Strain into cocktail glass.

BACARDI. 1 jigger of Bacardi White Label, juice of ½ lemon or lime, ½ teaspoonful of Grenadine. Shake with cracked ice. Strain into cocktail glass.

CUBA LIBRE. 1 jigger of White or Gold Label and juice of ½ lime in a collins glass. Add lime shell, ice cubes. Fill with cola. Stir slightly.

RUM AND SODA. 1 jigger of Gold Label in a highball glass. Add ice cubes, fill with soda. Stir slightly.

RUM COLLINS. 1 jigger of Gold Label, juice of ½ lemon, 1 teaspoonful of sugar in a collins glass. Add ice cubes, fill with soda. Stir slightly. Add cherry. Decorate with a slice of lemon.

PLANTER'S PUNCH. 2 jiggers of Jamaica rum (or other heavy-bodied rum), juice of 2 limes, 2 teaspoonsful of sugar, 3 dashes of aromatic bitters. Shake well in mixing glass. Pour unstrained into a 12-ounce collins glass. Fill with soda. Stir slightly. Decorate with slice of lemon. Dust with nutmeg.

RUM MANHATTAN. ⅔ Gold Label, ⅓ sweet vermouth, dash of bitters. Stir with cracked ice. Strain into cocktail glass.

ZOMBIE. 1 ounce of Jamaica rum, 2 ounces of Gold Label rum, 1 ounce of White Label rum, ½ ounce of apricot-flavored brandy, ¾ ounce of papaya juice, ¾ ounce of pineapple juice (unsweetened), 1 teaspoonful of sugar, juice of 1 lime. Shake with cracked ice. Pour unstrained into 14-ounce glass. Splash 151 proof Jamaica rum on top. Decorate with slice of orange and sprig of mint. Sprinkle with powdered sugar.

HOT RUM PUNCH (*16 servings*). With muddler, macerate 3 grated lemon rinds and ¼ pound of sugar. Add juice of 3 lemons, 1 tablespoonful of ground ginger. Mix, place in heated bowl. Add 1 pint of Gold Label, 1 pint of brandy, ½ pint of sherry, 1 quart of boiling water. Mix, set near heat for twenty minutes. Pour into punch cups. Dust with nutmeg.

TOM AND JERRY. Beat white and yolk of 1 egg separately, then mix in goblet. Add ½ jigger of Jamaica rum, ½ jigger of whiskey or brandy, 1 tablespoonful of sugar. Fill with hot milk or water. Stir. Dust with nutmeg.

HOT BUTTERED RUM. To 2 dashes of bitters in a glass add 3 ounces of Gold Label. Place teaspoonful of butter into the glass. Do not withdraw spoon. Add hot water. Sprinkle on cloves. Stir, let steep.

Vodka Drinks

Vodka may be taken straight, but is most frequently used in mixed drinks, and has proved to be particularly versatile. Vodka may be mixed with soft drinks, fruit juices, tomato juice, coffee, tea and other beverages and mixers.

MOSCOW MULE. 1 jigger of vodka, juice of ½ lime and ice cubes in the special mug used for this drink (or use any tall glass). Fill with ginger beer.

BLOODY MARY. 1 jigger of vodka, 3 ounces of heavy tomato juice, ½ ounce of lemon juice, 4 drops of Worcestershire sauce, dash of pepper. Shake in cracked ice.

SCREWDRIVER. 1 jigger of vodka in an 8-ounce glass. Add ice cubes. Fill with orange juice. Stir. Decorate with slice of orange.

VODKA MARTINI. ⅔ vodka, ⅓ dry vermouth. Stir in cracked ice and strain into cocktail glass. Add a twist of lemon peel.

CHAPTER ELEVEN

Marketing and Advertising Law

Mandatory and prohibited practices in liquor marketing and advertising are set forth by federal, state and local laws and regulations; and, in the case of liquor advertising in particular, by industry resolutions and by advertising media. We will discuss liquor marketing and advertising from national, state and local viewpoints.

1. Marketing Law

FEDERAL MARKETING LAW. We have already discussed to some extent the provisions of federal laws and regulations which control or otherwise affect liquor marketing and merchandising. We will briefly review these provisions, and enlarge upon those which are most important in day-to-day marketing and merchandising. In addition, we will set forth provisions which have not heretofore been mentioned.

It will be recalled that federal law prohibits, with respect to liquors in interstate or foreign commerce, trade practices by any industry member which exclude or restrict the sale of products of other industry members. In this connection, the law specifically prohibits producers, importers, wholesalers, or other vendors from establishing exclusive retail outlets, effecting "tied house" arrangements, or engaging in commercial bribery or consignment selling.

a. *Exclusive retail outlet.* No retailer may be required to sell the products of one industry member to the exclusion, complete or partial, of other industry members.

b. *Commercial bribery.* No industry member may exclude, or restrict the sale of, competitive products by commercial bribery or "by offering or giving any bonus, premium, or compensation to any officer, or employee, or representative of the trade buyer."

c. *Consignment sales.* Purchase or sale is prohibited on a consignment or conditional sale basis with the privilege of return. Only bona fide sales are permitted. When merchandise has been sold on a bona fide basis, bona fide return of this merchandise is permitted.

d. *"Tied house."* Industry members are prohibited from excluding or restricting the sale of competitive products by any of the following practices:

"By acquiring or holding (after the expiration of any existing license) any interest in any license with respect to the premises of the retailer."

"By acquiring any interest in real or personal property owned, occupied, or used by the retailer in the conduct of his business."

"By paying or crediting the retailer for any advertising, display, or distribution service."

"By guaranteeing any loan or the repayments of any financial obligation of the retailer."

"By extending to the retailer credit for a period in excess of the credit period usual and customary to the industry [30 days] for the particular class of transactions, as ascertained by the Secretary of the Treasury and prescribed by regulations by him."

"By requiring the retailer to take and dispose of a certain quota of products."

"By furnishing, giving, renting, lending, or selling to the retailer, any equipment, fixtures, signs, supplies, money, services or other thing of value, subject to such exceptions as the Secretary of the Treasury shall by regulation prescribe." This is an important provision. The following are the important exceptions prescribed by the Secretary of the Treasury, provided they are not conditioned on the purchase of spirits (or on the purchase of wine or malt beverages):

1. *Samples.* Not more than one pint of any brand of spirits may be given as a sample to any retailer who has not previously purchased the brand in question. However, two quarts may be given as a sample to any state agency or political subdivision which has not previously purchased the brand.

2. *Merchandise.* Merchandise, usually of the type which is intended for re-sale to the consumer, e.g., groceries and drugs, may be sold to a retailer by an industry member who operates as a bona fide vendor of such merchandise. This merchandise must be sold in accordance with open market prices and may not be sold in combination with distilled spirits.

3. *Point-of-sale display material, consumer and retail adver-*

tising specialties, retailer mat services, the use of dealer names in advertisements placed by industry members. These exceptions will be dealt with in detail in this chapter in the section on advertising.

The following federal liquor marketing legislation is also in effect:

A wholesaler may not sell spirits in quantities of less than five gallons (otherwise he may be taxed as a retailer).

A retailer may not sell spirits in quantities of five gallons or more to the same person at the same time (otherwise he may be taxed as a wholesaler).

Spirits may not be shipped through the mails.

Spirits may not be sold at U.S. immigration stations.

Spirits may not be sold on vessels of war.

Spirits may not be sold by the bottle at armed forces' clubs, messes, package stores, etc. on federal property.

Other important federal legislation which has been enacted to cover the marketing and merchandising activities of all industries applies also, of course, to the liquor industry. Legislation of this kind was mentioned in Chapter III. One type, re-sale price maintenance, was discussed in detail in Chapter VIII.

In the light of the many laws and regulations governing liquor marketing and merchandising, it is obvious that great care must be taken to avoid pitfalls when planning selling campaigns. Practices which are permitted in other industries are specifically ruled out in the liquor industry, either by the letter or the spirit of the law. For example, 1¢ sales, bottle-top promotions and other merchandising devices which are almost routine in other industries necessarily go by the board when it comes to marketing spirits.

STATE AND LOCAL MARKETING LAW. In our discussion of marketing channels in Chapter VI we touched upon certain phases of marketing covered by state and local legislation. For example, we learned that private wholesalers are prohibited in monopoly states; that on-premise retailing is prohibited in certain states, both open and monopoly; that direct selling and merchandising to monopoly state stores is prohibited; that certain types of retail outlets, both off-premise and on-premise, are permitted in some states but prohibited in others.

With respect to trade practices, individual states have enacted legislation which duplicates or enlarges upon federal legislation. Thus, states have ruled on Fair Trade and on the "tied house" and other methods of unfair competition.

A large body of state and local law concerns itself with liquor retailing. The following provisions appear most frequently on the statute books (not all provisions apply in all states):

Provisions as to hours of sale.

Prohibition of sales on Sundays, holidays, election days.

Prohibition of retail outlets near schools, churches and government buildings.

Provisions as to container sizes in which spirits may be sold.

Prohibition of sales to minors.

Prohibition of sales to intoxicated persons.

Prohibition of sales to women at bars.

Prohibition of employment of minors and women.

Provisions as to the maximum quantity of spirits which may be sold to one person at one time.

Provisions concerning retail premises—equipment, fixtures, booths, visibility of the interior from the street, etc.

Provisions as to serving customers in on-premise outlets, e.g., whether customers may be served standing, or whether they must be seated; whether spirits may be sold with or without food, etc.

2. Advertising Law

FEDERAL ADVERTISING LAW. Federal law sets forth specific provisions concerning liquor advertising. The pertinent section of the Federal Alcohol Administration Act states that it is "unlawful for any person engaged in business as a distiller, brewer, rectifier, blender, or other producer, or as an importer or wholesaler, of distilled spirits, wine, or malt beverages, or as a bottler, or warehouseman and bottler of distilled spirits, directly or indirectly or through an affiliate: To publish or disseminate or cause to be published or disseminated by radio broadcast, or in any newspaper, periodical, or other publication or by any sign or outdoor advertisement or any other printed or graphic matter, any advertisement of distilled spirits, wine, or malt beverages, if such advertisement is in, or is calculated to induce sales in, interstate or foreign commerce, or is disseminated by mail, unless such advertisement is in conformity with such regulations, to be prescribed by the Secretary of the Treasury,

1. as will prevent deception of the consumer with respect to the products advertised and as will prohibit, irrespective of falsity, such statements relating to age, manufacturing processes, analyses, guarantees, and scientific or irrelevant matters as the Secretary finds to be likely to mislead the consumer;

2. as will provide the consumer with adequate information as to the identity and quality of the products advertised, the alcoholic content thereof . . . and the person responsible for the advertisement;

3. as will require an accurate statement, in the case of distilled spirits (other than cordials, liqueurs and specialties) produced by blending or rectification, if neutral spirits have been used in the production thereof, informing the consumer of the percentage of neutral spirits so used and of the name of the commodity from which such neutral spirits have been distilled, or in case of neutral spirits or of gin produced by a process of continuous distillation, the name of the commodity from which distilled;

4. as will prohibit statements that are disparaging of a competitor's products or are false, misleading, obscene or indecent;

5. as will prevent statements inconsistent with any statement on the labeling of the products advertised."

Article VI of Regulations No. 5 under the FAA Act goes into detail on each point covered by the Act.

The following must appear in liquor advertising:

a. *Responsible advertiser.* The name and address of the permittee must appear. Street number and name may be omitted, e.g., "National Distillers Products Corporation, New York, N.Y."

b. *Class and type.* Class and type, corresponding to the class and type on the label, must appear conspicuously, e.g., "blended whiskey," "straight bourbon whiskey," "apricot brandy." In an advertisement for a blended whiskey, if the word "whiskey" appears anywhere in the ad without the qualifying type designation, "blended," then the complete class and type designation, "blended whiskey," must appear elsewhere in the ad, and must be equal in size to the unqualified word "whiskey." If the word "whiskey" is in upper and lower case, the class and type designation, "blended whiskey," may be in capitals no smaller than the lower case letters. If the word "whiskey" appears more than once in the ad, the rule for the class and type designation applies to the word in its largest size.

c. *Alcoholic content.* This must be stated in terms of proof, e.g., "86 proof." In the case of cordials, cocktails, highballs, bitters and some other specialties, alcoholic content may be stated either in terms of proof or in terms of percentage by volume, e.g., "30% alcohol by volume."

d. *Neutral spirits.* In blended and rectified products containing neutral spirits, the percentage of neutral spirits must be stated, together with the name of the product from which distilled, e.g., "65%

grain neutral spirits." The percentage of the other ingredient, e.g., straight whiskey, need not be stated. In the case of a gin not produced by continuous distillation, a typical statement of neutral spirits is as follows: "100% grain neutral spirits." In the case of a gin produced by continuous distillation, the percentage of spirits need not be stated. However, the name of the product from which distilled must be stated, e.g., "Distilled from grain."

e. *Statements of age.* In some instances, age must be stated in advertisements. This occurs when an advertisement is for a product which (legally) carries an age statement on the label, and when the advertisement for such a product carries a reference to, or a representation of age.

As we have learned, age statements are required on the labels of all whiskies and brandies, with the exception of the following, for which age statements are optional:

bottled in bond whiskies straight whiskies blends of straights Scotch whiskies Canadian whiskies Irish whiskies	4 or more years old
brandy—2 or more years old	

An age statement on the label is also optional in the case of rum.

In the case of any of the foregoing products (except rum), whether or not an age statement appears on the label, general inconspicuous representations of age may be made in the advertisement without an accompanying age statement.

When an age statement appears in an advertisement it must be identical with the age statement on the label.

EXAMPLES:

An advertisement for a 3-year-old straight bourbon states that the whiskey is matured in charred oak barrels (with or without mention of the number of years aged). The advertisement must carry the following age statement, "This whiskey is 3 years old."

An advertisement for a 3-year-old straight bourbon makes no stated reference to age, but contains an illustration of a barrel, hourglass or other age or time symbol. The advertisement must carry the age statement, "This whiskey is 3 years old."

An advertisement for a spirit blend containing 40% six-year-old whiskey contains a reference to, or a representation of age. In conjunction with this, the following statement must be reproduced in the advertisement (and must be of equal and conspicuous size throughout): "The straight whiskey in this product is 6 years old. 40% straight whiskey. 60% grain neutral spirits."

Age statements are prohibited in advertisements in certain instances. This matter will be discussed, along with other prohibited advertising practices, later in this chapter.

* * * * *

If an advertisement refers to the class, but not to the type of any given brand, then only the name of the responsible advertiser is mandatory in the advertisement. For example, if an advertisement for a brand of blended whiskey omits reference to the fact that it is a blend, if in addition it omits an illustration of a label or a recognizable label, omits prices and sizes, and contains no reference to or representation of age, then no mention need be made of type of spirits, proof, or grain neutral spirits.

* * * * *

The following are examples of usual minimum mandatory statements in advertisements for several types of distilled spirits:

"Blended whiskey. 86 proof. 65% grain neutral spirits. John Doe Distilling Co., Peoria, Ill." (If the advertisement does not represent or refer to age.)

"Straight bourbon whiskey. 86 proof. John Doe Distilling Company, Peoria, Ill." (For a straight bourbon of any age, when the advertisement does not represent or refer to age, and in the case of a whiskey four years or more old, when the advertisement carries a general inconspicuous representation of age.)

"Straight bourbon whiskey. 86 proof. This whiskey is 3 years old. John Doe Distilling Company, Peoria, Ill." (If the advertisement refers to or represents age.)

"Straight bourbon whiskey. 100 proof. John Doe Distilling Company, Peoria, Ill." (For a bonded bourbon, and in the case of a free-bottled 100 proof straight bourbon 4 years or more old, when the advertisement does not refer to or represent age, or when the advertisement makes a general inconspicuous representation of age. Also, in the case of a free-bottled 100 proof straight bourbon less than four years old, when the advertisement does not refer to or represent age.)

"Blended Scotch whisky. 86 proof. John Doe Import Company, New York, N. Y." (For a Scotch of any age when the advertisement does not refer to or represent age, and for a Scotch four years or more old, when the advertisement carries a general inconspicuous representation of age.)

"Brandy. 86 Proof. John Doe Distilling Company, San Francisco, Cal." (For a grape brandy of any age, when the advertisement does not refer to or represent age, and a brandy two years or more old, when the advertisement carries a general inconspicuous representation of age.)

"Peach Liqueur. 60 proof. John Doe Distilling Company, Cincinnati, Ohio." Or: "Peach Liqueur. 30% alcohol by volume. John Doe Distilling Company, Cincinnati, Ohio." (No reference to, or representation of age, may be made in the advertisement.)

"Distilled dry gin. 90 proof. 100% grain neutral spirits. John Doe Distilling Company, Newark, N. J." (No reference to, or representation of, age may be made in the advertisement.)

"Puerto Rican Rum. 86 proof. John Doe Import Co., New York, N. Y." (For a rum of any age, when the advertisement does not refer to, or represent, age.)

"Puerto Rican Rum. 86 Proof. This rum is ____ years old. John Doe Import Co., New York, N. Y." (For a rum of any age, when the advertisement makes any reference to, or representation of, age.)

"Vodka. 80 proof. 100% grain neutral spirits. John Doe Distilling Company, New Haven, Conn." (No reference to, or representation of, age may be made in the advertisement.)

All mandatory statements must appear on a contrasting background in type or lettering not smaller than 8 point Gothic caps. In advertising other than periodical advertising and direct mail, where the size of the advertisement is relatively large (e.g., 24 sheet posters and large point-of-sale pieces), mandatory statements must also be relatively large so as to be readily legible to the consumer.

The following are prohibited in liquor advertising:

a. "Any statement that is false and misleading in any material particular." In actual practice, this regulation refers both to statements and to illustrations. Government rulings regarding the use of statements and illustrations concerning athletics afford a good example. The underlying principle behind these rulings is to prevent any interpretation by the consumer that the advertised brand will aid him physically or help him to perform better athletically. Thus, the following are banned: testimonials by amateur or professional athletes; illustrations of athletes (actual or imaginary persons) engaged in any form of athletics in which the average man does not engage. For example, football players, baseball players, boxers, hockey players and track and field athletes may not be shown in liquor advertisements. However, illustrations of athletic action in which the average man engages are permitted. Thus, illustrations of tennis players and golfers are permitted (but not illustrations of champion tennis players and champion golfers). Also permitted are scenes of athletic events, provided the athletes themselves are not shown, e.g., spectators at a football game are permitted, provided the players are not visible. Still-life illustrations are also permitted, e.g., trophies, boxing gloves, tennis rackets, goal posts, etc.

Other examples of false and misleading statements or visual devices:

Medals and awards which have not in fact been given to a product.

The statement, "100% straight whiskies," when the product is less than 100 proof.

The statement, "fine bourbon whiskey is made only in Kentucky."

The words "genuine" or "friendly" when applied to a product.

The statement, when applied to a domestic product, "furnished to His Majesty, the King of –"

"Distilled from a scientifically controlled fermentation under laboratory control."

b. "Any statement that disparages a competitor's products." Examples:

"Contains no neutral spirits."

"Matured naturally, not heat treated."

"Not a compound, but a delicious distilled dry gin."

"Should not be confused with imitations that are made from neutral spirits."

"Contains no headaches."

c. "Any statement, design, device or representation which is obscene or indecent."

d. "Any statement, design, device or representation of or relating to analyses, standards, or tests, irrespective of falsity, which the

Deputy Commissioner finds to be likely to mislead the consumer." Examples:

"From 20 to 30 scientific determinations are required for each bottle tested."

"Analyzed by State laboratories and found to be pure and free from deleterious ingredients."

"The – Laboratories, recognized expert authority, tests and judges John Doe Brand."

"Tested and approved," signed by "The – Research Institute."

e. "Any statement, design, device or representation of or relating to any guaranty, irrespective of falsity, which the Deputy Commissioner finds to be likely to mislead the consumer." Examples:

"Guaranteed to consumer by –"

"Warranted to be the best product in its price range."

"Certified to be pure and free from deleterious matter."

"Guaranteed to be 10 years old."

"Guaranteed to be distilled in the State of –"

"Attested to be made by modern, scientific manufacturing processes."

An enforceable money-back guarantee is, however, permitted, provided it takes substantially this form:

"We will refund the purchase price to the purchaser if he is in any manner dissatisfied with the contents of this package." (Signed by name of permittee making the guarantee.)

f. "Any statement that the distilled spirits are distilled, blended, made, bottled or sold under or in accordance with any municipal, state or Federal authorization, law or regulation; and if a municipal, state or Federal permit number is stated, such permit number shall not be accompanied by any additional statement relating thereto."

Although it may be stated that a bonded whiskey is "bottled in bond under the supervision of the U. S. Government," it may not be stated that a bonded whiskey is made or bottled in accordance with federal law.

g. The words "bond," "bonded," "bottled in bond," "aged in bond," or phrases containing these or synonymous terms, may not be used for any product except bottled in bond spirits.

h. The word "pure" is prohibited (unless it is part of the bona fide name of a permittee, or a retailer for whom the distilled spirits are bottled).

i. The terms "double distilled," "triple distilled" and similar terms may not be used.

j. Statements of age, references to age, or representations of age are prohibited for gin, cordials, vodka, prepared mixed drinks, bitters and specialties. They are also prohibited for spirit blends as a finished product, although they are permitted in connection with the whiskey content of spirit blends.

k. Curative and therapeutic effects. Advertising "shall not contain any statement, design, or device representing that the use of any distilled spirits has curative or therapeutic effects, if such statement is untrue in any particular, or tends to create a misleading impression." Liquor advertisers scrupulously avoid all reference to therapeutic or curative effects, e.g., "no hangovers in John Doe Brand."

l. Place of origin. Advertising "shall not represent that the distilled spirits were manufactured in or imported from a place or country other than that of their actual origin, or were produced or processed by one who was not in fact the actual producer or processor." For example, if a line of domestic cordials has a French name, and if the advertisement contains illustrations of French scenes, dress, etc., then the phrase, "Made in U. S. A." must appear prominently in the advertisement.

m. Confusion of brands. "Two or more different brands or lots of distilled spirits shall not be advertised in one advertisement (or in two or more advertisements in one issue of a periodical or newspaper, or in one piece of other written, printed or graphic matter) if the advertisement tends to create the impression that representations made as to one brand or lot apply to the other or others, and if as to such latter the representations contravene any provision of this article or are in any respect untrue."

n. Flags, seals, coats of arms, crests, and other insignia. None of these is permitted to represent or relate to the flag or the armed forces of the United States, or to any emblem, seal, insignia, or decoration associated with them. Nor may any other similar type of pictorial device be used relating to or representing any government, organization, family or individual if this device is likely to mislead the consumer into believing that the product has been endorsed, made, or used by them.

o. No advertisement for a product may contain any statement which is inconsistent with any statement on the label.

In our discussion of liquor marketing law, mention was made of certain advertising material and practices concerning the retailer which are not considered in violation of federal "tied house" provisions. Advertising material and practices are permitted as follows, if they are not conditioned on the sale of spirits to the retailer, and if they comply with federal requirements as indicated:

a. *Point-of-sale interior display material.* A producer, importer or other industry member may give, rent, lend or sell such material to a retailer, provided (1) it has value to the retailer only as advertising; (2) the total dollar value of this material in any one retail establishment at any one time does not exceed $15 for window displays, and does not exceed $30 for display material for the interiors of stores or bars; (3) the cost of installation does not exceed that which is usual and customary in the locality in question; (4) the vendor does not pay the retailer for displaying the material, and does not defray any expense incidental to its operation.

The above provisions represent a liberalization of federal regulations which, prior to August, 1954, stipulated that the sum of $10 might not be exceeded for window and other display material combined, this $10 to include the cost of installation.

Exterior signs may not be furnished to retailers.

It will be observed that the vendor has strict limitations imposed upon him as compared with those in other industries. As one example, the renting of window display space, and the manufacture and installation of elaborate and costly window displays, which are accepted practice in some other industries, are ruled out in the liquor industry.

b. *Dealer names in advertising.* "The names and addresses of retailers selling the product of any industry member may be listed in the advertisement of such industry member; if such listing is the only reference to any retailer in the advertisement and is relatively inconspicuous in relation to the advertisement as a whole." This ruling in effect bans the use in consumer advertising of testimonials by retailers, and photographs of retailers or their premises (e.g., hotels, cocktail lounges). However, the name and photograph of a bartender may be used in consumer advertising, provided the name or address of his employer is not used. The ban does not apply to advertising by an industry member in trade papers, inasmuch as such advertising cannot create consumer business for the retailer, and is therefore not a thing of value provided to him.

c. *Consumer advertising specialties.* Ash trays, bottle openers, matches, recipe booklets, etc. which carry advertising matter may be furnished or sold to the retailer for distribution to the public, provided the retailer is not paid or credited for this service.

d. *Retailer advertising specialties.* Trays, coasters, menu cards, napkins, etc. which carry advertising matter may be furnished or sold to the retailer, provided the cost to the vendor does not exceed $10 in any one calendar year.

e. *Retailer mat services.* These are legal. Industry members may furnish retailers with mats, cuts, etc. which are to be used in local retailer advertising.

STATE AND LOCAL ADVERTISING LAW. We will consider this subject in the light of requirements and restrictions which must be observed in addition to those set forth by federal law. In some cases, states have no provisions concerning liquor advertising. However, in the majority of cases, the states (and, to some extent, smaller political subdivisions) have enacted laws which supplement federal law, and which, in a few instances, are severely restrictive. State advertising restrictions stem, of course, from concern by officials over sociological problems as they see them in their particular areas. We will discuss state advertising laws from the viewpoints of submission of advertising for approval, advertising copy, and advertising media.

a. *Submission of advertising for state approval.* Distilled spirits advertisers are not required to submit advertising copy for federal approval, although the government will review copy on request. Many advertisers voluntarily submit copy on this basis as general routine. As in the case of the federal government, most states do not require submission of copy for approval. States which have such a requirement are listed below. This list may not be expected to change radically or quickly:

Georgia	North Carolina
Idaho	Oregon
Kentucky	Tennessee
Michigan	Utah
Minnesota	Virginia
Montana	Washington
Nebraska	West Virginia
New Hampshire	Wyoming

b. *State laws concerning advertising copy.* The following subjects are the basis of the bulk of state advertising provisions which do not appear in federal laws and regulations, and which are not covered in self-imposed industry regulations. The listing is in the approximate order of frequency of appearance in state laws:

Prices
Code numbers
Santa Claus
Religious references
Drinking scenes
Recipes
References to state monopoly stores
Public characters, historical characters, U.S. presidents
Testimonials
Contests and prizes

Infrequently appearing in state laws are provisions regarding the number of brands in one ad; athletic contests; reference to legal holidays; references to, or illustrations of, banks and money.

When preparing campaigns, liquor advertisers automatically omit the following:

References to, or illustrations of, Santa Claus.

Religious references or illustrations, e.g., religious figures and themes. The words "Christmas" and "Easter" are not ordinarily used in liquor advertising.

References to, or illustrations of, presidents or living ex-presidents, or living federal, state or municipal government officials.

References to, or illustrations of, state monopoly stores.

The important remaining subjects covered by state laws, once we have eliminated the foregoing, are:

Prices
Code numbers
Drinking scenes
Recipes
Public and historical characters
Testimonials
Contests and prizes

When planning advertising campaigns, it is important to bear the above subjects in mind. For example, a campaign which is based primarily on any of the above might be outlawed in enough important markets to make it impractical.

Of the above subjects, two are of basic importance insofar as any advertising campaign is concerned: prices and drinking scenes. Price information in advertising is important, of course, and for obvious reasons. Drinking scenes, because they show the product in use, are also obviously important. As a result, liquor advertisers are concerned with these two subjects on a day-to-day basis in the preparation of advertising copy.

1. *Price information.* Each of the following provisions is in effect in one state or another:

(a) Prices may be shown in advertising, but reference to them is not permitted.
(b) Prices may be shown, and reference to them is permitted.
(c) Prices may not be shown, and reference to them is not permitted.
(d) Prices may not be shown, but reference to them is permitted.
(e) The word "price" may not be used, but words like "value," "bargain" and "buy" are permitted.
(f) If prices are shown, only the brand name and federal mandatory requirements may also appear in the advertisement.
(g) Prices may be shown, but they are not to be shown in type larger than a stated size.

(Similar provisions are in effect with respect to monopoly code numbers.)

In some instances, the advertiser finds it inadvisable, for one reason or other, to show prices, even though state law permits him to do so. For example, the advertiser will ordinarily elect not to show prices in advertising in cut-price markets.

It is clear that in the preparation of a campaign where prices and reference to price are an important factor, special ads must often be made which are variants from the basic campaign.

2. *Drinking scenes.* Five states prohibit illustrations showing the product in use: Georgia, North Carolina, Utah, Virginia and Washington. If drinking scenes are planned for a campaign, they must of course be eliminated in advertising intended for any of these states.

Two of these states, Virginia and North Carolina, have especially severe and stringent laws concerning distilled spirits copy in general. The advertiser is advised to make a thorough study of the liquor advertising laws of these states.

c. *State laws concerning media.* All wet states permit magazine and newspaper advertising. Most wet states also permit radio advertising. Outdoor advertising, transportation advertising and direct mail are also permitted in a majority of the states; however, one or more of them is prohibited in a sufficient number to justify a thorough study of the situation before proceeding at length in the preparation of advertising plans.

In the matter of point-of-sale material, the advertiser must also proceed cautiously. In some states, display material is prohibited. In other states display material is permitted, provided it conforms with federal and state marketing and advertising laws as discussed above. In still other states, display material is permitted, but in addition to complying with general marketing and advertising law, must meet one or more of the following requirements, among others, depending upon the state: (1) the size of display material must be limited to a specified size; (2) the value of display material must not exceed a specified dollar amount; (3) display material must meet certain requirements for off-premise outlets, and a different set of requirements for on-premise outlets; (4) display material must carry no mention of the brand name.

Consumer and retailer advertising specialties are also the subjects of state laws and regulations. Some states permit them; some permit them only under certain conditions, some prohibit them outright.

INDUSTRY ADVERTISING RESOLUTIONS. We have just explored in detail the many musts and taboos concerning liquor advertising which are established by federal and local law. In addition to these musts and taboos, rules have been imposed by the industry upon itself. These rules are in the form of advertising resolutions as set forth by the board of directors of the Distilled Spirits Institute.

a. No liquor advertising is to be placed in any publication carrying a Sunday date-line.

b. No liquor advertising is to be carried by radio or by television.

c. No liquor advertising is to be placed in religious publications.

d. No liquor advertising is to be placed in any publication which is owned or sponsored by any association, the membership of which is composed of wholesalers, retailers, or other trade buyers.

e. No liquor advertising is to contain references to, or illustrations of, women. References to, or illustrations of, children and infants are of course also ruled out in connection with liquor advertising.

f. No liquor advertising is to be placed on billboards or other media in the immediate vicinity of military or naval reservations.

In addition, the Distilled Spirits Institute has passed a resolution against the employment by industry members of paid agents to secure "plugs" or mention or showing of their products on radio, television, in motion pictures or on the legitimate stage.

Generally speaking, the industry also observes the following practices:

Advertising is not run during Holy Week, on national or religious holidays, in school publications, or in dry territory (even though local media may accept liquor advertising). Moreover, copy does not attempt to convert non-drinkers into drinkers, does not attempt to sell minors, and does not promote quantity buying.

MEDIA RESTRICTIONS ON LIQUOR ADVERTISING. It should be remembered that while federal law does not prohibit the industry from using any type of advertising medium, and while the industry itself chooses not to use radio and television (the latter, on their part, generally do not accept liquor advertising), certain magazines and newspapers refuse liquor copy (as do certain outdoor and transportation companies, even though laws of their states permit liquor copy in their particular media).

Most magazines accept liquor advertising. There are two notable exceptions, among general mass-circulation magazines: the *Saturday Evening Post* and the *Reader's Digest*. Certain women's magazines, e.g., *Ladies Home Journal*, also refuse liquor advertising.

Although all wet states permit liquor advertising in newspapers, there are some newspapers which refuse it. In certain cases, important markets are affected, e.g., Charlotte, N. C.; Des Moines, Iowa; Gary, Ind.; Kansas City, Mo.; Minneapolis, Minn.; Rochester, N. Y.; Salt Lake City, Utah; South Bend, Ind.; Spokane, Wash.; Utica, N. Y.; Worcester, Mass.

CHAPTER TWELVE

Marketing and Advertising Procedure

Reduced to barest essentials, liquor marketing and advertising procedure consists of selling a given brand of spirits to middlemen; obtaining the fullest possible support from these middlemen in moving the brand through marketing channels to the consumer; and building the greatest possible consumer acceptance and demand by means of advertisements in carefully selected media.

We will now observe the basic procedural steps in liquor marketing and advertising.

1. Marketing Procedure

DEVELOPING THE MARKETING AND MERCHANDISING PLAN. As in projects of any kind, it is necessary in liquor marketing and merchandising to agree, first of all, upon a realizable goal, to state and understand the obstacles to it, and to decide upon a course of action which will overcome these obstacles and reach the goal.

The ultimate goal, of course, is to conduct a marketing and advertising operation which will yield the largest possible net profit. To achieve this primary goal, other goals must be achieved, e.g., the establishment or continued maintenance of a strong brand name, the sale of a given volume of merchandise, etc.

Obstacles to marketing and advertising goals may range from production problems to middlemen resistance, from poor packaging design to poor pricing, from unfavorable business conditions and sales trends to heavy competition, etc.

Once having reached a clear understanding of goals and obstacles to achieving them, a detailed plan of marketing strategy must be developed, and action taken accordingly.

a. *Research.* Before goals can be determined, before obstacles can be evaluated, and before marketing strategy can be planned, it is vital to acquire all pertinent factual information concerning the brand, its competition, marketing channels, markets, sales, sales trends, the consumer, etc. Research departments of producers, importers, advertising agencies and advertising media are assigned the task of obtaining the necessary information. Independent research organizations are also available for this task. When all the facts are in, marketing and advertising skill is required to analyze and interpret the facts correctly, and creative marketing and advertising talent is required to deduce from them the wisest procedure.

Published information on distilled spirits is available for the industry as a whole as follows:

1. *Annual Statistical Review.* This publication presents a statistical report covering public revenues, tax rates, production, withdrawals, inventories, bottled output, apparent consumption, imports, exports, local option elections, etc. Published annually by the Distilled Spirits Institute.

2. *Corrado's Handbook of Liquor Marketing.* This publication offers a complete and comprehensive annual review—statistical, analytical and interpretative—of the liquor industry, in terms of sales, markets, prices, production, withdrawals, consumption, advertising, etc. First issued in 1954, and published by Benjamin W. Corrado, Marketing Consultants.

3. *Red Book Encyclopaedic Directory of the Wine and Liquor Industries* is published bi-annually by Liquor Publications, Inc., and contains lists of distillers, rectifiers, importers, vintners, brewers, distilleries, wineries, warehouses, bottling houses, wholesalers, brokers; sources of equipment and supplies; federal and state laws; etc.

Published information on distilled spirits is available on specific subjects as follows:

1. *Federal law.* Laws and regulations concerning production, standards of identity, warehousing, bottling, packaging, marketing, advertising, taxation, etc., are available through the U. S. Government Printing Office.

2. *State law.* Laws and regulations are available through state liquor units.

3. *Production, withdrawals, bottling, inventories.* Statistical reports, classified by states, on production, withdrawals from bonded

warehouses, bottling, and inventories of leading classes and types of spirits, are published monthly and annually by the Alcohol and Tobacco Tax Division of the Treasury Department. Reports on these and related subjects are also published monthly, annually and otherwise periodically by the Distilled Spirits Institute.

4. *Government revenue.* Reports on current federal internal revenue collections are published monthly and annually by the Internal Revenue Service. Reports on current state tax collections are published monthly and annually by state liquor units. Federal and state revenue is detailed at length in the annual report of the Distilled Spirits Institute, "Public Revenues from Alcoholic Beverages."

5. *Imports and exports.* Reports of current imports and exports by classes and types of spirits are published monthly by the Bureau of Foreign and Domestic Commerce. The National Association of Alcoholic Beverage Importers also issues information, e.g., statistics concerning entries into, and withdrawals from, customs bonded warehouses.

6. *Sales reports (open and monopoly states).* Sales reports by vendors, classes, types and brands are published monthly by the Distilled Spirits Institute for the following thirteen open states: Arizona, Colorado, Delaware, Indiana, Kansas, Louisiana, Missouri, Nebraska, New Mexico, Rhode Island, South Carolina, South Dakota, Texas. Similar sales reports for each of the seventeen monopoly states are published monthly and annually by the National Alcoholic Beverage Control Association.

Magazines, newspapers and trade papers are important sources of liquor research. Many publications, particularly newspapers, publish valuable periodic reports for individual states and cities on sales, market trends, etc.

Among magazines which issue or have issued reports on spirits are *Argosy, Collier's, Ebony, Esquire, Field & Stream, Life, Newsweek, The New Yorker, True.* Among newspapers: *Arkansas Dailies, Inc., Baltimore News-Post, Boston Record-American, Charleston Daily Mail, Cincinnati Enquirer, Cincinnati Post, Cleveland Plain Dealer, Detroit News, Detroit Times, Duluth Herald & News Tribune, Los Angeles Examiner, Los Angeles Herald Express, Milwaukee Journal, New York Journal-American, New York Mirror, New York News, Pittsburgh Post-Gazette, Pittsburgh Press, Pittsburgh Sun-Telegraph, Providence Journal-Bulletin, Seattle Post-Intelligencer, Seattle Times, San Francisco Call-Bulletin, San Francisco Examiner, Toledo Blade Times.*

Major Market Distillations, a report on sales activity in leading liquor markets, is issued monthly by the Hearst Advertising Service. *Beverage Media Blue Book,* published annually by Beverage Media, Ltd., is a reference manual for New York State licensees. This publication contains cost, mark-up and profit charts; trade directories; information concerning federal and New York State law; information concerning taxes and customs duties; etc.

Also a valuable research source are the many liquor trade papers, national, regional and state. Many of the state publications provide, in addition to local industry news, monthly listings of wholesale and retail prices by wholesalers, classes, types, brands and sizes, plus listings of price changes and current discounts.

Aside from published data, the brand owner also obtains information from local company personnel, from wholesalers, from retailers and from surveys which he himself undertakes.

b. *Brand name.* If a brand is being marketed for the first time, great care must be taken in selecting a name for it. The brand name should be easy to pronounce, easy to read, and short enough to appear legibly on the label. In addition, it should be distinctive and suggest character, personality and authority. It should also suggest, if feasible, tradition and age. In this latter connection, the word "old" as part of the brand name is a point to be considered.

Thought must also be given to the selection of a name which is easily illustrated, e.g., Seagram's 7 Crown is illustrated by the numeral 7 on top of a crown; Black & White Scotch is illustrated by two Scotties, one black and one white.

A brand name for a new product has a definite advantage if it is the brand name for a successful product of another type of spirits, or if it contains the name of a well-known distiller. Seagram's Ancient Bottle Gin is an example of this point. This brand followed Seagram's 7 Crown on the market after the latter achieved its tremendous success. A more recent example is PM straight bourbon, which in 1954 successfully joined on the market its namesake, PM blended whiskey, which has long been one of the nation's largest selling brands.

c. *Package, carton and case.* As mentioned in Chapter V, it is of vital importance to market brands in carefully designed packages, cartons and cases. Sometimes market conditions indicate that revisions in designs are called for in the case of an established brand, either to help halt a downward sales trend, or to help accelerate a rising sales trend.

In recent years decanters have become increasingly popular, especially during the Christmas and New Year's season. At this time of the year, brands which are marketed in decanters are usually sold simultaneously in their regular containers. Decanters are a proven device for increasing holiday business. Moreover, surveys reveal that a new decanter each year for a given brand is generally more effective than a repeat of a previous decanter. This suggests that the decanter represents style merchandising in the liquor industry.

d. *Pricing.* The importance of correct pricing has been discussed in Chapter VIII.

e. *Sales quotas.* Sales quotas must be established for a given brand of spirits nationally and by states and other local markets. The importance of sales quotas has been discussed in Chapter VIII.

f. *Markets.* When introducing a new brand to the market, the producer or importer may be in a position to enter all markets. On the other hand, he may have to limit geographically his initial distribution. In the case of a new brand of Scotch, for example, he will probably want to market his brand at first only in the larger metropolitan areas. In the case of a new brand of straight bourbon, as another example, he will probably consider it best to begin distribution in states where bourbons outsell blends or where bourbons are especially strong sales-wise, even though outsold by blends.

In most instances, a brand owner will want to conduct a test marketing campaign before attempting all-out distribution and sales.

If a brand is already established nationally, the producer or importer will check periodically on its sales progress in all markets. Such a check may suggest the advisability of revising marketing and advertising plans in certain areas. In some instances, the removal of the brand from a given market, or the halting of advertising may be indicated.

g. *Middlemen.* A producer or importer may be in the position of seeking wholesalers for a new brand, or of reviewing the merits of present wholesalers of an established brand. Some of the questions which must be answered with respect to wholesalers, and also with respect to monopoly states, are as follows:

1. *Open states.* What wholesalers are available? Do they handle competing brands? What is their past and current performance? What is their reputation with retailers in connection with deliveries, service, etc.? How quickly can they be expected to accomplish effective distribution? How many salesmen does each employ?

2. *Monopoly states.* Will all monopoly states list the brand? If not, which monopolies will? Are these monopolies satisfactory markets for the brand? How long will it take to obtain a listing? After

each listing, how long will it take to accomplish effective distribution (as a general rule in the monopolies, 100% distribution in state stores can be expected very quickly after a listing)?

With respect to both open and monopoly states, the producer or importer will take into account the type of retail outlets in those states in which he markets his brand. He must know of course whether there are on-premise outlets in the states in which he is interested, whether spirits are marketed in exclusive liquor stores, supermarkets, chains, hotels, restaurants, clubs, etc.

h. *Determining the appropriation.* Knowing the manufacturer's mark-up and anticipated sales volume (see Chapter VIII), management, sales and advertising executives are able to estimate annual gross profit for a given brand. Following this calculation, the task is to determine what percentage of gross profit is to be allocated to sales and advertising costs. Once this has been determined, the resulting dollar appropriation must be broken down into its component parts, which, as we have learned, are the following: sales expense (sales personnel salaries, sales branch offices, sales meetings, etc.); marketing expenses (allowances to wholesalers); advertising expenses; sales promotion expenses.

Annual sales expense may ordinarily be estimated fairly closely. When this is calculated, the remainder of the overall appropriation is broken down into marketing, advertising and sales promotion expenses. This breakdown depends upon the circumstances attending the brand in question. For example, marketing expenditures, the purpose of which is to increase trade support, may be slight for a brand which is a strong consumer call item. In another instance, when a new brand is being launched, marketing expense may account for a substantial part of the overall sales and advertising expenditure. In still another instance, the profit margin to the trade for a low-priced brand may be so small, or the competition may be dealing so heavily, that marketing expenses may necessarily be high.

Against requirements for marketing expense must be weighed requirements for advertising and sales promotion. If the brand in question sells in mass volume nationally, magazine and local advertising will doubtless be required. If the brand is a high-priced product with thin national distribution, only magazine advertising may be indicated, with perhaps some local advertising, if the budget permits, in a few primary markets. If the brand has consumer acceptance, but little consumer demand, magazine advertising may be called for in order to obtain continued brand name support, but it may be considered wise to devote most, if not all, funds in local markets to point-of-sale material.

Generally speaking, the advertising appropriation substantially exceeds the sales promotion appropriation. The industry as a whole spends in the proportion of approximately 75% for advertising, 25% for sales promotion. Individual brands spend in proportions which vary, depending upon the brand, anywhere from 90%-10% to 50%-50%.

Marketing, advertising and sales promotion expenditures may be viewed in terms of the total appropriation for each, or in terms of the expenditure per case for each. For example, the sales quota for a given brand may be 500,000 cases. If the marketing appropriation is, let us say, $400,000, the marketing expense is 80¢ per case.

Executing the marketing and merchandising plan. Once the overall marketing and merchandising plan has been developed, the producer or importer goes into action. His sales department, gearing its activities with the production and traffic departments, contacts and sells wholesalers in open states and liquor buying units in monopoly states; orders shipments; determines local marketing policies (e.g., allowances); conducts sales meetings of company and wholesaler personnel; furnishes salesmen with material for indoctrination purposes and for retail calls; notifies the advertising, sales promotion and publicity departments when distribution warrants the release of advertising, point-of-sale and publicity material.

At one time in the not too distant past, the producer or importer considered his job finished once he had filled a middleman's order and once he had launched a consumer and trade advertising campaign. His attitude was that it was thereafter up to the wholesaler to worry about moving the brand to the retailer, and up to the retailer to worry about moving the brand to the consumer. Overzealous brand owners, clinging to this attitude, devoted their full energies to moving stocks into wholesaler warehouses. As may have been expected, this mode of selling often boomeranged. If the retailer did not succeed in moving a brand, the wholesaler could not obtain repeat orders; and if the wholesaler failed in this respect, he was not in a position to re-order from the brand owner.

Today the brand owner takes it upon himself to do all he can to help both wholesalers and retailers to sell his brand. Not only does he place consumer and trade advertising, but he assists wholesalers in their efforts to sell retailers, and assists retailers in their efforts to sell the consumer.

Brand owners today engage in the following marketing and merchandising activities:

a. *Open states*

1. *Company sales personnel.* Local representatives of producers and importers have the job of selling wholesalers, and of assisting and winning the support of both wholesalers and retailers.

2. *Consumer advertising.* Advertising in magazines, newspapers and other media helps the retailer directly, and the wholesaler indirectly.

3. *Allowances.* Producers and importers give allowances to the wholesaler to induce him to put pressure on the brand in question. These allowances may be dictated by competitive dealing. Or the activities of the competition may not be a factor; the producer or importer of a brand of gin, for example, may offer allowances in cold weather (off-season) months, but may withdraw these allowances when the big summer gin season is at hand.

4. *Sales meetings.* The producer or importer sends his representatives to sales meetings to address wholesaler's salesmen and impel them to action.

5. *Direct mail.* The producer or importer sends broadsides, letters and other types of mailings to wholesaler executives, wholesaler salesmen and key retailers.

6. *Salesmen's kits.* The producer or importer furnishes sales kits to wholesaler's salesmen. These kits contain, for example, advertising proofs and media schedules, and are used by salesmen on retail calls.

7. *Contests, prizes and bonuses.* The producer or importer helps the wholesaler conduct contests for best selling performances by salesmen, with prizes in the form of cash, vacation trips, etc. In addition, special bonuses may be awarded.

8. *Truck panel advertising.* The producer or importer furnishes artwork for advertising to be painted on the sides or back of wholesaler delivery trucks.

9. *Sales promotion material.* The producer or importer furnishes window displays and other point-of-sale material to the retailer, and checks up periodically to determine whether this material continues in use.

10. *Mat services.* The producer or importer furnishes mat services to wholesalers and retailers in order to encourage advertising in local newspapers and trade papers. In addition, prepared copy for wholesaler-to-retailer and retailer-to-consumer direct mail is made available.

11. *Trade advertising.* The producer or importer places trade advertising in national and local trade papers which are directed to retailers.

12. *Trade publicity.* The producer or importer releases news items concerning his brand to newspapers, trade papers, and newspaper trade supplements.

13. *Merchandising by media.* The producer or importer obtains the services of national magazines and local media in merchandising his advertising campaign to wholesalers and retailers.

14. *Distribution checks.* By retailer surveys in a given market, the producer or importer determines the percentage of his overall distribution, determines whether retailers have full or token stocks of his brand, determines whether retailers have all sizes or only one or two. On the basis of this information, the brand owner can better assist the wholesaler, or if necessary, call him to task.

Producers and importers also activate their own local sales personnel with many of the methods mentioned above, i.e., through sales meetings, direct mail, salesmen's kits, contests, prizes and bonuses.

b. *Monopoly states.* In monopoly states, as we have observed, the brand owner may sell only to state liquor buying units. In Chapter VI we noted the selling problems which the brand owner must solve in his contacts with monopoly officials. In addition, we learned that local company personnel may make calls, by and large, only on bars and on privately owned package stores. Outside of these specialized marketing and merchandising activities which obtain in the monopolies, other activities, similar to those in open states, are open to the brand owner. Thus, he places consumer and trade advertising, releases consumer and trade publicity, installs point-of-sale material (where legal), etc. In addition, he activates his sales force, using the same methods employed in open states to activate his own and wholesalers' salesmen. For example, he conducts sales meetings, prepares selling kits, conducts direct mail campaigns, initiates contests, awards prizes and bonuses.

2. Advertising Procedure

THE SCOPE OF LIQUOR ADVERTISING. Before undertaking a study of the development and execution of the advertising and sales promotion plan, let us glance briefly at the overall industry advertising picture in which each individual brand owner operates.

As an advertiser, the liquor industry today ranks among the nation's leaders. In the four major consumer media open to the industry

—newspapers, magazines, outdoor and transportation—expenditures by producers and importers have approximated $75 million annually. Expenditures for trade paper advertising, point-of-sale material, direct mail, advertising by wholesalers and retailers, etc., account for many more millions of dollars.

With respect to the four principal media, more than 50% of liquor expenditures are in newspapers; magazine advertising accounts for about 30%; outdoor advertising for about 15%; and transportation advertising for about 2%.

Expenditures throughout the year roughly approximate sales curves, with largest outlays during October, November and December.

DEVELOPING THE ADVERTISING AND SALES PROMOTION PLAN. Like other phases of the overall marketing and merchandising operation, advertising and sales promotion must contribute their share to the goal of building sales and producing the largest possible net profit. What is the nature of the contribution which advertising and sales promotion must make to this goal? This naturally depends upon the specific circumstances in each case. A highly successful brand may require only a continuation in volume of what amounts to little more than reminder copy. At the other extreme, a new and struggling brand may require powerful selling copy strategically placed in a few carefully selected markets. As another example, advertising may be placed in important consumer media, e.g., *Life, Look, Collier's, Coronet,* not so much for its effect on the consumer as for its value as a merchandising tool when selling the trade. Moreover, advertising may be called upon to produce sales immediately, e.g., when a price reduction goes into effect, or, as is more often the case, it may be expected to build a brand name over an extended period of time.

Whatever an advertising and sales promotion campaign is expected to achieve, the purpose must be stated clearly at the outset, and must be adhered to carefully.

a. *Advertising agencies.* The brand owner who does business in any sort of volume must, of course, utilize the services of an advertising agency, and for the same major reasons that dictate this move by those who market volume brands in other industries. Among these reasons are the following:

1. Good advertising agencies are not only experts in the preparation, placement and merchandising of advertising campaigns, but are also experts in all phases of the marketing and merchandising operation.

2. It costs the national advertiser no more to buy space (and time) through an advertising agency than if he were to buy direct. Agencies are allowed a discount when buying space from media which is not allowed to other buyers. Hence the advertiser pays 100% of media national rates, whether he pays the agency or makes payment directly to media. The standard agency discount is 15% (outdoor plant operators allow 16⅔%).

When the producer or importer is in the market for an advertising agency, he must choose carefully. Because of legal restrictions, sociological problems and other aspects peculiar to the liquor industry, liquor advertising has become a highly specialized operation, and is best handled by advertising experts who are also experts on distilled spirits.

b. *Research.* As in the case of liquor marketing and merchandising, consumer and trade research is important in developing and executing liquor advertising and sales promotion campaigns. Many of the sources of research listed elsewhere in this chapter are useful to the liquor advertising and sales promotion man.

c. *The appropriation.* We discussed the determination of advertising and sales promotion appropriations in the previous section. We will proceed now on the assumption that these appropriations have already been established for a given brand of spirits, and that the problem at this point is to determine how to handle each. With regard to the advertising appropriation, decisions must be made as to which markets and media to choose and how much to spend in each. With regard to the sales promotion appropriation, decisions must be made as to which markets to choose, what items to produce for each, and how much to spend in each.

1. *The advertising appropriation.* Let us assume that we have a brand budget large enough to cover most markets adequately in all major media open to the liquor industry. Let us also assume that the brand in question is well established, has good national distribution, sells in mass volume and is comparatively stable sales-wise. Let us assume further that the goal is to increase sales by continuing to build consumer and trade confidence, acceptance and demand. With a set of conditions like this, magazine advertising is a must. After a decision to use magazines is made, the next task is to determine how much of the total advertising appropriation is to be allocated to this medium. Generally speaking, magazine space will be considered as a long-term investment, the purpose of which will be to establish the brand name more strongly and more favorably in the consumer mind.

The requirements in this direction must be judged carefully in relation to requirements for more immediate consumer motivation. The latter is of course provided by advertising in newspapers and other local media.

As noted previously, magazine advertising accounts for about 30% of total spirits expenditures in the four major consumer media available to liquor advertisers.

Choice of magazines, and the size and type of schedule in each, will depend upon the product, its price, distribution and similar factors. Primary magazines for a mass liquor brand are *Life, Look, Collier's* and *Coronet.* Magazines of general, smaller or specialized circulation will be chosen in accordance with the problem at hand, e.g., *American, American Legion, Argosy, Cosmopolitan, Ebony, Esquire, Field & Stream, Fortune, Gourmet, Holiday, Newsweek, the New Yorker, Outdoor Life, Promenade, Redbook, Social Spectator, Sports Afield, TV Guide, Time, Town & Country, True.*

If the magazine budget is substantial, attention must be given to the problem of 4 colors vs. 2 colors vs. black & white, and the number of insertions which may be purchased of each (or of a combination of two or all three) in full pages and in fractional pages. The problem of inside pages vs. covers will also require study.

Once the magazine budget and the magazine schedule have been worked out, it is important to know how much of the expenditure is chargeable to each state (magazine charges to each state may be considered as proportionate to magazine circulation in each state). Individual state advertising budgets will be reduced in each instance by the magazine charge, leaving the amount which may be expended for local advertising.

How are state advertising budgets determined to begin with? The usual method is to allocate to each state, based on the total advertising appropriation, a percentage which is approximately equivalent to each state's percentage of the total national sales quota (or each state's percentage of current total national sales).

Once local advertising budgets are determined for individual states, budgets for markets within each state must be established, and will also be based on percentages of sales quotas or current sales.

In the case of most brands, the major portion of local advertising funds will go to newspapers, inasmuch as this medium has proved itself to be the strongest local advertising force for distilled spirits. The media buyer will select newspapers which are most suitable in terms of the advertising problem. Moreover, he will evaluate the following: color vs. black & white; position (r.o.p., sports page, etc.); larger ads vs. greater frequency; larger schedules per market vs. a larger number of markets; hot weather vs. cold weather scheduling; pre-holiday scheduling; days of insertion (most liquor advertisers avoid Mondays, Saturdays and food days, and rule out Sundays and holidays).

As we have noted, more than 50% of total spirits' advertising is allocated to newspapers.

What about outdoor advertising and transportation advertising? These media must, in general, be considered as supplementary to newspapers, to be scheduled only after adequate newspaper coverage is achieved, except, of course, in those markets where newspapers do not accept liquor advertising.

With respect to outdoor, liquor advertisers use spectaculars, painted bulletins and 24-sheet posters, and, to a smaller extent, painted walls, 3-sheets and other posters. In buying outdoor it is wise to keep in mind that spectaculars, painted bulletins and painted walls incur extended fixed commitments as compared to posters.

Transportation advertising is an obvious choice in markets where the consumer makes substantial use of street cars, buses, ferries or railroads, as, for example, in New York and Chicago. The media buyer will carefully consider (1) interior cards (side-space and end-space positions; the standard 11″ x 28″ size and smaller and larger sizes); (2) exterior cards (traveling displays); (3) station posters (1-sheets, 2-sheets and 3-sheets).

Also to be considered under the classification of local media are local magazines and theatre programs, e.g., *Cue, Fortnight, Playbill.*

We have been discussing the major media which the liquor advertiser uses in reaching the consumer. Provision must also be made for advertising to local company executives and salesmen, to wholesaler executives and salesmen, to monopoly executives and to retailers. Direct mail is generally used to reach company and wholesaler personnel; trade papers are generally used to reach monopoly executives and the retailer.

The following is a listing of liquor trade publications.

National publications for liquor executives:

Monopoly State Review—directed to monopoly states commissioners, administrators, supervisors, state store managers, state agents and S.D.D.'s

Spirits—directed to distillers, rectifiers, vintners, importers, plant managers, purchasing agents, wholesalers, monopoly state officials, etc.

Ed Gibb's Newsletter
Frank Kane's Weekly Letter
Red Book Directory of the Wine and Liquor Industry
Corrado's Handbook of Liquor Marketing

National publications for retailers:

Bar Management—directed to on-premise retailers
Bar-Restaurant section of *Institutional Feeding*—directed to on-premise retailers
Frank Kane's Licensed Beverage Review—directed to on-premise and off-premise retailers.
Liquor Store—directed to off-premise retailers
Package Store Management—directed to off-premise retailers
The Server—directed to off-premise and on-premise retailers

Liquor Store provides a special service to wholesalers, whereby circulation may be directed to retailers selected by the wholesaler. Advertisements by the latter are limited to the retailer circulation in which they are interested. Copy for brand advertisements is usually furnished by the producer or importer.

Regional and state publications for retailers (when not part of the name of the publication, the state or states receiving primary coverage are indicated):

Alaska Beverage Analyst
Allied Food & Beverage Magazine—Washington
Arizona Beverage Journal
Beverage Bulletin—California
Beverage Dealer News—Illinois, Indiana, Minnesota, Missouri, North Dakota, South Dakota, Wisconsin
Beverage Industry News—California
Beverage Market Guide—New York, New Jersey
Beverage Media—New York, New Jersey
Beverage Media Blue Book—New York, New Jersey
Beverage Register—California
Beverage Retailer Weekly—New York, New Jersey
Beverage Times—New York, New Jersey
Buckeye Tavern—Ohio
California Beverage Journal

California Beverage Price Bulletin
Club Review—Washington
Connecticut Beverage Journal
Hawaii Beverage Guide
Illinois Beverage Journal
Indiana Beverage Life
Kansas Beverage Analyst
Kentucky Beverage Journal
Maryland-Washington-Delaware Beverage Journal
Massachusetts Beverage Journal
Michigan Beverage News
Michigan Table Topper
Missouri Beverage Journal
National Reviewer and Connecticut Items of Interest
Nebraska Beverage Analyst
Nevada Beverage Index
New Jersey Beverage Journal
New Mexico Beverage Journal
Northwest Beverage Journal—Minnesota, North Dakota, South Dakota
Observer—Pennsylvania
Ohio Tavern News
Oregon Licensee
Patterson's California Beverage Gazetteer
Rhode Island Beverage Journal
Rocky Mountain Beverage Analyst—Colorado, New Mexico, western Texas
Seaboard Beverage Journal—Delaware, Maryland, Washington, D. C.
Southern States Beverage Journal—Arkansas, Florida, Georgia, Kentucky, Louisiana, South Carolina, Tennessee, Texas
Tap & Tavern—Pennsylvania
Tavern Keeper—Illinois
Western States Beverage Analyst—Idaho, Montana, Oregon, Utah, Washington, Wyoming
Wisconsin Beverage Journal

A list of media commonly used by liquor advertisers follows:

Magazines—national, local; mass and class; weekly, bi-weekly, monthly; general, specialized, Negro.

Newspapers—daily, weekly; general, Negro, foreign language.

Outdoor—spectaculars, painted bulletins, painted walls, 24-sheet posters, 3-sheet posters.

Transportation—interior cards, traveling displays, station posters.

Trade papers—national, local; weekly, semi-monthly, monthly; executive, on-premise, off-premise.

Direct mail—letters, broadsides, etc.

Point-of-sale

Newspaper trade supplements

Match books

Wholesaler trucks

Cartons

Cases

2. *The sales promotion appropriation.* The sales promotion man must determine the type of items to produce and the quantity of each. In addition, he must develop a plan of distribution based on the size and legal requirements of individual markets. Moreover, he must see to it that the advertising copy campaign theme is carried out, if possible, in sales promotion material. The following are typical point-of-sale pieces used for distilled spirits:

awnings
bar stool covers
book matches
bottle attachments, e.g., caps, neckpiece cutouts
bottle caps
bottle reproductions, e.g., cardboard, dummy
cash register signs
change mats
circulars
clocks
coasters
cologne sticks
counter bottle bins
counter cards
cut-case cards
cut-out figures
drink reproductions (cardboard, dummy)
folders
floor mass display stands
half-gallon racks
key chains

lamps (bottle is base, shade carries advertising)
license holders
lighters
lipsticks
memo pads
menu clips
menus
mobiles
napkins
pourers
price cards, tags, signs
puzzles
recipe booklets
shelf strips
sports schedules (baseball, football, etc.)
stickers
stirrers
table tents
trays
wall panels
window displays
window streamers

d. *Advertising copy.* Considering legal restrictions, both federal and local, and considering the fact that few brands have a clear-cut product advantage over similarly priced competitive brands, it becomes clear that creative talent of the highest order is required to produce powerful and effective copy for most brands of spirits. In general, the ultimate function of most liquor advertising and promotion campaigns is to increase sales by building a distinctive personality, atmosphere or feeling about a brand. If this is accomplished, an equity is created which is one of the brand's most valuable properties. Thus, as for products of other industries, establishment of a strong brand name becomes the underlying principle for long-term success in liquor marketing and advertising. More immediate situations must be handled by copy, e.g., the announcement of a new package, an increase in age, a price reduction; nevertheless the basic job of brand building must constantly be borne in mind.

How does the copywriter go about the job of creating a campaign which will endow the brand with character, authority and personality? He will, of course, attempt first of all to find attributes of the brand (if any) which cannot be claimed by the competition. In seeking such attributes, he will look into the particular history and tradition (if any) of the brand, into the matter of sales leadership (if it exists), into the particular distinctiveness or attractiveness (if any) of the package, into any usable qualities inherent in the brand name or the trademark, into the matter of age (if the age is significant or greater than that of competitive brands), and into the matter of price (if the price suggests marked value).

Whether or not the copywriter discovers any particular attributes of the brand among the foregoing, he will probably give serious attention nevertheless to the idea of creating a symbol and a slogan. In some instances he may find either or both on the brand label.

Having arrived at an approach which will establish a distinctive character for the brand, the copywriter must consider slanting his campaign in terms of psychological appeals. As we have noted, certain appeals are automatically eliminated from liquor advertising, e.g., sex, romance, curative or therapeutic effects, absence of ill effects, claims based on scientific testing, discounts for quantity buying. Among the direct appeals which the liquor copywriter may use are the following: enjoyment of taste and quality; value; prestige; popularity; usefulness for gift and entertaining purposes; cooling refreshment in hot weather (provided the drinks, not the spirits, are represented as having a cooling effect).

Testimonials, contests and recipes are among familiar advertising devices which may be used as vehicles for presenting copy appeals to the consumer.

Special problems arise for all brands from time to time. In these instances, advertising must be tailor-made to the problem at hand.

Copy must be varied, as in the case of non-liquor products, for each type of media used. Magazine advertising will generally be considered most important for brand-building purposes. Newspaper advertising will also be considered as contributing to brand-building, but copy will attempt to prompt more immediate action. Outdoor advertising, traveling displays and station posters will keep the copy message to a minimum, and will try to convey only one salient point in connection with the brand. Interior bus and car cards will go into less detail than magazine or newspaper advertising, but will present lengthier copy, if feasible or so desired, than outdoor advertising and other forms of transportation advertising.

EXECUTING THE ADVERTISING AND SALES PROMOTION CAMPAIGN. Once the appropriation, media plan and copy campaign are agreed upon, the producer or importer and his advertising agency go into action. The advertising campaign is submitted for federal approval (if any doubts concerning federal approval are entertained, the campaign will be submitted at an earlier stage). In addition, variations in the campaign are prepared to meet individual state copy requirements, whereupon these variations are submitted for approval to liquor authorities in states which require this procedure.

Following federal and state copy approvals, advertising is mechanically produced to meet the requirements of the media schedule, which has meanwhile been prepared in complete detail in accordance with the basic media plan. Next, insertion orders together with plates, mats or artwork (as the case may be) are transmitted to all media on the schedule.

While the above process has been going on, the sales promotion man has been determining point-of-sale pieces for individual markets, has gone into production, and has arranged for shipments to individual markets. Also while the above process is going on, direct mail is prepared and forwarded to company and wholesaler executives and salesmen and to key retailers.

In addition, plans are made for merchandising the advertising and sales promotion campaign:

MERCHANDISING THE ADVERTISING AND SALES PROMOTION CAMPAIGN. Advertising and sales promotion campaigns are merchandised by the producer or importer, by wholesalers and by media.

a. *Merchandising by the producer or importer.* The brand owner, aided by his advertising agency, merchandises his campaign to his executives and salesmen, to wholesaler executives and salesmen, and to retailers as follows:

1. *Sales meetings.* At both distiller and wholesaler sales meetings, advertising and sales promotion campaigns are presented to executives and to salesmen in an effort to win interest, enthusiasm and support. Sales promotion pieces are put on display; advertising proofs, media schedules and sales kits are distributed.

2. *Direct mail.* Letters, broadsides and other direct mail pieces which merchandise the campaign are sent to company and wholesaler executives and salesmen and to important retailers.

3. *Trade advertising.* Advertisements featuring and merchan-

dising consumer advertising and sales promotion campaigns are placed in retailer trade papers and released to newspaper trade supplements.

4. *Trade publicity.* Announcements of advertising and sales promotion campaigns are released to retailer trade papers and to newspaper trade supplements.

5. *Retail calls.* Company salesmen present and merchandise campaigns during personal calls on retailers.

b. *Merchandising by wholesalers.* The wholesaler merchandises advertising and promotion campaigns, using methods employed by the producer or importer. Thus, the wholesaler will present and merchandise campaigns at his sales meetings, will make mailings to retailers, will place advertisements in local trade papers and newspaper trade supplements, will release announcements to local trade papers and newspaper trade supplements, will direct his salesmen to merchandise the campaign to retailers.

c. *Merchandising by media.* The advertising agency, working through media representatives, calls upon magazines, newspapers, outdoor plant operators, transportation advertising companies and trade papers to merchandise advertising and promotion campaigns to company and wholesaler personnel and to retailers. In some instances, this merchandising may take the form of personal calls, but more often consists of mailings. For example, national magazines may send a letter or other mailing piece, accompanied by a proof of a magazine advertisement for the brand in question, to company and wholesaler executives and salesmen. As another example, newspapers may make a mailing, accompanied by a proof of a newspaper advertisement for the brand, to local retailers.

PUBLICITY. A corollary to the advertising and promotion campaign is the publicity campaign. We have already touched upon publicity from the viewpoint of publicizing, and hence merchandising, advertising and promotion campaigns in trade papers and newspaper trade supplements. Other types of brand publicity are open to the producer or importer, to be developed by his publicity department, by the publicity department of his advertising agency, or by a publicity organization retained for this purpose.

The following are examples of publicity for a specific brand or for a producer or importer:

a. *Consumer publicity*

1. *Media.* Publicity may be released to newspapers and other

consumer media concerning the introduction of a brand, or concerning any other news in connection with a brand, or in connection with a producer or importer.

2. *"Plants."* These may be arranged in publication editorial matter, e.g., in popular newspaper columns.

3. *Special events.* Floats for parades, as well as other striking contrivances, have won publicity not only locally but through publication reporting.

4. *Manufactured news.* A special occasion or incident is created, with possibilities for publicity as the motivating idea.

b. *Trade publicity.* Consumer publicity as outlined above constitutes material for trade publications. In addition, together with publicity concerning advertising and sales promotion campaigns, publicity on the following subjects, among others, is released to the trade press in the form of stories or photographs or both:

1. News of producers, importers, wholesalers and retailers at the management level.

2. Appointments of new wholesalers and new personnel.

3. News concerning local sales meetings.

4. News concerning local wholesalers and retailers, e.g., the opening of a new warehouse.

5. News of visits to local areas of producer or importer executives from the home office.

Appendices

APPENDIX A

The 21st Amendment

This amendment, which brought Prohibition to an end, originated in the 72nd Congress and was incorporated into a joint resolution by the Senate and House of Representatives (approved by the Senate on February 16, 1933 by a vote of 63 to 23, and approved by the House on February 20, 1933 by a vote of 289 to 121). On February 21st, Secretary of State Cordell Hull sent copies of the resolution to the governors of each state. Utah became the 36th state to ratify. The amendment went into effect on December 5, 1933.

ARTICLE XXI

SECTION 1

The eighteenth article of amendment to the Constitution of the United States is hereby repealed.

SECTION 2

The transportation or importation into any State, Territory, or Possession of the United States for delivery or use therein of intoxicating liquors, in violation of the laws thereof, is hereby prohibited.

SECTION 3

This article shall be inoperative unless it shall have been ratified as an amendment to the Constitution by convention in the several States, as provided in the Constitution, within seven years from the date of the submission hereof to the States by the Congress.

APPENDIX B

Federal Alcohol Administration Act

AN ACT

To further protect the revenue derived from distilled spirits, wine, and malt beverages, to regulate interstate and foreign commerce and enforce the postal laws with respect thereto, to enforce the twenty-first amendment, and for other purposes.

Be it enacted by the Senate and House of Representatives of the United States of America in Congress assembled, That this Act may be cited as the "Federal Alcohol Administration Act."

Sec. 2. (a) Appropriations to carry out powers and duties of the Secretary of the Treasury shall be available for expenditure, among other purposes, for personal services and rent in the District of Columbia and elsewhere, expenses for travel and subsistence, for law books, books of reference, magazines, periodicals, and newspapers, for contract stenographic reporting services, for subscriptions for library services, for purchase of samples for analysis or use as evidence, and for holding conferences of State and Federal liquor control officials.

(b) The Secretary of the Treasury may, with the consent of the department or agency affected, utilize the services of any department or other agency of the Government to the extent necessary to carry out his powers and duties and authorize officers and employees thereof to act as his agents.

(c) The provisions, including penalties, of sections 9 and 10 of the Federal Trade Commission Act, as now or hereafter amended, shall be applicable to the jurisdiction, powers, and duties of the Secretary of the Treasury, and to any person (whether or not a corporation) subject to the provisions of laws administered by the Secretary of the Treasury.

(d) The Secretary of the Treasury is authorized to require, in such manner and form as he shall prescribe, such reports as are necessary to carry out his powers and duties.

UNLAWFUL BUSINESSES WITHOUT PERMIT

Sec. 3. In order effectively to regulate interstate and foreign commerce in distilled spirits, wine, and malt beverages, to enforce the twenty-first amendment, and to protect the revenue and enforce the postal laws with respect to distilled spirits, wine, and malt beverages:

(a) It shall be unlawful, except pursuant to a basic permit issued under this Act by the Secretary of the Treasury—

(1) to engage in the business of importing into the United States distilled spirits, wine, or malt beverages; or

(2) for any person so engaged to sell, offer or deliver for sale, contract to sell, or ship, in interstate or foreign commerce, directly or indirectly or through an affiliate, distilled spirits, wine, or malt beverages so imported.

(b) It shall be unlawful, except pursuant to a basic permit issued under this Act by the Secretary of the Treasury—

(1) to engage in the business of distilling distilled spirits, producing wine, rectifying or blending distilled spirits or wine, or bottling, or warehousing and bottling, distilled spirits; or

(2) for any person so engaged to sell, offer or deliver for sale, contract to sell, or ship, in interstate or foreign commerce, directly or indirectly or through an affiliate, distilled spirits or wine so distilled, produced, rectified, blended, or bottled, or warehoused and bottled.

(c) It shall be unlawful, except pursuant to a basic permit issued under this Act by the Secretary of the Treasury—

(1) to engage in the business of purchasing for resale at wholesale distilled spirits, wine, or malt beverages; or

(2) for any person so engaged to receive or to sell, offer or deliver for sale, contract to sell, or ship, in interstate or foreign commerce, directly or indirectly or through an affiliate, distilled spirits, wine, or malt beverages so purchased.

This section shall not apply to any agency of a State or political subdivision thereof or any officer or employee of any such agency, and no such agency or officer or employee shall be required to obtain a basic permit under this Act.

PERMITS

Sec. 4. (a) The following persons shall, on application therefor, be entitled to a basic permit:

(1) Any person, who, on May 25, 1935, held a basic permit as distiller, rectifier, wine producer, or importer issued by an agency of the Federal Government.

(2) Any other person unless the Secretary of the Treasury finds (A) that such person (or in case of a corporation, any of its officers, directors, or principal stockholders) has, within five years prior to date of application, been convicted of a felony under Federal or State law or has, within three years prior to date of application, been convicted of a misdemeanor under any Federal law relating to liquor, including the taxation thereof; or (B) that such person is, by reason of his business experience, financial standing, or trade connections, not likely to commence operations within a reasonable period or to maintain such operations in conformity with Federal law; or (C) that the operations proposed to be conducted by such person are in violation of the law of the State in which they are to be conducted.

(b) If upon examination of any application for a basic permit the Secretary of the Treasury has reason to believe that the applicant is not entitled to such permit, he shall notify the applicant thereof and, upon request by the applicant, afford him due notice and opportunity for hearing on the application. If the Secretary of the Treasury, after affording such notice and opportunity for hearing, finds that the applicant is not entitled to a basic permit hereunder, he shall by order deny the application stating the findings which are the basis for his order.

(c) The Secretary of the Treasury shall prescribe the manner and form of all applications for basic permits (including the facts to be set forth therein) and the form of all basic permits, and shall specify in any basic permit the authority conferred by the permit and the conditions thereof in accordance with the provisions of this Act. To the extent deemed necessary by the Secretary of the Treasury for the efficient administration of this Act, separate applications and permits shall be required by the Secretary of the Treasury with respect to distilled spirits, wine, and malt beverages, and the various classes thereof, and with respect to the various classes of persons entitled to permits hereunder. The issuance of a basic permit under this Act shall not operate to deprive the United States of its remedy for any violation of law.

(d) A basic permit shall be conditioned upon compliance with the requirements of section 5 (relating to unfair competition and unlawful practices) and of section 6 (relating to bulk sales and bottling), with the twenty-first amendment and laws relating to the enforcement thereof, and with all other Federal laws relating to distilled spirits, wine, and malt beverages, including taxes with respect thereto.

(e) A basic permit shall by order of the Secretary of the Treasury, after due notice and opportunity for hearing to the permittee, (1) be revoked, or suspended for such period as the Secretary of the Treasury deems appropriate, if the Secretary of the Treasury finds that the permittee has willfully violated any of the conditions thereof, provided that for a first violation of the conditions thereof the permit shall be subject to suspension only; or (2) be revoked if the Secretary of the Treasury finds that the permittee has not engaged in the operations authorized by the permit for a period of more than two years; or (3) be annulled if the Secretary of the Treasury finds that the permit was procured through fraud, or misrepresentation, or concealment of material fact. The order shall state the findings which are the basis for the order.

(f) Orders of the Secretary of the Treasury with respect to any denial of application, suspension, revocation, annulment, or other proceedings, shall be served (1) in person by any officer or employee of the Secretary of the Treasury designated by the Secretary of the Treasury or any internal revenue or customs officer authorized by the Secretary of the Treasury for the purpose, or (2) by mailing the order by registered mail, addressed to the applicant or respondent at his last known address in the records of the Secretary of the Treasury.

(g) A basic permit shall continue in effect until suspended, revoked, or annulled as provided herein, or voluntarily surrendered; except that (1) if leased, sold or otherwise voluntarily transferred, the permit shall be automatically terminated thereupon, and (2) if transferred by operation of law or if actual or legal control of the permittee is acquired, directly or indirectly, whether by stock-ownership or in any other manner, by any person, then such permit shall be automatically terminated at the expiration of thirty days thereafter:

Provided, That if within such thirty-day period application for a new basic permit is made by the transferee or permittee, respectively, then the outstanding basic permit shall continue in effect until such application is finally acted on by the Secretary of the Treasury.

(h) An appeal may be taken by the permittee or applicant for a permit from any order of the Secretary of the Treasury denying an application for, or suspending, revoking, or annulling, a basic permit. Such appeal shall be taken by filing, in the circuit court of appeals of the United States within any circuit wherein such person resides or has his principal place of business, or in the United States Court of Appeals for the District of Columbia, within sixty days after the entry of such order, a written petition praying that the order of the Secretary of the Treasury be modified or set aside in whole or in part. A copy of such petition shall be forthwith served upon the Secretary of the Treasury, or upon any officer designated by him for that purpose, and thereupon the Secretary of the Treasury shall certify and file in the court a transcript of the record upon which the order complained of was entered. Upon the filing of such transcript such court shall have exclusive jurisdiction to affirm, modify, or set aside such order, in whole or in part. No objection to the order of the Secretary of the Treasury shall be considered by the court unless such objection shall have been urged before the Secretary of the Treasury or unless there were reasonable grounds for failure so to do. The finding of the Secretary of the Treasury as to the facts, if supported by substantial evidence, shall be conclusive. If any party shall apply to the court for leave to adduce additional evidence, and shall show to the satisfaction of the court that such additional evidence is material and that there were reasonable grounds for failure to adduce such evidence in the proceeding before the Secretary of the Treasury, the court may order such additional evidence to be taken before the Secretary of the Treasury and to be adduced upon the hearing in such manner and upon such terms and conditions as to the court may seem proper. The Secretary of the Treasury may modify his findings as to the facts by reason of the additional evidence so taken, and he shall file with the court such modified or new findings, which, if supported by substantial evidence, shall be conclusive, and his recommendation, if any, for the modification or setting aside of the original order. The judgment and decree of the court affirming, modifying, or setting aside, in whole or in part, any such order of the Secretary of the Treasury shall be final, subject to review by the Supreme Court of the United States upon certiorari or certification as provided in sections 239 and 240 of the Judicial Code, as amended (U.S.C., title 28, secs. 346 and 347). The commencement of proceedings under this subsection shall, unless specifically ordered by the court to the contrary, operate as a stay of the Secretary's order.

(i) No proceeding for the suspension or revocation of a basic permit for violation of any condition thereof relating to compliance with Federal law shall be instituted by the Secretary of the Treasury more than eighteen months after conviction of the violation of Federal law, or, if no conviction has been had, more than three years after the violation occurred; and no basic permit shall be suspended or revoked for a violation of any such condition thereof if the alleged violation of Federal law has been compromised by any officer of the Government authorized to compromise such violation.

UNFAIR COMPETITION AND UNLAWFUL PRACTICES

Sec. 5. It shall be unlawful for any person engaged in business as a distiller, brewer, rectifier, blender, or other producer, or as an importer or wholesaler, of distilled spirits, wine, or malt beverages, or as a bottler, or warehouseman and bottler, of distilled spirits, directly or indirectly or through an affiliate:

(a) Exclusive outlet: To require, by agreement or otherwise, that any retailer engaged in the sale of distilled spirits, wine, or malt beverages, purchase any such products from such person to the exclusion in whole or in part of distilled spirits, wine, or malt beverages sold or offered for sale by other persons in interstate or foreign commerce, if such requirement is made in the course of interstate or foreign commerce, or if such person engages in such practice to such an extent as substantially to restrain or prevent transactions in interstate or foreign commerce in any such products, or if the direct effect of such requirement is to prevent, deter, hinder, or restrict other persons from selling or offering for sale any such products to such retailer in interstate or foreign commerce; or

(b) "Tied house": To induce through any of the following means, any retailer, engaged in the sale of distilled spirits, wine, or malt beverages, to purchase any such products from such person to the exclusion in whole or in part of distilled spirits, wine, or malt beverages sold or offered for sale by other persons in interstate or foreign commerce, if such inducement is made in the course of interstate or foreign commerce, or if such person engages in the practice of using such means, or any of them, to such an extent as substantially to restrain or prevent transactions in interstate or foreign commerce in any such products, or if the direct effect of such inducement is to prevent, deter, hinder, or restrict other persons from selling or offering for sale any such products to such retailer in interstate or foreign commerce: (1) By acquiring or holding (after the expiration of any existing license) any interest in any license with respect to the premises of the retailer; or (2) by acquiring any interest in real or personal property owned, occupied, or used by the retailer in the conduct of his business; or (3) by furnishing, giving, renting, lending, or selling to the retailer, any equipment, fixtures, signs, supplies, money, services, or other thing of value, subject to such exceptions as the Secretary of the Treasury shall by regulation prescribe, having due regard for public health, the quantity and value of articles involved, established trade customs not contrary to the public interest and the purposes of this subsection; or (4) by paying or crediting the retailer for any advertising, display, or distribution service; or (5) by guaranteeing any loan or the repayment of any financial obligation of the retailer; or (6) by extending to the retailer credit for a period in excess of the credit period usual and customary to the industry for the particular class of transactions, as ascertained by the Secretary of the Treasury and prescribed by regulations by him; or (7) by requiring the retailer to take and dispose of a certain quota of any of such products; or

(c) Commercial bribery: To induce through any of the following means, any trade buyer engaged in the sale of distilled spirits, wine, or malt beverages, to purchase any such products from such person to the exclusion in whole or in part of distilled spirits, wine, or malt beverages sold or offered for sale by other persons in interstate or foreign commerce, if such inducement is made in the course of interstate or foreign commerce, or if such person engages in the practice of using such means, or any of them, to such an extent as substantially to restrain or prevent transactions in interstate or foreign commerce in any such products, or if the direct effect of such inducement is to prevent, deter, hinder, or restrict other persons from selling or offering for sale any such products to such trade buyer in interstate or foreign commerce: (1) By commercial bribery; or (2) by offering or giving any bonus, premium, or compensation to any officer, or employee, or representative of the trade buyer; or

(d) Consignment sales: To sell, offer for sale, or contract to sell to any trade buyer engaged in the sale of distilled spirits, wine, or malt beverages, or for any such trade buyer to purchase, offer to purchase, or contract to purchase, any such products on consignment or under conditional sale or with the privilege of return or on any basis otherwise than a bona fide sale, or where any part of such transaction involves, directly or indirectly, the acquisition by such person from the trade buyer or his agreement to acquire from the trade buyer other distilled spirits, wine, or malt beverages—if such sale, purchase, offer, or contract is made in the course of interstate or foreign commerce, or if such person or trade buyer engages in such practice to such an extent as substantially to restrain or prevent transactions in interstate or foreign commerce in any such products, or if the direct effect of such sale, purchase, offer, or contract is to prevent, deter, hinder, or restrict other persons from selling or offering for sale any such products to such trade buyer in interstate or foreign commerce: *Provided,* That this subsection shall not apply to transactions involving solely the bona fide return of merchandise for ordinary and usual commercial reasons arising after the merchandise has been sold; or

(e) Labeling.—To sell or ship or deliver for sale or shipment, or otherwise introduce in interstate or foreign commerce, or to receive therein, or to remove from customs custody for consumption, any distilled spirits, wine, or malt beverages in bottles, unless such products are bottled, packaged, and labeled in conformity with such regulations, to be prescribed by the Secretary of the Treasury, with respect to packaging, marking, branding, and labeling and size and fill of container (1) as will prohibit deception of the consumer with respect to such products or the quantity thereof and as will prohibit, irrespective of falsity, such statements relating to age, manufacturing processes, analyses, guarantees, and scientific or irrelevant matters as the Secretary of the Treasury finds to be likely to mislead the consumer; (2) as will provide the consumer with adequate information as to the identity and quality of the products, the alcoholic content thereof (except that statements of, or statements likely to be considered as statements of, alcoholic content of malt beverages are hereby prohibited unless required by State law and except that, in case of wines, statements of alcoholic content shall be required only for wines containing more than 14 per centum of alcohol by volume), the net contents of the package, and the manufacturer or bottler or importer of the product; (3) as will require an accurate statement, in the case of distilled spirits (other than cordials, liqueurs, and specialties) produced by blending or rectification, if neutral spirits have been used in the production thereof, informing the consumer of the percentage of neutral spirits so used and of the name of the commodity from which such neutral spirits have been distilled, or in case of neutral spirits or of gin produced by a process of continuous distillation, the name of the commodity from which distilled; (4) as will prohibit statements on the label that are disparaging of a competitor's products or are false, misleading, obscene, or indecent; and (5) as will prevent deception of the consumer by use of a trade or brand name that is the name of any living individual of public prominence, or existing private or public organization, or is a name that is in simulation or is an abbreviation thereof, and as will prevent the use of a graphic, pictorial, or emblematic representation of any such individual or organization, if the use of such name or representation is likely falsely to lead the consumer to believe that the product has been indorsed, made, or used by, or produced for, or under the supervision of, or in accordance with the specifications of, such individual or organization: *Provided,* That this clause shall not apply to the use of the name of any person engaged in business as a distiller, brewer, rectifier, blender, or other producer, or as an importer, wholesaler, retailer, bottler, or warehouseman, of distilled spirits, wine, or malt beverages, nor to the use by any person of a trade or brand name used by him or his predecessor in interest prior to the date of the enactment of this Act; including regulations requiring, at time of release from customs custody, certificates issued by foreign governments covering origin, age, and identity of imported products: *Provided further,* That nothing herein nor any decision, ruling, or regulation of any Department of the Government shall deny the right of any person to use any trade name or brand of foreign origin not presently effectively registered in the United States Patent Office which has been used by such person or predecessors in the United States for a period of at least five years last past, if the use of such name or brand is qualified by the name of the locality in the United States in which the product is produced, and, in the case of the use of such name or brand on any label or in any advertisement, if such qualification is as conspicuous as such name or brand.

It shall be unlawful for any person to alter, mutilate, destroy, obliterate, or remove any mark, brand, or label upon distilled spirits, wine, or malt beverages held for sale in interstate or foreign commerce or after shipment therein, except as authorized by Federal law or except pursuant to regulations of the Secretary of the Treasury authorizing relabeling for purposes of compliance with the requirements of this subsection or of State law.

In order to prevent the sale or shipment or other introduction of distilled spirits, wine, or malt beverages, in interstate or foreign commerce, if bottled, packaged, or labeled in violation of the requirements of this subsection, (1) no bottler of distilled spirits, no producer, blender, or wholesaler of wine, or proprietor of a bonded wine storeroom, and no brewer or wholesaler of malt beverages shall bottle, and (2) no person shall remove from customs custody, in bottles, for sale or any other commercial purpose, distilled spirits, wine, or malt beverages, respectively, after such date as the Secretary of the Treasury fixes as the earliest practicable date for the application of the provisions of this subsection to any class of such persons (but not later than August 15, 1936, in the case of distilled spirits, and December 15, 1936, in the case of wine and malt beverages, and only after thirty days' public notice), unless, upon application to the Secretary of the Treasury, he has obtained and has in his possession a certificate of label approval covering the distilled spirits, wine, or malt beverages, issued by the Secretary of the Treasury in such manner and form as he shall by regulations prescribe: *Provided,* That any such bottler of distilled spirits, or producer, blender, or wholesaler of wine, or proprietor of a bonded wine storeroom, or brewer or wholesaler of malt beverages shall be exempt from the requirements of this subsection if, upon application to the Secretary of the Treasury, he shows to the satisfaction of the Secretary of the Treasury, that the distilled spirits, wine or malt beverages to be bottled by the applicant are not to be sold, or offered for sale, or shipped or delivered for shipment, or otherwise introduced, in interstate or foreign commerce. Officers of internal revenue are authorized and directed to withhold the release of distilled spirits from the bottling plant unless such certificates have been obtained, or unless the application of the bottler for exemption has been granted by the Secretary of the Treasury; and customs officers are authorized and directed to withhold the release from customs custody of distilled spirits, wine, and malt beverages, unless such certificates have been obtained. The District Courts of the United States, the District Court of the United States for the District of Columbia, and the United States court for any Territory shall have jurisdiction of suits to enjoin, annul, or suspend in whole or in part any final action by the Secretary of the Treasury upon any application under this subsection; or

(f) Advertising: To publish or disseminate or cause to be published or disseminated by radio broadcast, or in any newspaper, periodical or other publication or by any sign or outdoor advertisement or any other printed or graphic matter, any advertisement of distilled spirits, wine, or malt beverages, if such advertisement is in, or is calculated to induce sales in, interstate or foreign commerce, or is disseminated by mail, unless such advertisement is in conformity with such regulations, to be prescribed by the Secretary of the Treasury (1) as will prevent deception of the consumer with respect to the products advertised and as will prohibit, irrespective of falsity, such statements relating to age, manufacturing processes, analyses, guarantees, and scientific or irrelevant matters as the Secretary of the Treasury finds to be likely to mislead the consumer; (2) as will provide the consumer with adequate information as to the identity and quality of the products advertised, the alcoholic content thereof (except that statements of, or statements likely to be considered as statements of, alcoholic content of malt beverages and wines are prohibited), and the person responsible for the advertisement; (3) as will require an accurate statement, in the case of distilled spirits (other than cordials, liqueurs, and specialties) produced by blending or rectification, if neutral spirits have been used in the production thereof, informing the consumer of the percentage of neutral spirits so used and of the name of the commodity from which such neutral spirits have been distilled, or in case of neutral spirits or of gin produced by a process of continuous distillation, the name of the commodity from which distilled; (4) as will prohibit statements that are disparaging of a competitor's products or are false, misleading, obscene, or indecent; (5) as will prevent statements inconsistent with any statement on the labeling of the products advertised. This subsection shall not apply to outdoor advertising in place on June 18, 1935, but shall apply upon replacement, restoration, or renovation of any such advertising. The prohibitions of this subsection and regulations thereunder shall not apply to the publisher of any newspaper, periodical, or other publication, or radio broadcaster, unless such publisher or radio broadcaster is engaged in business as a distiller, brewer, rectifier, or other producer, or as an importer or wholesaler, of distilled spirits, wine, or malt beverages, or as a bottler, or warehouseman and bottler, of distilled spirits, directly or indirectly or through an affiliate.

The provisions of subsections (a), (b), and (c) shall not apply to any act done by an agency of a State or political subdivision thereof, or by any officer or employee of such agency.

In the case of malt beverages, the provisions of subsections (a), (b), (c), and (d) shall apply to transactions between a retailer or trade buyer in any State and a brewer, importer, or wholesaler of malt beverages outside such State only to the extent that the law of such State imposes similar requirements with respect to similar transactions between a retailer or trade buyer in such State and a brewer, importer, or wholesaler of malt beverages in such State, as the case may be. In the case of malt beverages, the provisions of subsections (e) and (f) shall apply to the labeling of malt beverages sold or shipped or delivered for shipment or otherwise introduced into or received in any State from any place outside thereof, or the advertising of malt beverages intended to be sold or shipped or delivered for shipment or otherwise introduced into or received in any State from any place outside thereof, only to the extent that the law of such State imposes similar requirements with respect to the labeling or advertising, as the case may be, of malt beverages not sold or shipped or delivered for shipment or otherwise introduced into or received in such State from any place outside thereof.

The Secretary of the Treasury shall give reasonable public notice, and afford to interested parties opportunity for hearing, prior to prescribing regulations to carry out the provisions of this section.

BULK SALES AND BOTTLING

Sec. 6 (a) It shall be unlawful for any person—

(1) To sell or offer to sell, contract to sell, or otherwise dispose of distilled spirits in bulk except, under regulations of the Administrator, for export or to the following, or to import distilled spirits in bulk except, under such regulations, for sale to or for use by the following: A distiller, rectifier of distilled spirits, person operating a bonded warehouse qualified under the internal-revenue laws or a class 8 bonded warehouse qualified under the customs laws, a winemaker for the fortification of wines, a proprietor of an industrial alcohol plant, or an agency of the United States or any State or political subdivision thereof.

(2) To sell or offer to sell, contract to sell, or otherwise dispose of warehouse receipts for distilled spirits in bulk unless such warehouse receipts require that the warehouseman shall package such distilled spirits, before delivery, in bottles labeled and marked in accordance with law, or deliver such distilled spirits in bulk only to persons to whom it is lawful to sell or otherwise dispose of distilled spirits in bulk.

(3) To bottle distilled spirits unless the bottler is a person to whom it is lawful to sell or otherwise dispose of distilled spirits in bulk.

(b) Any person who violates the requirements of this section shall, upon conviction thereof, be fined not more than $5,000 or imprisoned for not more than one year or both, and shall forfeit to the United States all distilled spirits with respect to which the violation occurs and the containers thereof.

(c) The term "in bulk" means in containers having a capacity in excess of one wine gallon.

PENALTIES

Sec. 7. The District Courts of the United States, the District Court of the United States for the District of Columbia, and the United States court for any Territory, of the District where the offense is committed or threatened or of which the offender is an inhabitant or has his principal place of business, are hereby vested with jurisdiction of any suit brought by the Attorney General in the name of the United States, to prevent and restrain violations of any of the provisions of this Act. Any person violating any of the provisions of section 3 or 5 shall be guilty of a misdemeanor and upon conviction thereof be fined not more than $1,000 for each offense.

The Secretary of the Treasury is authorized, with respect to any violation of this Act, to compromise the liability arising with respect to such violation (1) upon payment of a sum not in excess of $500 for each offense, to be collected by the Secretary of the Treasury and to be paid into the Treasury as miscellaneous receipts, and (2) in case of repetitious violations and in order to avoid multiplicity of criminal proceedings, upon agreement to a stipulation that the United States may, on its own motion upon five days' notice to the violator, cause a consent decree to be entered by any court of competent jurisdiction enjoining the repetition of such violation.

INTERLOCKING DIRECTORATES

Sec. 8. (a) Except as provided in subsection (b), it shall be unlawful for any individual to take office, after the date of the enactment of this Act, as an officer or director of any company, if his doing so would make him an officer or director of more than one company engaged in business as a distiller, rectifier, or blender of distilled spirits, or of any such company and of a company which is an affiliate of any company engaged in business as a distiller, rectifier, or blender of distilled spirits, or of more than one company which is an affiliate of any company engaged in business as a distiller, rectifier, or blender of distilled spirits, unless, prior to taking such office, application made by such individual to the Secretary of the Treasury, has been granted and after due showing has been made to him that service by such individual as officer or director of all the foregoing companies of which he is an officer or director together with service in the company with respect to which application is made will not substantially restrain or prevent competition in interstate or foreign commerce in distilled spirits. The Secretary of the Treasury shall, by order, grant or deny such application on the basis of the proof submitted to him and his finding thereon. The District Courts of the United States, the District Court of United States for the District of Columbia, and the United States court for any Territory shall have jurisdiction of suits to enjoin, annul, or suspend in whole or in part any final action by the Secretary of the Treasury upon any application under this subsection.

(b) An individual may, without regard to the provision of subsection (a), take office as an officer or director of a company described in subsection

(a) while holding the position of officer or director of any other such company if such companies are affiliates at the time of his taking office and if—

(1) Such companies are affiliates on the date of the enactment of this Act; or

(2) Each of such companies has been organized under the law of a State to comply with a requirement thereof under which, as a condition of doing business in such State, such company must be organized under the law of such State; or

(3) One or more such companies has been organized under the law of a State to comply with a requirement thereof under which, as a condition of doing business in such State, such company must be organized under the laws of such State, and the other one or more of such companies not so organized, is in existence on the date of the enactment of this Act; or

(4) One or more of such companies has been organized under the law of a State to comply with a requirement thereof under which, as a condition of doing business in such State, such company must be organized under the law of such State, and not more than one of such companies is a company which has not been so organized and which has been organized after the date of the enactment of this Act.

(c) As used in this section, the term "company" means a corporation, joint stock company, business trust, or association, but does not include any agency of a State or political subdivision thereof or any officer or employee of any such agency.

(d) Any individual taking office in violation of this section shall be punished by a fine of not exceeding $1,000.

DISPOSAL OF FORFEITED ALCOHOLIC BEVERAGES

Sec. 9. (a) All distilled spirits, wine, and malt beverages forfeited summarily or by order of court, under any law of the United States, shall be delivered to the Secretary of the Treasury to be disposed of as hereinafter provided.

(b) The Secretary of the Treasury shall dispose of all distilled spirits, wine, and malt beverages which have been delivered to him pursuant to subsection (a)—

(1) By delivery to such Government agencies as, in his opinion, have a need for such distilled spirits, wine, or malt beverages for medicinal, scientific, or mechanical purposes; or

(2) By gift to such eleemosynary institutions as, in his opinion, have a need for such distilled spirits, wine, or malt beverages for medicinal purposes; or

(3) By destruction.

(c) No distilled spirits, wine, or malt beverages which have been seized under any law of the United States, may be disposed of in any manner whatsoever except after forfeiture and as provided in this section.

(d) The Secretary of the Treasury is authorized to make all rules and regulations necessary to carry out the provisions of this section.

(e) Nothing in this section shall affect the authority of the Secretary of the Treasury, under the customs or internal-revenue laws, to remit or mitigate the forfeiture, or alleged forfeiture, of such distilled spirits, wines, or malt beverages, or the authority of the Commissioner of Internal Revenue, with the approval of the Secretary of the Treasury, to compromise any civil or criminal case in respect of such distilled spirits, wines, or malt beverages prior to commencement of suit thereon, or the authority of the Secretary of the Treasury to compromise any claim under the customs laws in respect of such distilled spirits, wines, or malt beverages.

FEDERAL ALCOHOL CONTROL ADMINISTRATION

Sec. 10. The Federal Alcohol Control Administration established by Executive order under the provisions of Title I of the National Industrial Recovery Act is hereby abolished. All papers, records, and property of such Federal Alcohol Control Administration are hereby transferred to the Administrator. This section shall take effect on the date that the Administrator first appointed under this Act takes office.

(Sections 11, 12, 13, 14, 15, and 16 are omitted from this print of the Federal Alcohol Administration Act since they contain amendments to the Internal Revenue Laws and do not relate to the powers or duties otherwise conferred or imposed by the Act.)

MISCELLANEOUS

Sec. 17. (a) As used in this Act—

(1) The term "Secretary" means the Secretary of the Treasury.

(2) The term "United States" means the several States and Territories and the District of Columbia; the term "State" includes a Territory and the District of Columbia; and the term "Territory" means Alaska, Hawaii, and Puerto Rico.

(3) The term "interstate or foreign commerce" means commerce between any State and any place outside thereof, or commerce within any Territory or the District of Columbia, or between points within the same State but through any place outside thereof.

(4) The term "person" means individual, partnership, joint stock company, business trust, association, corporation, or other form of business enterprise, including a receiver, trustee, or liquidating agent and including an officer or employee of any agency of a State or political subdivision thereof; and the term "trade buyer" means any person who is a wholesaler or retailer.

(5) The term "affiliate" means any one of two or more persons if one of such persons has actual or legal control, directly or indirectly, whether by stock ownership or otherwise, of the other or others of such persons; and any one of two or more persons subject to common control, actual or legal, directly or indirectly, whether by stock ownership or otherwise.

(6) The term "distilled spirits" means ethyl alcohol, hydrated oxide of ethyl, spirits of wine, whiskey, rum, brandy, gin, and other distilled spirits, including all dilutions and mixtures thereof, for non-industrial use.

(7) The term "wine" means (1) wine as defined in section 610 and section 617 of the Revenue Act of 1918, (U.S.C., title 26, secs. 441 and 444) as now in force or hereafter amended, and (2) other alcoholic beverages not so defined, but made in the manner of wine, including sparkling and carbonated wine, wine made from condensed grape must, wine made from other agricultural products than the juice of sound, ripe grapes, imitation wine, compounds sold as wine, vermouth, cider, perry and sake; in each instance only if

containing not less than 7 per centum and not more than 24 per centum of alcohol by volume, and if for non-industrial use.

(8) The term "malt beverage" means a beverage made by the alcoholic fermentation of an infusion or decoction, or combination of both, in potable brewing water, of malted barley with hops, or their parts, or their products, and with or without other malted cereals, and with or without the addition of unmalted or prepared cereals, other carbohydrates or products prepared therefrom, and with or without the addition of carbon dioxide, and with or without other wholesome products suitable for human food consumption.

(9) The term "bottle" means any container, irrespective of the material from which made, for use for the sale of distilled spirits, wine, or malt beverages at retail.

(b) The right to amend or repeal the provisions of this Act is expressly reserved.

(c) If any provision of this Act, or the application of such provision to any person or circumstance, is held invalid, the remainder of the Act and the application of such provision to persons or circumstances other than those as to which it is held invalid, shall not be affected thereby.

Standards of Identity for Distilled Spirits

(Article II, Regulations No. 5, FAA Act)

SEC. 20. APPLICATION OF STANDARDS. The standards of identity for the several classes and types of distilled spirits set forth herein shall be applicable only to distilled spirits for beverage or other non-industrial purposes. Nothing contained in these standards of identity shall be construed as authorizing the non-industrial use of any distilled spirits produced in an industrial alcohol plant, except that "alcohol" or "neutral spirits," as herein defined, may be so used if produced pursuant to the basic permit requirements of the Federal Alcohol Administration Act.

SEC. 21. THE STANDARDS OF IDENTITY. Standards of identity for the several classes and types of distilled spirits set forth herein shall be as follows:

CLASS 1. *Neutral spirits or alcohol.* "Neutral spirits" or "alcohol" are distilled spirits distilled from any material at or above 190° proof, whether or not such proof is subsequently reduced. During the period of the unlimited national emergency proclaimed by the President on May 27, 1941, the term "neutral spirits" shall also include any spirits distilled at less than 190° proof, which are so distilled, or so treated in the process of distillation, or so refined by other processes after distillation, as to lack the taste, aroma, and other characteristics of whisky, brandy, rum, or other potable beverage spirits, but the containers of such product shall not be labeled as "alcohol."

(a) "Vodka" is neutral spirits distilled from any material at or above 190° proof, reduced to not more than 110° proof and not less than 80° proof and, after such reduction in proof, so treated by one of the following methods as to be without distinctive character, aroma or taste.

(1) By causing the distillate to flow continuously through a tank or a series of tanks containing at least 1½ pounds of charcoal for each gallon of distillate contained therein at any one time so that the distillate is in intimate contact with the charcoal for a period of not less than 8 hours, not less than 10% of the charcoal being replaced by new charcoal at the expiration of each 40 hours of operation, at a rate which will replace at least 6 pounds of charcoal for every 100 gallons of spirits treated;

(2) By keeping the distillate in constant movement by mechanical means

in contact for not less than 8 hours with at least 6 pounds of new charcoal for every 100 gallons of distillate;

(3) By purifying or refining the distillate by any other method which the Deputy Commissioner finds will result in a product equally without distinctive character, aroma or taste, and which has been approved by him.

After such treatment the distillate is stored in metal, porcelain or glass containers or paraffin-lined tanks, and bottled at not less than 80° proof. If any flavoring material is added to the distillate it shall be designated "flavored vodka" and may be further qualified with the name of the flavoring material used.

CLASS 2. *Whisky.* "Whisky" is an alcoholic distillate from a fermented mash of grain distilled at less than 190° proof in such manner that the distillate possesses the taste, aroma, and characteristics generally attributed to whisky, and withdrawn from the cistern room of the distillery at not more than 110° and not less than 80° proof, whether or not such proof is further reduced prior to bottling to not less than 80° proof; and also includes mixtures of the foregoing distillates for which no specific standards of identity are prescribed herein. Those types of whisky specified in sub-sections (a) through (j) below shall be deemed "American type" whiskies.

(a) "Rye whisky," "bourbon whisky," "wheat whisky," "malt whisky," or "rye malt whisky" is whisky which has been distilled at not exceeding 160° proof from a fermented mash of not less than 51 percent rye grain, corn grain, wheat grain, malted barley grain, or malted rye grain, respectively, and, if produced on or after March 1, 1938, stored in charred new oak containers; and also includes mixtures of such whiskies where the mixture consists exclusively of whiskies of the same type. "Corn whisky" is whisky which has been distilled at not exceeding 160° proof from a fermented mash of not less than 80 percent corn grain, stored in uncharred oak containers or reused charred oak containers, and not subject, in the process of distillation or otherwise, to treatment with charred wood; and also includes mixtures of such whisky.

(b) "Straight whisky" is an alcoholic distillate from a fermented mash of grain distilled at not exceeding 160° proof and withdrawn from the cistern room of the distillery at not more than 110° and not less than 80° proof, whether or not such proof is further reduced prior to bottling to not less than 80° proof, and is—

(1) Aged for not less than 12 calendar months if bottled on or after July 1, 1936, and before July 1, 1937; or

(2) Aged for not less than 18 calendar months if bottled on or after July 1, 1937, and before July 1, 1938; or

(3) Aged for not less than 24 calendar months if bottled on or after July 1, 1938.

The term "straight whisky" also includes mixtures of straight whisky which, by reason of being homogeneous, are not subject to the rectification tax under the internal revenue laws.

(c) "Straight rye whisky" is straight whisky distilled from a fermented mash of grain of which not less than 51 percent is rye grain.

(d) (1) "Straight bourbon whisky" is straight whisky distilled from a fermented mash of grain of which not less than 51 percent is corn grain.

(2) "Straight corn whisky" is straight whisky distilled from a fermented mash of grain of which not less than 80 percent is corn grain, aged for the required period in uncharred oak containers or reused charred oak containers, and not subjected, in the process of distillation or otherwise, to treatment with charred wood.

(e) "Straight wheat whisky" is straight whisky distilled from a fermented mash of grain of which not less than 51 percent is wheat grain.

(f) "Straight malt whisky" and "straight rye malt whisky" are straight whiskies distilled from a fermented mash of grain of which not less than 51 percent of the grain is malted barley or malted rye, respectively.

(g) "Blended whisky" (whisky—a blend) is a mixture which contains at least 20 percent by volume of 100° proof straight whisky and, separately or in combination, whisky or neutral spirits, if such mixture at the time of bottling is not less than 80° proof.

(h) "Blended rye whisky" (rye whisky—a blend), "blended bourbon whisky" (bourbon whisky—a blend), "blended corn whisky" (corn whisky—a blend), "blended wheat whisky" (wheat whisky—a blend), "blended malt whisky" (malt whisky—a blend), or "blended rye malt whisky" (rye malt whisky—a blend) is blended whisky which contains not less than 51 percent by volume of straight rye whisky, straight bourbon whisky, straight corn whisky, straight wheat whisky, straight malt whisky, or straight rye malt whisky, respectively.

(i) "A blend of straight whiskies" (blended straight whiskies), "a blend of straight rye whiskies" (blended straight rye whiskies), "a blend of straight bourbon whiskies" (blended straight bourbon whiskies), "a blend of straight corn whiskies" (blended straight corn whiskies), "a blend of straight wheat whiskies" (blended straight wheat whiskies), "a blend of straight malt whiskies" (blended straight malt whiskies), and "a blend of straight rye malt whiskies" (blended straight rye malt whiskies) are mixtures of only straight whiskies, straight rye whiskies, straight bourbon whiskies, straight corn whiskies, straight wheat whiskies, straight malt whiskies, or straight rye malt whiskies, respectively.

(j) "Spirit whisky" is a mixture (1) of neutral spirits and not less than 5 percent by volume of whisky, or (2) of neutral spirits and less than 20 percent by volume of straight whisky, but not less than 5 percent by volume of straight whisky, or of straight whisky and whisky, if the resulting product at the time of bottling be not less than 80° proof.

(k) "Scotch whisky" is a distinctive product of Scotland, manufactured in Scotland in compliance with the laws of Great Britain regulating the manufacture of Scotch whisky for consumption in Great Britain, and containing no distilled spirits less than 3 years old: *Provided,* That if in fact such product as so manufactured is a mixture of distilled spirits, such mixture is "blended Scotch whisky" (Scotch whisky—a blend). "Scotch whisky" shall not be designated as "straight."

(l) "Irish whisky" is a distinctive product of Ireland, manufactured either in the Irish Free State or in Northern Ireland, in compliance with the laws of those respective territories regulating the manufacture of Irish whisky for consumption in such territories, and containing no distilled spirits less than 3 years old: *Provided,* That if in fact such product as so manufactured is a mixture of distilled spirits, such whisky is "blended Irish whisky" (Irish whisky —a blend). "Irish whisky" shall not be designated as "straight."

(m) "Canadian whisky" is a distinctive product of Canada, manufactured in Canada in compliance with the laws of the Dominion of Canada regulating the manufacture of whisky for consumption in Canada, and containing no distilled spirits less than 2 years old: *Provided,* That if in fact such product as so manufactured is a mixture of distilled spirits, such whisky is "blended Canadian whisky" (Canadian whisky—a blend). "Canadian whisky" shall not be designated as "straight."

(n) "Blended Scotch type whisky" (Scotch type whisky—a blend) is a mixture made outside Great Britain and composed of—

(1) Not less than 20 percent by volume of 100° proof malt whisky or whiskies distilled in pot stills at not more than 160° proof (whether or not such proof is subsequently reduced prior to bottling to not less than 80° proof) solely from a fermented mash of malted barley dried over peat fire and aged for not less than 3 years in new plain, or reused, oak containers, and

(2) Not more than 80% by volume of whisky distilled at more than 180° proof (whether or not such proof is subsequently reduced prior to bottling to not less than 80° proof) aged for not less than 3 years in new plain, or reused, oak containers.

CLASS 3. *Gins.* (a) "Distilled gin" is a distillate obtained by original distillation from mash, or by the redistillation of distilled spirits, over or with juniper berries and other aromatics customarily used in the production of gin, and deriving its main characteristic flavor from juniper berries and reduced at time of bottling to not less than 80° proof; and includes mixtures solely of such distillates.

(b) "Compound gin" is the product obtained by mixing neutral spirits with distilled gin or gin essence or other flavoring materials customarily used in the production of gin, and deriving its main characteristic flavor from juniper berries and reduced at time of bottling to not less than 80° proof; and includes mixtures of such products.

(c) "Dry gin," "London dry gin," "Hollands gin," "Geneva gin," "Old Tom gin," "Tom gin," and "buchu gin" are the types of gin known under such designations, and shall be further designated as "distilled" or "compound," as the case may be.

CLASS 4. *Brandies.* "Brandy" is a distillate, or a mixture of distillates, obtained solely from the fermented juice, mash, or wine, of fruit, or from the residue thereof, distilled at less than 190° proof in such manner as to possess the taste, aroma, and characteristics generally attributed to the product, and bottled at not less than 80° proof; and shall also include such distillates, aged for a period of not less than 50 years, and bottled at not less than 72° proof, in cases where the reduction in proof below 80° is due solely to losses resulting from natural causes during the period of aging. Brandy, or mixtures thereof, not conforming to any of the following standards shall be designated as "brandy," and such designation shall be qualified by a truthful and adequate statement of composition in direct conjunction therewith.

(a) "Fruit brandy" is brandy distilled solely from the juice or mash of whole, sound, ripe fruit, or from standard grape, citrus, or other fruit wine, having a volatile acidity, calculated as acetic acid and exclusive of sulphur dioxide, not in excess of 0.20 gram per 100 cubic centimeters (20° C.), with or without the addition of not more than 20 percent by weight of the pomace of such juice or wine, or 30 percent by volume of the lees of such wine, or both (calculated prior to the addition of water to facilitate fermentation or distillation), and shall include mixtures of such brandy with not more than 30 percent (calculated on a proof basis) of lees brandy. Fruit brandy, derived exclusively from grapes, shall be designated as "grape brandy" or "brandy." Fruit brandy, other than grape brandy, derived exclusively from one variety of fruit, shall be designated by the word "brandy" qualified by the name of such fruit (e.g., "peach brandy," "apple brandy," "orange brandy,") except that "apple brandy" may be designated "applejack." Fruit brandy derived from more than one variety of fruit shall be designated as "fruit brandy," qualified by a truthful and adequate statement of composition (e.g., "fruit brandy—a blend of 90 percent grape brandy and 10 percent blackberry brandy").

(b) "Cognac" or "Cognac (grape) brandy" is grape brandy distilled in the Cognac region of France, which is entitled to be so designated by the laws and regulations of the French Government.

(c) "Dried fruit brandy" is brandy that conforms to the standard for fruit brandy except that it has been derived from sound, dried fruit, or from the standard wine of such fruit. Brandy derived from raisins, or from raisin wine, shall be designated as "raisin brandy." Other brandies defined in this paragraph shall be designated in the same manner as fruit brandy from the corresponding variety or varieties of fruit except that the name of the fruit shall be qualified by the word "dried."

(d) "Lees brandy" is brandy distilled from the lees of standard grape, citrus, or other fruit wine, and shall be designated as "lees brandy," qualified by the name of the fruit from which such lees are derived.

(e) "Pomace brandy," or "marc brandy," is brandy distilled from the skin and pulp of sound, ripe grapes, citrus or other fruit, after the withdrawal of the juice or wine therefrom, and shall be designated as "pomace brandy," or "marc brandy," qualified by the name of the fruit from which derived. Grape pomace brandy may be designated as "grappa" or "grappa brandy."

(ee) "Residue brandy" is brandy distilled wholly or in part from the residue of fruit or wine, and shall be designated as "residue brandy," qualified by the name of the fruit from which derived. Brandy distilled wholly or in part from residue materials which conforms to any of the standards set forth in subsections (a), (c), (d), and (e) hereof, may, regardless of such fact, be designated "residue brandy" by the distiller thereof; but the use of this designation shall be conclusive, precluding any later change of designation.

(f) "Neutral brandy" is any brandy distilled on or after July 1, 1941, at more than 170° proof. Brandy so distilled shall be designated in the same manner as if distilled at a lower proof, except that the designation shall be qualified by the word "neutral" in the same size and kind of type, e.g., "neutral brandy," "neutral grape lees brandy," or "neutral grape pomace brandy."

(g) "Substandard brandy" shall bear as a part of its designation the word "substandard," and shall include—

(1) Any brandy distilled from juice, mash, or wine having a volatile acidity calculated as acetic acid and exclusive of sulphur dioxide, in excess

of 0.20 gram per 100 cubic centimeters (20° C.); measurements of volatile acidity under this paragraph shall be calculated exclusive of water added to facilitate distillation.

(2) Any brandy which has been distilled from unsound, moldy, diseased, or decomposed juice, mash, wine, lees, pomace or residue, or which shows in the finished product any taste, aroma, or characteristic associated with products distilled from such material.

CLASS 5. *Rum.* (a) "Rum" is any alcoholic distillate from the fermented juice of sugarcane, sugarcane sirup, sugarcane molasses, or other sugarcane by-products, distilled at less than 190° proof (whether or not such proof is further reduced prior to bottling to not less than 80° proof) in such manner that the distillate possesses the taste, aroma, and characteristics generally attributed to rum; and includes mixtures solely of such distillates.

(b) "New England rum" is rum as above defined, except that it is produced in the United States, is distilled at less than 160° proof, and is a straight rum and not a mixture of rums.

(c) Puerto Rico, Cuba, Demerara, Barbados, St. Croix, St. Thomas, Virgin Islands, Jamaica, Martinique, Trinidad, Haiti, and San Domingo rum are not distinctive types of rum. Such names are not generic but retain their geographic significance. They may not be applied to rum produced in any other place than the particular region indicated in the name, and may not be used as a designation of a product as rum, unless such product is rum as defined in subsection (a).

CLASS 6. *Cordials and liqueurs.* (a) Cordials and liqueurs are products obtained by mixing or redistilling neutral spirits, brandy, gin, or other distilled spirits with or over fruits, flowers, plants, or pure juices therefrom, or other natural flavoring materials, or with extracts derived from infusions, percolations, or maceration of such materials, and to which sugar or dextrose or both have been added in an amount not less than 2½ percent by weight of the finished product. Synthetic or imitation flavoring materials shall not be included.

(b) "Sloe gin" is a cordial or liqueur with the main characteristic flavoring derived from sloe berries.

(c) Cordials and liqueurs shall not be designated as "distilled" or "compound."

(d) *Dry cordials and dry liqueurs.*—The designation of a cordial or liqueur may include the word "dry" if the added sugar and dextrose are less than 10 percent by weight of the finished product.

(e) *Rye liqueur, bourbon liqueur.*—"Rye liqueur," "bourbon liqueur," (rye, bourbon cordial) are liqueurs bottled at not less than 60° proof, in which not less than 51%, on a proof basis, of the distilled spirits used are, respectively, rye or bourbon whisky, straight rye or straight bourbon whisky, or whisky distilled from a rye or bourbon mash, and which possesses a predominant characteristic bourbon or rye flavor derived from such whisky.

(f) *Rock and rye, rock and bourbon, rock and brandy, rock and rum.* "Rock and rye," "rock and bourbon," "rock and brandy" and "rock and rum" are liqueurs, bottled at not less than 48° proof, in which, in the case of rock and rye and rock and bourbon, not less than 51%, on a proof basis, of the distilled spirits used are, respectively, rye or bourbon whisky, straight rye or straight bourbon whisky, or whisky distilled from a rye or bourbon mash, and, in the case of rock and brandy, and rock and rum, the distilled spirits used are all grape brandy, distilled at not in excess of 170° proof, or rum, respectively; containing rock candy or sugar syrup, with or without the addition of fruit, fruit juices or other natural flavoring materials, and possessing, respectively, a predominant characteristic rye, bourbon, brandy or rum flavor derived from the distilled spirits used.

CLASS 7. *Imitations.*—Imitations shall bear, as a part of the designation thereof, the word "imitation" and shall include the following:

(a) Any class or type of distilled spirits to which has been added coloring or flavoring material of such nature as to cause the resultant product to simulate any other class or type of distilled spirits;

(b) Any class or type of distilled spirits (other than distilled spirits required under section 34, Article III, of these regulations to bear a distinctive or fanciful name and a truthful and adequate statement of composition) to which has been added synthetic flavoring material;

(c) Any class or type of distilled spirits (other than distilled spirits required under section 34, Article III, of these regulations to bear a distinctive or fanciful name and a truthful and adequate statement of composition) to which has been added a natural flavoring material which simulates or enhances, or is used by the trade or in the particular product to simulate or enhance, the characteristics of any other flavoring material, if the labeling of such distilled spirits creates the impression that such other flavoring material has been employed in the manufacture of the product;

(d) Any class or type of distilled spirits (except cordials, liqueurs, and specialties marketed under labels which do not indicate, or infer, that a particular class or type of distilled spirits was used in the manufacture thereof) to which has been added any whisky essence, brandy essence, rum essence, or similar essence or extract which simulates or enhances, or is used by the trade or in the particular product to simulate or enhance, the characteristics of any class or type of distilled spirits;

(e) Any type of rum to which neutral spirits or other distilled spirits than rum have been added;

(f) Any type of brandy to which neutral spirits or other distilled spirits than brandy have been added; and

(g) Any brandy to the distilling material for which has been added any amount of sugar other than the kind and amount of sugar expressly authorized for the amelioration of standard wine.

CLASS 8. *Geographical designations.*—(a) Geographical names for distinctive types of distilled spirits (other than names found by the Deputy Commissioner under subsection (b) to have become generic) shall not be applied to distilled spirits produced in any other place than the particular region indicated by the name, unless (1) in direct conjunction with the name there appears the word "type" or the word "American," or some other adjective indicating the true place of production, in lettering substantially as conspicuous as such name, and (2) the distilled spirits to which the name is applied conform to the distilled spirits of that particular region. The following are examples of distinctive types of distilled spirits with geographical names that have not become generic: Eau de Vie de Dantzig (Danziger goldwasser), Ojen, Swedish punch, blended Scotch whisky, blended Irish whisky, blended Canadian whisky.

Geographical names for distinctive types of distilled spirits shall be used to designate only distilled spirits conforming to the standard of identity, if any, for such type specified in this article, or if no such standard is so specified, then in accordance with the trade understanding of that distinctive type. Such geographical names for distinctive types of distilled spirits shall not be used as the name or a part of the name for distilled spirits not of that distinctive type.

(b) Only such geographical names for distilled spirits as the Deputy Commissioner finds have by usage and common knowledge lost their geographical significance to such extent that they have become generic, shall be deemed to have become generic. The following are examples of distinctive types of distilled spirits with geographical names that have become generic: London dry gin, Geneva gin, Hollands gin, tequila.

(c) Geographical names that are not names for distinctive types of distilled spirits, and that have not become generic, shall not be applied to distilled spirits produced in any other place than the particular place or region indicated in the name. The following are examples of geographical names for distilled spirits that are not generic and are not names for distinctive types of distilled spirits: Cognac, Armagnac, Greek brandy, Pisco brandy, Jamaica rum, Kentucky straight bourbon whisky, Maryland straight rye whisky.

(d) The words "Scotch," "Scots," "Highland" or "Highlands" and similar words connoting, indicating, or commonly associated with Scotland, shall not (except for the use of the word "Scotch" in the type designation "blended Scotch type whisky") be used to designate any product not wholly produced in Scotland.

CLASS 9. *Products without geographical designations but distinctive of a particular place.*—(a) The whiskies of the types specified in paragraphs (a) to (j), inclusive, of Class 2 of this article, are distinctive products of the United States and, if produced in a foreign country, shall be designated by the applicable designation prescribed in such paragraph, together with the words "American type" or the words "produced (distilled, blended) in . . . ," the blank to be filled in with the name of the foreign country. If whisky of any of these types is composed in part of whisky or whiskies produced in a foreign country there shall be stated on the government label the percentage of such whisky and the country of origin thereof. Such statement shall appear as a part of, or in direct conjunction with, any age or percentage statement which may be required under Section 39 (27 CFR 5.39).

(b) The name for other distilled spirits which are distinctive products of a particular place or country shall not be given to the product of any other place or country unless the designation for such product includes the word "type" or any adjective such as "American" or the like, clearly indicating the true place of production. This paragraph shall not apply to designations which by usage and common knowledge have lost their geographical significance to such an extent that they have become generic, provided the approval of the Deputy Commissioner is obtained prior to using such designation. An example of a product which is a distinctive product of a particular place or country and which has not become generic is the following: Habanero. Examples of products which have lost their geographical significance to such an extent that they are no longer distinctive products of a particular place or country, but have become generic, are the following: Vodka, slivovitz, zubrovka, aquavit, arrack, and kirschwasser.

SEC. 22. ALTERATION OF CLASS AND TYPE: HARMLESS COLORING, FLAVORING, AND BLENDING MATERIALS.–Except as otherwise provided in this section, the addition of any coloring, flavoring, or blending materials whatsoever, to any class or type of distilled spirits shall be deemed to alter the class and type thereof. If the class or type of any distilled spirits shall be so altered, and if there is no class or type designation for the product as so altered, either specified in this article or in accordance with trade understanding, such distilled spirits shall be designated with a distinctive or fanciful name, together with a truthful and adequate statement of composition in accordance with section 34, Article III, of these regulations. There may be added to any class or type of distilled spirits, without changing the class or type thereof, (1) such harmless coloring, flavoring, or blending materials as are an essential component part of the particular class or type of distilled spirits to which added, and (2) harmless coloring, flavoring, or blending materials, such as caramel, straight malt or straight rye malt whiskies, fruit juices, sugar, or wine, which are not an essential component part of the particular distilled spirits to which added, but which are customarily employed therein in accordance with established trade usage, if such coloring, flavoring or blending materials do not total more than 2½ percent by volume of the finished product.

"Harmless coloring, flavoring, and blending materials" shall not include (1) any material which would render the product to which it is added an imitation, or (2) any material whatsoever in the case of straight whisky or in the case of neutral spirits, or (3) any material, other than caramel and sugar, in the case of cognac brandy.

Nothing herein shall be construed as in any manner modifying the standards of identity for cordials and liqueurs, or as authorizing any product which is defined in class 7 as an imitation to be otherwise designated.

APPENDIX D

Advertising of Distilled Spirits

(Article VI, Regulations No. 5, FAA Act)

SEC. 60. APPLICATION OF THIS ARTICLE.—No person engaged in business as a distiller, rectifier, importer, wholesaler, or warehouseman and bottler of distilled spirits, directly or indirectly, or through an affiliate, shall publish or disseminate or cause to be published or disseminated by radio broadcast, or in any newspaper, periodical, or other publication, or by any sign or outdoor advertisement, or any other printed or graphic matter, any advertisement of distilled spirits if such advertisement is in, or is calculated to induce sales in, interstate or foreign commerce, or is disseminated by mail, unless such advertisement is in conformity with this article: *Provided,* That this article shall not apply to outdoor advertising in place on June 18, 1935, but shall apply upon replacement, restoration, or renovation of any such advertising: *And provided further,* That this article shall not apply to the publisher of any newspaper, periodical, or other publication, or radio broadcaster, unless such publisher or radio broadcaster is engaged in business as a distiller, rectifier, importer, wholesaler, or warehouseman and bottler of distilled spirits, directly or indirectly, or through an affiliate.

SEC. 61. DEFINITIONS.—As used in this article—

The term "advertisement" includes any advertisement of distilled spirits through the medium of radio broadcast; or of newspapers, periodicals, or other publications; or of any sign or outoor advertisement; or of any other printed or graphic matter, including trade booklets, menus, and wine cards—if such advertisement is in, or is calculated to induce sales in, interstate or foreign commerce, or is disseminated by mail; except that such terms shall not include

(1) Any label affixed to any bottle of distilled spirits, or any individual covering, carton, or other container of the bottle, or any written, printed, graphic, or other matter accompanying the bottle, which constitutes a part of the labeling under Article III of these regulations.

(2) Any editorial or other reading matter in any periodical or newspaper for the publication of which no money or other valuable consideration is paid or promised, directly or indirectly, by any permittee.

SEC. 62. MANDATORY STATEMENTS.—(a) *Responsible advertiser.*—The advertisement shall state the name and address of the permittee responsible for its publication or broadcast. Street number and name may be omitted in the address.

(b) *Class and type.* The advertisement shall contain a conspicuous statement of the class to which the product belongs and the type thereof corresponding with the statement of class and type which is required to appear on the label of the product.

(c) *Alcoholic content.*

(1) The alcoholic content by proof shall be stated for distilled spirits except as otherwise provided in paragraph (2) of this subsection.

(2) The alcoholic content in percentage by volume or by proof shall be stated for cordials and liqueurs, and gin fizzes, cocktails, highballs, bitters, and such other specialties as may be specified by the Deputy Commissioner from time to time.

(d) *Percentage of neutral spirits and name of commodity.*—

(1) In the case of distilled spirits (other than cordials, liqueurs and specialties) produced by blending or rectification, if neutral spirits have been used in the production thereof, there shall be stated the percentage of neutral spirits so used and the name of the commodity from which such neutral spirits have been distilled. The statement of percentage and the name of the commodity shall be made in substantially the following form: " . . . percent neutral spirits distilled from grain"; or " . . . percent neutral spirits distilled from cane products"; or ". . . percent neutral spirits distilled from fruit"; or " . . . percent grain (cane products) (fruit) neutral spirits."

(2) In the case of neutral spirits or of gin produced by a process of continuous distillation, there shall be stated the name of the commodity from which such neutral spirits or gin has been distilled. The statement of the name of the commodity shall be made in substantially the following form: "Distilled from grain," or "distilled from cane products," or "distilled from fruit."

SEC. 63. LETTERING.—Statements required under this article to appear in any written, printed, or graphic advertisement shall be in lettering or type of a size sufficient to render them both conspicuous and readily legible.

SEC. 64. PROHIBITED STATEMENTS.—(a) An advertisement of distilled spirits shall not contain—

(1) Any statement that is false or misleading in any material particular.

(2) Any statement that is disparaging of a competitor's products.

(3) Any statement, design, device, or representation which is obscene or indecent.

(4) Any statement, design, device, or representation of or relating to analyses, standards, or tests, irrespective of falsity, which the Deputy Commissioner finds to be likely to mislead the consumer.

(5) Any statement, design, device, or representation of or relating to any guaranty, irrespective of falsity, which the Deputy Commissioner finds to be likely to mislead the consumer. Nothing herein shall prohibit the use of an enforceable guaranty in substantially the following form: "We will refund the purchase price to the purchaser if he is in any manner dissatisfied with the contents of this package.

--"

(Blank to be filled in with name of the permittee making guaranty)

(6) Any statement that the distilled spirits are distilled, blended, made,

bottled, or sold under or in accordance with any municipal, State, or Federal authorization, law, or regulation; and if a municipal, State, or Federal permit number is stated, such permit number shall not be accompanied by any additional statement relating thereto.

(7) The words "bond," "bonded," "bottled in bond," "aged in bond," or phrases containing these or synonymous terms, unless such words or phrases appear, pursuant to Article III of these regulations, upon the labels of the distilled spirits advertised, and are stated in the advertisement in the manner and form in which they are required to appear upon the label.

(8) The word "pure" except as part of the bona fide name of a permittee or a retailer for whom the distilled spirits are bottled.

(9) The terms "double distilled," "triple distilled," or any similar terms.

(b) *Statements inconsistent with labeling.*—The advertisement shall not contain any statement concerning a brand or lot of distilled spirits that is inconsistent with any statement on the labeling thereof. This requirement shall become effective August 15, 1936.

(c) *Statements of age.*—The advertisement shall not contain any statement, design, or device directly or by implication concerning age or maturity of any brand or lot of distilled spirits unless a statement of age appears on the label of the advertised product. When any such statement, design, or device concerning age or maturity is contained in any advertisement, it shall include (in direct conjunction therewith and with substantially equal conspicuousness) all parts of the statement, if any, concerning age and percentages required to be made on the label under the provisions of Article III of these regulations. An advertisement for any whisky or brandy which is not required to bear a statement of age on the label may, however, contain general inconspicuous age, maturity or other similar representations even though the optional age statement does not appear on the label of the advertised product and in the advertisement itself.

(d) *Curative and therapeutic effects.* The advertisements shall not contain any statement, design, or device representing that the use of any distilled spirits has curative or therapeutic effects, if such statement is untrue in any particular, or tends to create a misleading impression.

(e) *Place of origin.* The advertisement shall not represent that the distilled spirits were manufactured in or imported from a place or country other than that of their actual origin, or were produced or processed by one who was not in fact the actual producer or processor.

(f) *Confusion of brands.* Two or more different brands or lots of distilled spirits shall not be advertised in one advertisement (or in two or more advertisements in one issue of a periodical or newspaper, or in one piece of other written, printed, or graphic matter) if the advertisement tends to create the impression that representations made as to one brand or lot apply to the other or others, and if as to such latter the representations contravene any provision of this article or are in any respect untrue.

(g) *Flags, seals, coats of arms, crests, and other insignia.*—No advertisement shall contain any statement, design, device, or pictorial representation of or relating to, or capable of being construed as relating to, the armed forces of the United States, or of the American flag, or of any emblem, seal, insignia, or decoration associated with such flag or armed forces; nor shall any advertisement contain any statement, device, design, or pictorial representation of or concerning any flag, seal, coat of arms, crest, or other insignia, likely to mislead the consumer to believe that the product has been endorsed, made, or used by, or produced for, or under the supervision of, or in accordance with the specifications of the government, organization, family, or individual with whom such flag, seal, coat of arms, crest, or insignia is associated.

Appendix E

Inducements Furnished To Retailers

(Regulations No. 6, FAA Act)

Subpart A—Scope of Regulations

Section 6.1 *Inducements furnished to retailers.* These regulations, "Regulations No. 6, Inducements Furnished to Retailers" (27 CFR Part 6), issued pursuant to section 5 of the Federal Alcohol Administration Act (27 U.S.C. 205), contain the substantive requirements relative to the furnishing of inducements to retailers of distilled spirits, wine, and malt beverages. No procedural requirements are prescribed.

Subpart B—Definitions

Sec. 6.5 *Meaning of terms.* As used in this part, unless the context otherwise requires, terms shall have the meanings ascribed in this subpart.

Sec. 6.6 *Retailer.* "Retailer" shall mean any person engaged in the sale of distilled spirits, wine, or malt beverages to consumers.

Sec. 6.7 *Retail establishment.* "Retail establishment" shall mean any premises where distilled spirits, wine, or malt beverages are sold or offered for sale to consumers, whether for consumption on or off the premises where sold.

Sec. 6.8 *Industry member.* "Industry member" shall mean any person engaged in business as a distiller, brewer, rectifier, blender, or other producer, or as an importer or wholesaler, of distilled spirits, wine, or malt beverages, or as a bottler, or warehouseman and bottler, of distilled spirits, but shall not include an agency of a State or political subdivision thereof, or an officer or employee of such agency.

Sec. 6.9 *Product.* "Product" shall mean distilled spirits, wine, or malt beverages, as defined in the Federal Alcohol Administration Act.

Sec. 6.10 *Other terms.* Any other term defined in the Federal Alcohol Administration Act and used in this part shall have the meaning assigned to it by such act.

Subpart C—Unlawful Inducements and Exceptions

Unlawful Inducements

Sec. 6.20 *Application.* Except as provided in this part, it is unlawful for any industry member to induce, by furnishing, giving, renting, lending, or selling any equipment, fixtures, signs, supplies, money, services, or other thing of value, directly or indirectly or through an affiliate, any retailer to purchase any products from such industry member to the exclusion in whole or in part of such products sold or offered for sale by other industry members in interstate or foreign commerce, if such inducement is made in the course of interstate or foreign commerce, or if such industry member engages in the practice of using such means to such an extent as substantially to restrain or prevent transactions in interstate or foreign commerce in any such products, or if the direct effect of such inducement is to prevent, deter, hinder, or restrict other industry members from selling or offering for sale any such products to such retailer in interstate or foreign commerce: *Provided,* That in the case of malt beverages, this part shall apply to transactions between a retailer in any State and a brewer, importer, or wholesaler of malt beverages outside such State only to the extent that the law of such State imposes requirements similar to the requirements of section 5 (b) of the Federal Alcohol Administration Act (27 U.S.C. 205 (b)), with respect to similar transactions between a retailer in such State and a brewer, importer, or wholesaler of malt beverages in such State, as the case may be; *Provided further,* That this part shall not operate to exempt any person from the requirements of any State law or regulation.

Exceptions

Sec. 6.21 *General.* An industry member may furnish to a retailer, under the conditions and within the limitations prescribed, the equipment, signs, supplies, services or other things of value specified in sections 6.22-6.31: *Provided,* That such furnishing is not conditioned directly or indirectly on the purchase of distilled spirits, wine, or malt beverages.

Sec. 6.22 *Equipment.* Tapping accessories, such as rods, vents, taps, hoses, washers, couplings, vent tongues, and check valves may be sold to a retailer and installed in his establishment if such tapping accessories are sold at a price not less than the cost thereof to the industry member selling the same, and if the price thereof is collected within 30 days of the date of sale.

Sec. 6.23 *Inside signs; wine and malt beverages.* Signs, posters, placards, designs, devices, decorations or graphic displays bearing advertising matter and for use in the windows or elsewhere in the interior of a retail establishment, may be given, rented, loaned, or sold to a retailer by an industry member engaged in business as a rectifier, blender, producer, bottler, importer or wholsaler, of wine, or as a brewer, importer or wholesaler, of malt beverages if they have no value to the retailer except as advertisements and if the total value of all such materials furnished by any industry member and in use at any one time in any retail extablishment does not exceed $10, including all expenses incurred directly or indirectly by any industry member in connection with the purchase, manufacture, transportation, assembly, and installation of such materials and of accessories thereto: *Provided,* That the industry member shall not directly or indirectly pay or credit the retailer for displaying such materials or for any expense incidental to their operation.

Sec. 6.23a *Inside signs; distilled spirits.* Signs, posters, placards, designs, devices, decorations or graphic displays, bearing advertising matter and for use in the windows or elsewhere in the interior of a retail establishment, may be given, rented, loaned, or sold to a retailer by an industry member engaged in business as a distiller, rectifier, blender, producer, importer, wholesaler, bottler, or warehouseman and bottler, of distilled spirits, (a) if they have no value to the retailer except as advertisements, (b) if the total value of all such materials furnished by any industry member and in use in any one retail establishment at any one time does not exceed $15 in the case of materials used in window displays, or does not exceed $30 in the case of materials used elsewhere than in the windows, and (c) if the cost of installation of such materials does not exceed that which is usual and customary in that locality: *Provided,* That the industry member shall not directly or indirectly pay or credit the retailer for displaying such materials or for any expense incidental to their operation.

Sec. 6.24 *Supplies.* Carbonic acid gas or ice may be sold to a retailer, if sold in accordance with the reasonable open market price thereof in the locality where sold, and if the price thereof is collected within 30 days of the date of sale.

Sec. 6.25 *Coil cleaning service.* Coil cleaning service may be furnished, given, or sold to a retailer of malt beverages.

Sec. 6.26 *Advertising service.* The names and addresses of retailers selling the products of any industry member may be listed in an advertisement of such industry member, if such listing is the only reference to any retailer in the advertisement and is relatively inconspicuous in relation to the advertisement as a whole.

Sec. 6.27 *Consumer advertising specialties.* Consumer advertising specialties, such as ash trays, bottle or can openers, corkscrews, paper shopping bags, matches, printed recipes, wine lists, leaflets, blotters, post cards, and pencils, which bear advertising matter, may be furnished, given, or sold to a retailer for unconditional distribution by him to the general public, if the retailer is not paid or credited in any manner directly or indirectly for such distribution service.

Sec. 6.28 *Retailer advertising specialties.* Retailer advertising specialties, such as trays, coasters, beer mats, menu cards, meal checks, paper napkins, foam scrapers, back bar mats, tap markers, thermometers, clocks, and calendars, which bear advertising matter, and which are primarily valuable to the retailer as point of sale advertising media, may be furnished, given, or sold to a retailer if the aggregate cost to any industry member of such retailer advertising specialties furnished, given, or sold in connection with any one retail establishment in any one calendar year does not exceed $10.

Sec. 6.29 *Samples.* Not more than 2 gallons of any brand of malt beverages, not more than 1 pint of any brand of distilled spirits, and not more than 1 gallon of any brand of wine, may be furnished or given as a sample to a retailer who has not previously purchased that particular product: *Provided,* That 2 quarts of any brand of distilled spirits may be furnished or given as a sample to any agency of a State or political subdivision thereof which has not purchased that particular product.

Sec. 6.30 *Newspaper cuts.* Newspaper cuts, mats, or engraved blocks for use in retailers' advertisements, may be furnished, given, rented, loaned, or sold by an industry member to a retailer selling his products.

Sec. 6.31 *Merchandise.* Merchandise, such as groceries and drugs, may be sold to a retailer, without limit as to quantity or value, by an industry member who is also engaged in business as a bona fide vendor of such merchandise, if such merchandise is sold in accordance with the reasonable open market price thereof in the locality where sold, and if such merchandise is not sold in combination with distilled spirits, wine, or malt beverages and is itemized separately on the industry member's invoices and other records: *Provided,* That equipment, fixtures, signs, supplies, and consumer and retailer advertising specialties may be furnished only as provided elsewhere in this part.

APPENDIX F

Chronology

1640	First spirits distilled from grain in America (by William Kieft, Director General of the colony of New Netherlands).
1733	Molasses Act. All West Indies molasses, except British, taxed prohibitively. Colony of Georgia outlaws importation of distilled spirits.
1750	New England-Africa-West Indies rum trade at its height.
1764	Sugar Act. British warships authorized to intercept colonial rum smugglers.
1789	First "temperance society" formed (Connecticut).
1790	Congress provides daily rum ration for U.S. soldiers.
1791	Alexander Hamilton's whiskey excise tax (7¢ per gallon).
1794	Whiskey Rebellion. Pennsylvania farmer-distillers fight excise tax.
1800	Excise tax repealed.
1808	African slave trade abolished; rum industry declines.
1812	Wartime excise tax levied.
1816	First prohibition law; Indiana outlaws Sunday sales.
1832	Aeneas Coffey patents the continuous still.
1846	First statewide prohibition law (Maine).
1862	First resumption since War of 1812 of excise tax (20¢ per gallon).
1869	National Prohibition Party formed.
1874	Women's Christian Temperance Union formed.
1891	First prohibition convention (Wisconsin).
1895	Anti-Saloon League formed.
1897	Bottling in Bond Act.
1909	Blends classified legally as whiskey.
1913	Webb-Kenyon Act.
1920	18th Amendment. Prohibition era begins. Volstead Act. Association Against Prohibition Amendment formed.
1925	St. Valentine's Day Massacre.
1933	3.2% wine and beer legalized. 21st Amendment. Prohibition era ends. Distilled Spirits Institute formed.
1934	National Association of Alcoholic Beverage Importers, Inc. formed. National Conference of State Liquor Administrators formed. Excise tax levied at $2 per gallon.
1935	Federal Alcohol Administration Act.

1938 National Alcoholic Beverage Control Association formed.
Excise tax increased to $2.25 per gallon.
1940 Alcohol Tax Unit replaces Federal Alcohol Administration.
Excise tax increased to $3 per gallon.
1941 Partial conversion to war production.
Excise tax increased to $4 per gallon.
1942 Total conversion to war production.
Excise tax increased to $6 per gallon.
1943 Puerto Rican Rum Institute formed.
1944 Excise tax increased to $9 per gallon.
1945 Beverage production resumed.
1946 Licensed Beverage Industries formed.
1951 Excise tax increased to $10.50 per gallon.
1952 Federal enforcement authority vested in Alcohol and Tobacco Tax Division of the Bureau of Internal Revenue.

APPENDIX G

Glossary

A

"A" *blend*—a spirit blend in the middle retail whiskey price bracket.
absinthe—a greenish liquor, made from oils of wormwood, anise and other aromatics; licorice flavor (absinthe may not be legally sold in the United States).
age—the period between distillation and bottling when distilled spirits are stored in wood containers.
agency—in monopoly states, a privately owned off-premise retail outlet.
akvavit—variant of aquavit.
alcohol—a colorless, inflammable, volatile liquid (C_2H_5OH). See *ethyl alcohol.*
aldehyde—a colorless, volatile liquid found in alcohol.
alembic—an early type of still.
anise—herb of the carrot family.
aniseed—seed of the anise, from which anise oil, a flavoring for cordials, is produced.
anisette—a colorless cordial flavored with aniseed.
applejack—apple brandy.
aquavit—a Scandinavian liquor with caraway flavoring.
aqua vitae—a Latin phrase meaning "water of life"; a former name for alcohol.
arak—variant of arrack.
Armagnac—a grape brandy, produced in France in the region southeast of Bordeaux.
aromatic bitters—a liquor consisting of a spirits base flavored with aromatic plants, seeds, etc. (used as an ingredient in mixed drinks).
arrack—a Dutch East Indies aromatic rum.
"A" *straight*—a straight whiskey in the middle retail whiskey price bracket.

B

bar—1. a counter across which liquors are served by the drink. 2. an on-premise outlet.
bar bourbon, bar gin, bar whiskey, etc.—the brand which a particular bar uses when the customer does not specify a brand.
"B" *blend*—a spirit blend in the lower retail whiskey price bracket.
bead—one of the small bubbles which forms on the surface of some liquors after pouring; particularly noticeable, for example, with higher proof whiskies.

Big Four, the—the four largest distilling organizations in the United States: Seagram, National Distillers, Schenley and Hiram Walker.
bitters—a liquor used as an ingredient in mixed drinks (there are two types: aromatic and flavoring bitters).
blend—a mixture of two or more distilled spirits (generally used as a synonym for *spirit blend*).
blended bourbon whiskey—a blend of whiskey and grain neutral spirits; at least 51% by volume of the blend is straight bourbon whiskey.
blended Canadian whiskey—a blend of whiskies distilled in Canada, all of which are two or more years old.
blended corn whiskey—a blend of whiskey and grain neutral spirits; at least 51% by volume of the blend is straight corn whiskey.
blended Irish whiskey—a blend of whiskies, all of which are three or more years old, distilled either in the Irish Free State or in Northern Ireland.
blended malt whiskey—a blend of whiskey and grain neutral spirits; at least 51% by volume of the blend is straight malt whiskey.
blended rye malt whiskey—a blend of whiskey and grain neutral spirits; at least 51% by volume of the blend is straight rye malt whiskey.
blended rye whiskey—a blend of whiskey and grain neutral spirits; at least 51% by volume of the blend is straight rye whiskey.
blended Scotch type whiskey—a domestic whiskey consisting of a blend of at least 20% by volume of 100 proof malt whiskey and not more than 80% by volume of whiskey distilled at over 180 proof; the malt whiskey is pot-stilled at 160 proof or less from a fermented mash of malted barley dried over peat fire; both whiskey components of the blend are aged for three or more years in new plain, or re-used oak containers.
blended Scotch whisky—a blend of whiskies distilled in Scotland, all of which are three or more years old.
blended straight bourbon whiskies—a blend of straight bourbon whiskies only.
blended straight corn whiskies—a blend of straight corn whiskies only.
blended straight malt whiskies—a blend of straight malt whiskies only.
blended straight rye malt whiskies—a blend of straight rye malt whiskies only.
blended straight rye whiskies—a blend of straight rye whiskies only.
blended straight wheat whiskies—a blend of straight wheat whiskies only.
blended straight whiskies—a blend of straight whiskies only.
blended wheat whiskey—a blend of whiskey and grain neutral spirits; at least 51% by volume of the blend is straight wheat whiskey.
blended whiskey—a whiskey containing at least 20% by volume of 100 proof straight whiskey, and not more than 80% by volume of neutral spirits (or other whiskey, or a mixture of neutral spirits and other whiskey).
blending agent—an ingredient, e.g., sherry, used in the blending process.
blend of straights—a blend of straight whiskies.
Bois communs dits à Terroir—one of the seven subdivisions of the Cognac region in France.
Bois Ordinaires—one of the seven subdivisions of the Cognac region in France.
bond—a bottled in bond liquor (the term is most commonly used in connection with bottled in bond whiskey).
bonded bourbon—a bottled in bond straight bourbon whiskey.
bonded rye—a bottled in bond straight rye whiskey.

bonded whiskey—a bottled in bond whiskey.

Bons Bois—one of the seven subdivisions of the Cognac region in France.

bootlegger—one who illegally produces or sells distilled spirits.

Borderies—one of the seven subdivisions of the Cognac region in France.

botanicals—plants and plant derivatives used for flavoring purposes in the production of distilled spirits (the term is commonly used in connection with gin).

bottled in bond whiskey—a straight whiskey which is entitled to a grain designation, and which is the product of one distillery and one distilling season, aged for four or more years, and bottled at 100 proof under federal government supervision at an internal revenue bonded warehouse.

bottling in bond department—that part of an internal revenue bonded warehouse which is set aside for the bottling of spirits which meet requirements for designation as "bottled in bond."

bourbon liqueur—a cordial with a bourbon whiskey flavor; at least 51% of the spirits content is bourbon whiskey, or straight bourbon whiskey, or whiskey distilled from a bourbon mash; proof is 60° or higher.

bourbon whiskey—whiskey distilled at 160 proof or lower from a fermented mash containing at least 51% corn grain, and stored in charred new oak containers.

bourbon whiskey—a blend—same as "blended bourbon whiskey."

brand label—the front label; on the brand label appear the brand name, class and type of spirits, and the name and address of the bottler, distiller, rectifier or importer.

brandy—1. one of the classes of distilled spirits; distilled at less than 190 proof from the fermented juice, mash or wine of fruit or from its residue, and bottled at 80 proof or higher. 2. grape brandy.

"B" straight—a straight whiskey in the lower retail price bracket.

bulk spirits—spirits in containers having a capacity of more than one wine gallon.

C

call item—a brand which sells primarily on the basis of consumer demand.

Calvados—a French apple brandy.

Campbeltown malt whisky—one of the four principal varieties of Scotch malt whisky; produced on the peninsula in Scotland which lies to the east of the island of Islay.

Canadian whiskey—a blend—same as "blended Canadian whiskey."

capsule—a device made of foil or other material, tubular in shape and closed at one end; used for bottle closures.

caramel—burnt sugar; used to color and to flavor distilled spirits.

caraway—an aromatic herb, the seeds of which are used for flavoring purposes.

carton—a container for a bottle of distilled spirits.

case—a shipping container for distilled spirits (for example, one type of whiskey case contains 12 bottles of fifths).

cask—a generic term for "barrel," "hogshead," "keg," etc.

cassia bark—Chinese cinnamon; the powdered, aromatic bark of a tree of the laurel family (used for flavoring purposes).

champagne Cognac—Cognac produced in either the Grande Champagne or the Petite Champagne.
charred barrel—a barrel, the inside of which is charred; used for aging distilled spirits.
chaser—a drink, e.g., water, taken after a straight drink of spirits.
cistern—a tank for distilled spirits.
class—one of the principal classifications of distilled spirits, e.g., whiskey, gin, brandy, etc.
closure—a device for closing the opening of a bottle.
cocktail—a short mixed drink.
cocktail glass—a glass ranging in size from 2 to 3½ ounces.
code number—in a monopoly state, the particular number assigned to each size of each brand sold in the state.
Cognac—grape brandy distilled in the Cognac region of France.
collins—a tall iced drink made with distilled spirits, sugar and lemon or lime juice.
collins glass—a glass ranging in size from 10 to 14 ounces.
column still—same as "continuous still."
compound gin—a gin produced by mixing neutral spirits with distilled gin, gin essence or other material carrying the characteristic juniper berry flavor.
congeners—substances which are contained in alcohol following distillation.
continuously distilled gin—non-rectified gin.
continuous still—a tall cylindrical still in which steam is used as the heating device to distill alcohol from the fermented substance.
cooler—a tall iced drink made with spirits, sugar, lemon juice and club soda.
cooper—a barrel-maker.
cooperage—casks, barrels, etc.
cordial—one of the classes of distilled spirits; made from a spirits base, natural flavoring materials and sweetening. At least 2½% by weight is sugar or dextrose.
cordial glass—a glass ranging in size from ¾ to 1 ounce.
coriander seeds—aromatic seeds used for flavoring purposes.
corn whiskey—whiskey distilled at 160 proof or lower from a fermented mash containing at least 80% corn, and stored in uncharred or re-used charred oak barrels.
corn whiskey—a blend—same as "blended corn whiskey."
crême d'ananas—a cordial made from pineapples.
crême de bananes—a cordial made from bananas.
crême de cacao—a cordial made from cocoa beans (two varieties: brown and white).
crême de cassis—a cordial made from black currants.
crême de fraises—a cordial made from strawberries.
crême de framboises—a cordial made from raspberries.
crême de menthe—a cordial made from mint (two varieties: green and white).
crême de noyaux—a cordial made from fruit stones.
crême de vanille—a cordial made from vanilla beans.
cuba libre—a tall iced drink made with White Label rum, cola and lime juice.
curacao—a cordial made with orange peel.

customs bonded warehouse—a warehouse, under federal government supervision, for storing imported spirits or spirits for export.

cut-case card—a point-of-sale display card affixed upright in back of a case which has been cut to display the bottles inside.

D

daiquiri—a cocktail made with White Label rum, sugar and lime juice.

daisy—a tall iced drink made with spirits, lemon juice, grenadine, and decorated with fruit.

dash—1/6 teaspoonful.

decanter—in the liquor industry, a specially designed bottle simulating non-commercial decanters.

delmonico glass—a glass ranging in size from 5 to 7 ounces.

Demerara rum—a sweet, dark, heavy-bodied rum from British Guiana.

Des Moines Warranty—a warranty that distillers, importers and vendors of spirits will not sell to any customer in the United States at a price lower than that to monopoly states.

distillation—the process by which alcohol is separated from a fermented liquid, mash or other substance.

distilled dry gin—a distilled, unsweetened gin.

distilled gin—1. a gin produced by distillation from mash, the alcohol passing through a gin head of botanicals before condensation. 2. a gin produced by the re-distillation of spirits, the alcohol passing through a gin head of botanicals before condensation. 3. a gin produced by distillation from a mash containing botanicals.

distilled London dry gin—same as "distilled dry gin."

distilled spirits—the general term for all distilled alcoholic beverages; defined by federal law as "ethyl alcohol, hydrated oxide of ethyl, spirits of wine, whiskey, rum, brandy, gin, and other distilled spirits, including all dilutions and mixtures thereof, for non-industrial use."

distillers feeds—livestock and poultry feeds, produced from the mash which remains after distillation.

distributor—a wholesaler.

dry—1. not sweet. 2. a person militantly opposed to the manufacture, sale and consumption of alcoholic beverages.

dry cordial—a cordial containing less than 10% by weight of sugar or dextrose.

dry county—a county in which prohibition is in effect.

dry gin—an unsweetened gin.

dry martini—a cocktail made from dry gin, dry vermouth, and containing an olive.

dry newspaper—a newspaper which does not accept liquor advertising.

dry state—a state in which prohibition is in effect (there are two dry states: Mississippi and Oklahoma).

dunder—a sugar-cane by-product, used in the production of Jamaica rum.

E

eau de vie—a French phrase meaning "water of life"; spirits distilled from wine; brandy.

ethyl alcohol—the type of alcohol common to all distilled spirits used for beverage purposes.

excise tax—a liquor excise tax is a per-gallon tax levied by federal and state governments on producers and importers.

F

Fair Trade law—a law concerning re-sale price maintenance. See "mandatory Fair Trade law" and "voluntary Fair Trade law."

fermentation—in the production of distilled spirits, the conversion of sugar by yeast into alcohol, prior to distillation.

fifth—a fifth of a gallon; 4/5 quart.

Fins Bois—one of the seven subdivisions of the Cognac region in France.

fizz—a tall iced drink, made with spirits, sugar, lemon juice and club soda.

flask—a broad flat bottle.

flavored brandy—a cordial-type of spirits, consisting primarily of a brandy base, fruit or other flavoring, and bottled at 70 proof.

flavored gin—a cordial-type of spirits, consisting primarily of a gin base, fruit or mint flavoring, and bottled at 70 proof.

flavoring bitters—bitters flavored with orange, lemon or lime (used as an ingredient in mixed drinks).

flip—a mixed drink made with spirits, sugar and an egg; served spiced.

Folle Blanche—the white grape from which Cognac is made.

frappé—a drink made by pouring spirits, usually a cordial, into a cocktail glass filled with shaved ice.

French vermouth—a dry vermouth.

fusel oil—an oily liquid found with ethyl alcohol (after distillation); amyl alcohol.

G

gallon—the United States gallon of 231 cubic inches of alcoholic beverage at 60° Fahrenheit; 128 fluid ounces.

gibson—a dry martini served with an onion instead of an olive.

gin—one of the classes of distilled spirits; produced as "distilled gin" or as "compound gin" and bottled at 80 proof or higher; has a juniper berry flavor.

gin head—in the production of gin, the container in which botanicals are placed, and through which distilled alcohol passes prior to condensation.

goblet—a glass ranging in size from 8 to 12 ounces.

golden gin—a gin with a pale golden color; the color is produced by storage in charred oak barrels.

Gold Label—one of two varieties of Puerto Rican, Cuban and other light-bodied rums; dark in color, sweet.

Government label—the back label; on the Government label appear the alcoholic content, net contents, artificial or excessive coloring or flavoring, percentage of neutral spirits and the name of the commodity from which distilled, age, state where distilled.

grain neutral spirits—neutral spirits distilled from grain.

Grande Champagne—one of the seven subdivisions of the Cognac region in France.

grappa—grappa brandy.
grappa brandy—grape pomace brandy.
green strip stamp—a strip stamp affixed only to bottles of bottled in bond spirits.
grenadine—a red syrup of pomegranates used as an ingredient in mixed drinks.

H

heads and tails—high and low wines; distillates containing one-half of 1% or more of aldehydes or 1% or more of fusel oil.
highball—a tall iced drink made with spirits and club soda or ginger ale.
highball glass—a glass ranging in size from 8 to 10 ounces.
Highland malt whisky—one of the four principal varieties of Scotch malt whisky; produced in northern Scotland.
high wines—see "heads and tails."

I

imperial gallon—British gallon of 277.274 cubic inches, equal to 1.2003 U.S. gallons.
internal revenue bonded warehouse—a warehouse, under federal government supervision, for the storage and aging of spirits.
Irish whiskey—a blend—same as "blended Irish whiskey."
Islay malt whisky—one of the four principal varieties of Scotch malt whisky; produced in Scotland on the island of Islay.
Italian vermouth—a sweet vermouth.

J

jigger—1½ ounces.
jigger cap—a bottle closure which also serves as a jigger glass.
julep—a tall iced drink made with whiskey (usually bourbon), sugar, mint leaves, and decorated with mint leaves and fruit.
juniper berry—the berry of the juniper evergreen, used to give to gin its characteristic flavor.

K

kirsch—cherry brandy.
kirschwasser—same as "kirsch."
kümmel—a cordial flavored with caraway seeds.

L

leaching—filtration of a liquor through a substance, e.g., charcoal, in order to remove undesirable properties.
lees—the sediment of wine.
lees brandy—brandy distilled from the lees of fruit wine.
lemon bitters—one of the varieties of flavoring bitters.
license—authorization from a government unit to operate as a vendor of distilled spirits.
license state—a state in which private wholesalers and retailers are licensed to operate as vendors of distilled spirits.

lime bitters—one of the varieties of flavoring bitters.
liqueur—same as "cordial."
liquor—popular name for a distilled alcoholic beverage.
listing—in a monopoly state, a place on the list of brands bought and sold by the state.
local option—the privilege of counties and smaller political units, as established by their law, to vote themselves from dry to wet or wet to dry.
London Dock rum—Jamaica rum which is stored and aged on the docks of London.
London dry gin—same as "distilled London dry gin."
Lowland malt whisky—one of the four principal varieties of Scotch malt whisky; produced in southern Scotland.
low wines—see "heads and tails"; when pot stills are used, the first distillation is called low wines.

M

maceration—in the production of cordials, the soaking of flavoring materials in the spirits base.
malt—grain, usually barley, which is steeped in water and then allowed to germinate.
malt whiskey—1. domestic whiskey distilled at 160 proof or lower from a fermented mash containing at least 51% barley malt, and stored in charred new oak containers. 2. Scotch malt whisky, distilled in accordance with Scottish law.
malt whiskey—a blend—same as "blended malt whiskey."
mandatory Fair Trade law—a state law which provides for fixed retail prices, and for automatic enforcement without requiring action on the part of the brand owner.
mandatory mark-up law—a law which establishes exact percentages of mark-up.
mandatory statement—a statement descriptive of a brand of spirits, required by law to appear on the label, in advertising, or both.
manhattan—a cocktail made with whiskey and vermouth, and containing a maraschino cherry.
maraschino—a cordial made from the marasca cherry.
maraschino cherries—cherries preserved in maraschino.
marc—see "pomace."
marc brandy—see "pomace brandy."
marry—to allow components of a blend to mix thoroughly over a period of time.
martini—a cocktail made with gin and vermouth.
mash—meal of grain steeped and stirred in water (fermented, and then distilled).
miniature—a small bottle of spirits (1 ounce, 1.6 ounces, or 2 ounces).
monopoly state—a state which functions as a wholesaler, buying spirits directly from producers and importers; nearly all monopoly states operate state-owned retail package stores; and wholesale to privately owned package stores and/or bars.

N

neutral brandy—brandy distilled at more than 170 proof.
neutral spirits—spirits distilled from any substance at or above 190 proof.

New England rum—a straight rum produced in the United States, and distilled at less than 160 proof.
nip—a miniature.

O

off-premise retailer—a retailer who sells by the bottle for off-premise consumption; a package store.
okolehao—an Hawaiian liquor made from molasses, rice lees, and the juice of the taro root.
Old Fashioned—a short iced drink made with spirits (usually whiskey), sugar, and decorated with fruit.
Old Fashioned glass—a glass ranging in size from 4 to 6 ounces.
Old Tom gin—a sweet gin.
on-premise retailer—a retailer who sells by the drink or by the bottle for on-premise consumption; tavern; bar.
on the rocks—a drink consisting of spirits poured over ice cubes.
open state—same as "license state."
orange bitters—one of the varieties of flavoring bitters.
original entry gallon—same as "original proof gallon."
original proof gallon—a proof gallon of spirits at the time it is placed in wood for aging.

P

package store—an off-premise retail outlet.
patent still—same as "continuous still."
pearl onion—a cocktail onion.
peppermint schnapps—a cordial made with mint.
percolation—in the production of cordials, the filtering of the spirits base through flavoring material.
Petite Champagne—one of the seven subdivisions of the Cognac region in France.
pomace—the crushed skin and pulp of fruit.
pomace brandy—brandy distilled from pomace after fruit juices are withdrawn.
pony—1 ounce.
pony glass—a glass containing 1 ounce.
pot still—a still consisting of a pot-shaped vessel with a tapering neck which connects to a tube in which alcohol, vaporized by heat, is collected.
pourer—a device, with a narrow spout, which fits into the mouth of a bottle, and which makes pouring easier and more accurate; commonly used in bars.
pouring bourbon, pouring gin, pouring whiskey, etc.—same as "bar bourbon," "bar gin," etc.
pouring spot—a bar; on-premise outlet.
prepared cocktail—a cocktail bottled under a brand name.
prohibition—the forbidding, by law, of the manufacture, sale, or both, of alcoholic beverages.
Prohibition—the period from January 16, 1920 to December 5, 1933 when the manufacture, sale or transportation of alcoholic beverages in the United States was prohibited.

prohibitionist—a dry.
proof—the alcoholic content by volume of distilled spirits, stated in terms of twice the percentage of alcoholic content, e.g., a whiskey containing 50% alcohol by volume is 100 proof whiskey.
proof gallon—a wine gallon of 100 proof spirits.
proof spirits—100 proof spirits.
punch—a beverage made from spirits (or wine) and other varied ingredients (mixed in a large bowl from which individual portions are served).
puncheon—a large cask of varying size.

Q

Quetsch—a French plum brandy.
quinine water—a carbonated water containing quinine sulphate (used primarily as a mixer for "gin and tonic").

R

rectification tax—a tax on rectified spirits, levied on a per-gallon basis.
rectified spirits—spirits whose natural composition is altered following distillation through closed pipes and vessels.
red strip stamp—a strip stamp affixed to all bottles of distilled spirits except bottled in bond spirits.
regauge proof gallon—a proof gallon of spirits when measured after aging.
Repeal—repeal of the Prohibition amendment (December 5, 1933).
residue brandy—brandy distilled from the residue of fruit or wine.
rickey—a tall iced drink made with spirits, lime juice, lime rind, and club soda.
rock and bourbon—a cordial containing bourbon whiskey, rock candy (or sugar syrup), and usually also containing fruit, fruit juices or other flavoring material. At least 51% of the spirits content is bourbon whiskey (or straight bourbon whiskey, or whiskey distilled from a bourbon mash); proof is 48° or higher.
rock and brandy—a cordial containing brandy, rock candy (or sugar syrup), and usually also containing fruit, fruit juices or other flavoring material. 100% of the spirits content is grape brandy distilled at 170 proof or less; proof is 48° or higher.
rock and rum—a cordial containing rum, rock candy (or sugar syrup), and usually also containing fruit, fruit juices or other flavoring material. 100% of the spirits content is rum; proof is 48° or higher.
rock and rye—a cordial containing rye whiskey, rock candy (or sugar syrup), and usually also containing fruit, fruit juices or other flavoring material. At least 51% of the spirits content is rye whiskey (or straight rye whiskey, or whiskey distilled from a rye mash); proof is 48° or higher.
rum—one of the classes of distilled spirits; made from the fermented juice of sugar-cane, sugar-cane syrup, sugar-cane molasses or other sugar-cane by-products; distilled at less than 190 proof and bottled at 80 proof or higher.
rye liqueur—a cordial with a rye whiskey flavor; at least 51% of the spirits content is rye whiskey, or straight rye whiskey, or whiskey distilled from a rye mash; proof is 60° or higher.

rye malt whiskey—whiskey distilled at 160 proof or lower from a fermented mash containing at least 51% rye malt, and stored in new charred oak containers.

rye malt whiskey—a blend—same as "blended rye malt whiskey."

rye whiskey—whiskey distilled at 160 proof or lower from a fermented mash containing at least 51% rye grain, and stored in charred new oak containers.

rye whiskey—a blend—same as "blended rye whiskey."

S

Scotch type whiskey—a blend—same as "blended Scotch type whiskey."

Scotch whisky—a blend—same as "blended Scotch whisky."

S.D.D.—Specially Designated Distributor.

size—bottle size: quart, fifth, etc.

sling—a tall iced drink made with spirits (usually gin), sugar, lemon peel, club soda.

slivovitz—plum brandy.

sloe gin—a cordial made from sloe berries.

smash—a short iced drink made with spirits, mint, sugar.

sour—a short drink made with spirits, lemon juice, sugar, and decorated with a slice of orange and a cherry.

sparkling water—carbonated water; club soda; seltzer.

Specially Designated Distributor—in Michigan, a privately owned package store.

spirit blend—a blend of whiskey and neutral spirits; at least 20% by volume is 100 proof straight whiskey, and not more than 80% by volume is neutral spirits.

spirits—same as "distilled spirits."

spirit whiskey—1. a mixture of neutral spirits and not less than 5% by volume of whiskey. 2. a mixture of neutral spirits and less than 20% by volume of straight whiskey, but not less than 5% by volume of straight whiskey, or of straight whiskey and whiskey.

standard liquor bottle—a bottle made, formed and filled in such a way as not to mislead the consumer.

standards of fill—bottle sizes, as established by federal law.

standards of identity—specifications, as established by federal law, for each class and type of spirits.

state store—in monopoly states, a package store which is state-owned and state-operated.

still—the apparatus used to distill alcohol from a fermented substance.

stillage—the mash which remains after alcohol has been distilled from it; used in the production of distillers feeds.

stirrer—a small rod for stirring mixed drinks.

storekeeper-gauger—a representative of the federal government at distilleries, warehouses, etc.

straight bourbon whiskey—straight whiskey distilled from a fermented mash containing at least 51% corn grain, and aged in charred new oak barrels.

straight corn whiskey—straight whiskey distilled from a fermented mash containing at least 80% corn grain, and aged in uncharred or re-used charred oak barrels.

straight malt whiskey—straight whiskey distilled from a fermented mash containing at least 51% barley malt, and aged in charred new oak barrels.
straight rum—New England rum.
straight rye malt whiskey—straight whiskey distilled from a fermented mash containing at least 51% rye malt, and aged in charred new oak barrels.
straight rye whiskey—straight whiskey distilled from a fermented mash containing at least 51% rye grain, and aged in charred new oak barrels.
straight wheat whiskey—straight whiskey distilled from a fermented mash containing at least 51% wheat grain, and aged in charred new oak barrels.
straight whiskey—whiskey distilled at 160 proof or less from a fermented grain mash, and aged for a minimum of two years.
strip stamp—a stamp affixed over the closure of each bottle of spirits, stating the net contents and indicating that federal excise tax has been paid. See "green strip stamp" and "red strip stamp."
swizzle—a drink made by placing spirits, and other ingredients, depending upon the type of swizzle, into a pitcher containing shaved ice; the contents are thoroughly agitated by twirling a swizzle stick (a stick with forked ends); swizzles are made equally well, if less dramatically, in the ordinary cocktail shaker.

T

table tent—a small point-of-sale display piece, folded in half, and placed tent-fashion on restaurant tables.
tax gallon—the unit of distilled spirits upon which the rate of tax prescribed by law is imposed.
tenth—a tenth of a gallon; 4/5 pint.
tequila—a Mexican liquor made from the century plant.
tied house—a retail outlet that has been induced by a producer or importer to exclude or restrict the sale of products of competing producers or importers (the tied house is illegal).
Tom Collins—a collins made with gin.
triple sec—a cordial made with orange peel.
tumbler—a glass ranging in size from 8 to 12 ounces.
type—one of the varieties within a given class of spirits.

U

usquebaugh—an ancient name for whiskey, meaning "water of life."

V

vermouth—a wine flavored with aromatic herbs, used primarily with whiskey in making the manhattan cocktail, and with gin, in making the martini cocktail (two varieties: dry and sweet).
vodka—one of the classes of distilled spirits; grain neutral spirits reduced to 80 to 110 proof and filtered through, or kept mechanically in motion against, charcoal; bottled at 80 proof or higher; colorless, tasteless, odorless.

voluntary Fair Trade law—a state law which provides for fixed retail prices, but which is not enforced unless the brand owner brings legal action.

W

warehouse receipt—a receipt issued by a warehouseman, containing a description of spirits stored with him (warehouse receipts are negotiable).
well—the place at a bar where the bar (pouring) gin or the bar (pouring) whiskey is kept for handy use.
wet county—a county where alcoholic beverages are legal.
wet newspaper—a newspaper which accepts liquor advertising.
wet state—a state where alcoholic beverages are legal.
wheat whiskey—whiskey distilled at 160 proof or lower from a fermented mash containing at least 51% wheat grain, and stored in charred new oak containers.
wheat whiskey—a blend—same as "blended wheat whiskey."
whiskey—one of the classes of distilled spirits; made from a fermented mash of grain distilled at less than 190 proof, withdrawn from the cistern room of the distillery at not more than 110 proof and not less than 80 proof, and bottled at 80 proof or higher.
whiskey—a blend—same as "blended whiskey."
whisky—the spelling used in connection with Scotch, also often used by brands of other imported whiskies, and sometimes by brands of domestic whiskies.
White Label—one of two varieties of Puerto Rican, Cuban and other light bodied rums; light in color, not overly sweet.
wine gallon—same as "gallon."
withdrawal—removal of spirits from a warehouse.

Y

yeast—a plant which induces fermentation in a liquid or other substance, through the action of an enzyme on sugar.

Z

zubrowka—a variety of vodka.
zymase—the enzyme in yeast which induces fermentation.

Bibliography

Corrado, Benjamin W. *Corrado's Handbook of Liquor Marketing.* 1954.

Distilled Spirits Institute. *Alcohol for War.* 1944.

Annual Statistical Review. 1953.

Public Revenues from Alcoholic Beverages. 1953.

Distillers Feed Research Council, Inc. *Distillers Feeds. Their importance to the U.S. economy.* 1951.

Grossman, Harold J. *Grossman's Guide to Wines, Spirits and Beer.* Charles Scribner's Sons. 1943.

Joyce, R. E. *Special Problems of the Whiskey Business.* Distilled Spirits Institute. 1949.

Liquor Store. *Knowing Alcoholic Beverages.* Conover-Mast Publications, Inc. June, 1954.

Red Book Encyclopaedic Directory of the Wine and Liquor Industries. Liquor Publications, Inc. 1953.

Rosenbloom, Morris Victor. *The Liquor Industry.* Ruffsdale Distilling Company. 1935.

U.S. Tariff Commission. *Summaries of Tariff Information, Vol. 8. Spirits, Wines, and other Beverages.* U.S. Gov't. Printing Office. 1948.

U.S. Treasury Department, Internal Revenue Service. *Bottling of Tax-Paid Distilled Spirits (Regulations No. 11).* U.S. Gov't. Printing Office. 1950.

Bulk Sales and Bottling of Distilled Spirits (Regulations No. 3).* U.S. Gov't. Printing Office. 1948.

Credit Period to be Extended to Retailers of Alcoholic Beverages (Regulations No. 8).* U.S. Gov't. Printing Office. 1949.

Federal Alcohol Administration Act. U.S. Gov't. Printing Office. 1949.

Importation of Distilled Spirits, Wines and Fermented Liquors (Regulations No. 21). U.S. Gov't. Printing Office. 1951.

Inducements Furnished to Retailers (Regulations No. 6).* U.S. Gov't. Printing Office. 1952.

Labeling and Advertising of Distilled Spirits (Regulations No. 5).* U.S. Gov't. Printing Office. 1948.

* under the provisions of the Federal Alcohol Administration Act.

Liquors and Articles from Puerto Rico and the Virgin Islands (*Regulations No. 24*). U.S. Gov't. Printing Office. 1952.

Non-Industrial Use of Distilled Spirits and Wine (*Regulations No. 2**). U.S. Gov't. Printing Office. 1935.

Production of Brandy (*Regulations No. 5*). U.S. Gov't. Printing Office. 1950.

Production of Distilled Spirits (*Regulations No. 4*). U.S. Gov't. Printing Office. 1950

Rectification of Spirits and Wines (*Regulations No. 15*). U.S. Gov't. Printing Office. 1950.

Stills and Distilling Apparatus (*Regulations No. 23*). U.S. Gov't. Printing Office. 1950.

Traffic in Containers of Distilled Spirits (*Regulations No. 13*). U.S. Gov't. Printing Office. 1950.

Warehousing of Distilled Spirits (*Regulations No. 10*). U.S. Gov't. Printing Office. 1950.

Wholesale and Retail Dealers in Liquors (*Regulations No. 20*). U.S. Gov't. Printing Office. 1949.

* under the provisions of the Federal Alcohol Administration Act.

Index

A

Administrators, state, 28

Advertising, 16-17, 150, 184
  agencies, 186-187
  copy for, 172-174, 193-194
  developing the plan, 186-194
  executing the plan, 195
  expenses and appropriations, 182-183
  FAA Act regulations, 224-227
  history of, 8-9
  industry-imposed resolutions, 175
  legal aspects, 21, 163-176
  meaning of, 2
  merchandising the campaign, 195-196
  scope of, 185-186
  specialties, 171
  submission for state approval, 172

Advocaat, 63

Africa, 4

Age, consumer preferences and, 148-149

Agencies, advertising, 186-187

Aging, 39, 148
  defined, 36
  label requirements, 72-74, 165-166
  problems created by, 25-27
  process of, 39
  of whiskey, 45

Akvavit (aquavit), 63, 120*n*

Alcoholic content, 148-149, 164

Alcoholism, 23, 25

Alcohol Tax Unit, 14

Alcohol and Tobacco Tax Division, 14, 179

Alexander, 156, 157

Allowances, to the wholesaler, 184

American Distilling Co., Inc., 116

Amer Picon, 56

Angostura bitters, 63

Anisette, 55

Annual Statistical Review, 178

Anti-Saloon League, 10

Apple brandies, 157

Applejack, 58, 142

Appropriation:
  for advertising, 187-192
  allocating of, 182-183
  sales promotion, 192-193

Apricot cordial, 55

Apricot-flavored brandy, 57

Aquavit (akvavit), 63, 120*n*

Armagnac, 57, 60

Aromatic bitters, 63

Arrow Liqueurs Corp., 116

Association Against the Prohibition Amendment, 12

Austin, Nichols & Co., Inc., 116

B

B & B, 56
Bacardi, 158
Bacardi Imports, Inc., 116
Barley, 41
Barrels, whiskey, 41
Bars, 17
  prices in, 105-106
"Bathtub gin," 15
Beam Distilling Co., James B., 116
Benedictine D. O. M., 56
Beverage Media Blue Book, 180
Big Four, The, 15, 114
Bitters, 63, 120*n,* 152
Black & White Scotch, 180
Blackberry cordial, 55
Blackberry-flavored brandy, 57
Blended Irish whiskey, 50
Blended Scotch whisky, 49
Blended whiskey, 9, 41, 47-49, 128, 150
Blends of straight whiskies, 46, 131
Bloody Mary, 159
Bonded whiskies, sales statistics, 130-131, 134-135
Bonuses, 184
Bootlegging, 11-12, 23, 25
  markets lost to, 92
Bottled in bond whiskies, 45-46
Bottling, 7-8, 40-41
  statistical reports on, 178-179
Bottling in Bond Act, 8
Bottling house, 37
Bourbon County, 6
Bourbon liqueur, 54, 55
Bourbon de Luxe, 47, 48
Bourbon whiskey, 6-8, 44-46
  meaning of term, 150
  sales statistics, 129-131
Brand names, 7-8, 17, 26
  label requirements, 70
  research for, 180
Brands:
  of brandy, 142
  of cordials, 139
  gin sales by, 137
  of rum, 144
  of vodka, 146
  of whiskey, 114-117, 133
Brandy, 15, 38, 56, 58
  drinks made with, 157
  labeling, 73
  prices of, 107-108
  production of, 57-60
  sales of, 120-125, 140-142
  see also Standards of Identity, etc.
Brandy Alexander, 157
Brandy and soda, 157
Bribery, commercial, 160
British Guiana, 60
Brokers associations, 31
Bronx (drink), 155
Brown-Forman Distillers Corp., 115
Buchu gin, 52
Bulk spirits, 21, 36
Bureau of Customs, 14, 20
Bureau of Foreign and Domestic Commerce, 179
By-products, 32-33

C

California, 41, 57, 99, 145
Calvados, 57, 60
Calvert, 16
Calvert Reserve, 16, 47

Campbeltown malt whiskies, 49
Canada, 13, 41
Canada Dry Ginger Ale, Inc., 116
Canadian Club, 132
Canadian whiskey, 48, 49, 51
 sales statistics, 132, 134-135
Carbonated water, 152
Carton, the, 75
 advertising on, 192
Case, the, 75-76
 advertising on, 192
Chartreuse, 56
Cherry cordial, 55
Cherry-flavored brandy, 57
Cherry Heering, 56
Cistern, 35
Climate, consumer buying and, 150
Closures, bottle, 67-68
Clover Club, 156
Cocktails, 120*n*, 151-152
 bottled, 63
 prices of, 108-111
Code numbers, monopoly, 174
Codes of Fair Competition, 13
Coffey, Aeneas, 35
Coffey still, 35
Cognac, 57, 59-60, 141, 142
Cointreau, 56
Cola, 152
Collins mixer, 152
Collinses, 151-152, 154
Colonies, American, in early liquor history, 4-5
Column still, 35
Commissioners, state, 28
Compound gin, 52
Compounding, 40
Congeners, 38-39
Connecticut, 10
Consignment sales, 161
Consumers:
 analysis of, as market, 85-90
 distilled spirits as used by, 151-159
 price reaction of, 95-96
 publicity for, 196-197
 reasons for buying, 147-150
Containers, 65-67
 research on, 180-181
 re-use of, 27
 size of, 148
Contests, 184, 194
Continuous still, 35, 72
Copy, advertising, 193-194
Cordials, 15, 51
 drinks made with, 156-157
 labeling, 70
 prices of, 107-108
 production of, 53-57
 sales statistics, 120-125, 137-140
  see also Standards of Identity, etc.
Corn, 41
Corn oil, 32
Corn whiskey, 44
Corrado, Benjamin W., Marketing Consultants, 178
Corrado's Handbook of Liquor Marketing, 178
Costs:
 manufacturer's, 99-101
 retailer's, 102
 wholesaler's, 101-102
Crême d'ananas, 55
Crême de bananes, 55
Crême de cacao, 55

Crême de cassis, 55
Crême de fraises, 55
Crême de framboises, 55
Crême de menthe, 55
Crême de noyaux, 55
Crême de vanille, 55
Crême de violette, 55
Crime, 11-12, 23
Crow, James, 7
Cuba Libre, 158
Cuban rum, 60-62, 142-144
Curaçao, 55
Customs bonded warehouse, 37

D

Daiquiri, 158
Danziger Goldwasser, 56
Decanters, 180-181
Demerara rum, 62
Denmark, 53, 140
Direct mail merchandising, 184, 192, 195
Discounting, 97-99
Display material, 171
Distillation, defined, 34
Distilled spirits, 1
  defined, 35-36
Distilled Spirits Institute, Inc. (DSI), 14, 24, 28-30, 33, 175
  publications of, 178, 179
Distiller's beer, 41
Distillers Company, Ltd. (DCL), 15
Distillers Corp.–Seagrams, Ltd., 15, 114-115
Distillers dried grains, 33
Distillers dried grains with solubles, 33
Distillers dried solubles, 33
Distillers Feed Research Council, 33
Distillers feeds, 32-33
Distilling, 38-39
  of brandy, 57-60
  by-products, 32-33
  of cordials, 53-57
  of gin, 51-53
  history of 6-7
  of rum, 60-62
  of vodka, 62-63
  of whiskey, 41-51
  see also Standards of Identity, etc.
Distribution, checks on, 185
Drambuie, 56
Dried fruit brandy, 58
Drinkers and non-drinkers (graph), 86
Drinking, 148
  advertising use of scenes of, 174
  age of consumers, 87
  consumer habits, 85-90
  urban, 87
Drinks:
  recipes, 153-159
  usage customs, 151-153
Drunken driving, 24, 25
Dryness:
  consumer preferences, 148-149
  meaning of term, 52, 54
Drys, 18
  areas of, 90-91
  war on liquor industry, 22-23
Dubonnet, 156
Dutch gins, 53

E

Earthenware containers, 67
Egg nog, 154

Eighteenth Amendment, 10-11
England, 53
Excise tax, 5-6
Exports, reports on, 179

F

Fair Trade, 22, 27, 97, 162
Farm whiskey, 5-6
Federal Alcohol Administration (FAA), 14
Federal Alcohol Administration Act (FAA Act), 14, 20-21, 69, 163-165
  advertising regulations, 224-227
  inducements to retailers regulated by, 228-231
  standards of identity regulations, 215-223
  text of, 202-214
Federal Alcohol Control Administration (FACA), 13
Federal law, 19-22
  advertising, 163-176
  marketing, 160-162
  see also FAA Act
Federal Trade Commission, 21
Fill, standards of, 65-66
Finland, 13
Flavor, consumer preferences, 148-149
Flavored brandies, 56
Flavored gins, 56
Flavoring bitters, 63
Floats, parade, 197
Floor taxes, 20
Florida, 57
Folle Blanche, 59
Forbidden Fruit, 56
Foreign-born population, drinking habits, 89-90
Forfeited alcoholic beverages, 21-22
France, 53, 57, 59-60, 140
French, 75, 156, 157
Fromm & Sichel, Inc., 116
Fruit brandy, 58
Fruit cordials, 54
Fruit juices, 152, 153
Fruits, 152
Fusel oil, 32

G

Gallon, meaning of term, 36-37
Geneva gin, 52, 53
George III, 4
Georgia, 9
Gibson, 155
Gin, 15, 38, 52, 74
  continuously distilled, 72
  distilled dry, 52
  distilled London dry, 52, 53
  drinks made with, 155-156
  prices of, 107-108
  production of, 51-53
  sales of, 120-125, 136-137
  see also Standards of Identity, etc.
Gin and bitters, 155
Gin daisy, 155
Gin fizz, 156
Ginger ale, 152
Ginger beer, 152
Ginger-flavored brandy, 57
Gin rickey, 155
Gin sling, 156
Gin and tonic, 155
Glass bottles, 65-67

Glasses, for drinks, 153
Glenmore Distilleries Corp., 115
Golden gins, 52
Gold Label rum, 61, 144
Grain, used in distilling, 32-33
Grain neutral spirits, 50
Grain whiskey, 50
Grand Marnier, 56
Grant, Ulysses S., 8
Grape pomace brandy, 59
Grapes, 57, 58
Grappa brandy, 59
Great Britain, 4-5, 53
Greece, 53, 57
Green strip stamps, 68

H

Hamilton, Alexander, 5
Hearst Advertising Service, 180
Heublein & Bro., Inc., G. F., 108, 115, 146
Highballs, 151, 153
Hill & Hill, 48
History, liquor, *see* Liquor history
Holidays, consumer buying and, 150
Holland, 53
Hollands gin, 52, 53
Home consumption, 17
Hot buttered rum, 159
Hot rum punch, 159
Hot toddy, 154
Hungary, 57

I

Ice, shaved, 151
Iceland, 13
Illinois, 41, 45
Imperial gallon, defined, 37
Imperial whiskey, 16
Importers:
  associations of, 30
  branch offices, 84
  leading, 114-117
  merchandising by, 195-196
Imports, reports on, 179
Income, drinking habits and, 87
Indiana, 41, 45
Indicia, bottle, 65, 67
Industry, liquor, *see* Liquor industry
Interlocking directorates, 21
Internal Revenue bonded warehouse, 37
Internal Revenue Service, 14, 20
  reports on, 179
Inventories, 27
  statistical reports on, 178-179
Ireland, 41
Irish Mist, 56
Irish whiskey, 48, 49, 50-51
  sales statistics, 132
Islay, island of, 49
Islay malt whiskies, 49
Italy, 53, 57

J

Jack Rose, 157
Jamaica, 60
Jamaica rum, 60-62, 142-144
Jefferson, Thomas, 5
Jiggers, 67
Joint Committee of the States to Study Alcoholic Beverage Laws, 28

K

Kentucky, 6, 7, 41, 45, 48, 60
Kentucky Blended Whiskey, 128
Kieft, William, 4
Kirsch (Kirschwasser), 59, 142
Kits, salesmen's, 184
Kummel, 55

L

Label:
information required on, 68-75, 164-165
see also Advertising
Ladies' Home Journal, 176
Law:
advertising, 163-176
industry regulating by, 19-22
marketing, 160-163
published information on, 178
see also FAA Act
Leaching, 39
Lee, General Henry, 6
Lees brandy, 58
Lemon bitters, 63
Lemon-flavored gin, 57
Licensed Beverage Industries, Inc. (LBI), 24, 31
Lime bitters, 63
Limousin casks, 59
Liqueurs, *see* Cordials *and note* on 120
Liquor history, 3-18
bootlegging, 11-12
chronology of, 232-233
post-repeal period, 13-18
pre-prohibition, 3-10
prohibition, 9-13
wartime, 16-18
Liquor industry, 2, 22-24
aging requirements and, 25-27
bottling, *see* Bottling
by-products, 32-33
history of, *see* Liquor history
legal aspects, 19-22, 69-75; *see also* FAA Act
markets, *see* Markets
national associations, 28-32
packaging, *see* Packaging
post-repeal, 14-18
production, *see* Production
public relations problem, 24
size of, 19
warehousing, *see* Warehousing
Liquor Publications, Inc., 178
Liquors, meaning of term, 1-2
Liquor Store, 190
London Dock rums, 62
London dry gin, 52, 53
Louisiana, 60

M

McGuire Act, 27, 96-97
McKesson & Robbins, Inc., 116
Magazines, 176
liquor advertising in, 185-188, 191, 194, 196
reports on spirits, 179-180
Maine, 10
Major Market Distillations, 179-180
Malt, 41
Malt whiskey, 44, 49-50
Manhattan (cocktail), 152, 153
Maraschino cordial, 55
Marc brandy, 58-59

Marketing, 16-17
channels of, 77-84
developing the plan, 177-183
executing the plan, 183-185
expenses and appropriations, 182-183
history of, 7-8
legal aspects, 21, 160-163
meaning of, 2
Markets, 26, 85-92
research on, 181
see also Sales
Mark-up, 101, 102
Martini, 152, 155
Maryland, 6, 41, 45
Mash, 33, 41
Massachusetts, 41, 60
Matchbook advertising, 192
Mat services, 172, 184
Measures, for drinks, 153
Meetings, sales, 184, 195
Mercantile System, British, 4
Merchandising:
developing the plan, 177-183
executing the plan, 183-185
see also Marketing
Michigan, 83
Middlemen, 181-182
Mineral water, 152
Mint-flavored gin, 57
Mint julep, 154
Missouri, 41
Mixed drinks, 63, 106, 151-159
Moderation, in drinking, 25
Molasses, in liquor history, 4-5
Molasses Act, 4-5
Monopoly State Review, 189
Monopoly states, 77
marketing and merchandising activities in, 82-84, 185
pricing in, 97-99, 103-105
sales in, 117, 120, 133, 136, 138, 141, 143, 145
Moscow Mule, 146, 159

N

National, *see* National Distillers Products Corp.
National Alcoholic Beverage Control Association (NABCA), 28, 179
National Association of Alcoholic Beverage Importers (NAABI), 30, 179
National associations, 28-32
National brands, 1
National Conference of State Liquor Administrators (NCSLA), 28
National Distillers Products Corp., 15, 115
National Industrial Recovery Act, 13
Nationality, in drinking, 89-90
National Licensed Beverage Association (NLBA), 31
National Prohibition Party, 10
National Retail Liquor Package Stores Association, Inc. (NRLPSA), 31
Neat drinks, 151
Nebraska, 10
Negro market, 88-89
Neutral spirits, 36, 38, 72, 164-165
New England rum, 4, 61
Newfoundland, 13
New Jersey, 57
New York Sun, 6
Newspapers, 176

advertising in, 185, 186, 188-189, 191, 194, 196-197
reports on spirits, 179-180
New York (State), 57, 70, 180
"Noble experiment," 11
North Carolina, 83
Northern straights, 45
Norway, 13

O

Occupational taxes, 20
Off-premise outlets, 31, 77-82, 83, 148
Ohio, 41
Old Crow, 7, 16, 129-130
Old-fashioned, 154
Old Grand-Dad, 46
Old Hermitage, 8
Old Sunny Brook, 16, 48
Old Tom gin, 52, 53
On-premise outlets, 31, 83, 148
On-the-rocks drinks, 151, 153
Open states:
marketing and merchandising activities, 77-82, 184-185
pricing in, 97-103
sales in, 117, 120, 133, 136, 138, 141, 143, 145
see also States
Orange bitters, 63
Orange blossom, 155
Orange-flavored gin, 57
Oregon, 57
Original proof (entry) gallon, 36
Outdoor advertising, 186, 189, 192, 194, 196
Ouzo, 56

P

Package goods, 1
Package stores, 83, 105
Packaging, 64-76, 150
label use requirements, 68-75
Parfait amour, 55
Patent still, 35
Peach brandy, 57
Peach cordial, 55
Peach-flavored brandy, 57
Pennsylvania, 6, 41, 45, 60
Peppermint schnapps, 55
Permits, 21
Pernod, 56
Pilgrims, prohibition and, 9
Pimm's Cup No. 1, 56
Pink lady, 156
Pittsburgh, 6
Planter's Punch, 158
"Plants," 197
PM whiskey, 16, 180
Point-of-sale advertising, 192
Pomace brandy, 58-59
Portugal, 57
Pot still, 34
Pousse café, 157
Price-fixing, 27
Prices:
advertising and, 174
bar, 105-106
classes of liquors and, 106-111
consumer buying and, 149-150
control of, 96-99
for maximum profit, 93-96
in monopoly states, 103-105
in open states, 94-103
package store, 105

post-repeal, 18
re-sale, 27
sales and, 128
see also separate spirits
Primary marketing channels (graph), 78
Prizes, 184
Producers:
associations of, 28-30
leading, 114-117
local offices of, 84
merchandising by, 195-196
Production, 37-40
statistical reports on, 178-179
see also separate spirits
Prohibition:
history of, 9-13
prospects for renewal, 18
Promotion:
expenses and appropriations, 182-183
plan for, 186-194
sales material for, 184
Proof, 35, 38-39, 44
Proof gallon, 36
Proof spirits, 36
Publications, history of, 189-193
Publicity, 150, 196-197
Publicker Industries, Inc., 115
Public relations, 24
associations, 31-32
"Public Revenues from Alcoholic Beverages," Distilled Spirits Institute, 179
Puerto Rican rum, 60-62, 142-144
Puerto Rican Rum Institute, 30

Q

Quality, consumer preferences and, 148-149
Quetsch, 60
Quinine water, 152

R

Race, in drinking, 88-89
Racketeering, 23
Reader's Digest, 176
Recipes, for drinks, 153-159, 194
Rectification, 20, 36, 39-40
Red Book Encyclopedic Directory of the Wine and Liquor Industries, 178
Re-distilled spirits, 40
Red strip stamps, 68
Renfield Importers, Ltd., 116
Repeal, 12-13; *see also* Twenty-first Amendment
Research:
for advertising and sales promotion, 187
for marketing information, 178-180
Residue brandy, 58, 59
Retailers:
associations of, 31
calls on, by producers, 196
exclusive, 160
in monopoly states, 83-84
in open states, 80
regulation of inducements to, 228-231
sales by, 120
sociological problems of, 24
types of, 148
Retail price:
breakdown of (chart), 98
control of, 96-99
determining the, 93-96
see also Prices

Revenue legislation, 20
Revolutionary War, 5
Rhode Island, 10
Rob Roy, 154
"Rock and," meaning of term, 55
Rock and bourbon, 55
Rock and brandy, 55
Rock and rum, 55
Rock and rye, 55
Rocks, meaning of term, 151
Rum, 3, 15, 17, 38
  drinks made with, 158-159
  in liquor history, 4-5
  prices of, 107-108
  production of, 60-62
  sales of, 120-125, 142-144
  see also Standards of Identity, etc.
Rum Collins, 158
Rum Manhattan, 158
Rum and soda, 158
Rural drinkers, 87
Russia, 13
"Rye" (as a blend), 150
Rye (grain), 41
Rye liqueur, 54, 55
Rye malt, 41
Rye malt whiskey, 44
Rye whiskey, 6, 7, 44-46, 129

S

"St. Valentine's Day Massacre," 12
Sales:
  of brandy, 140-142
  of classes of spirits, 120-125
  consumer preferences and, 147-150
  of cordials, 138-140
  expenses and appropriations, 182-183, 192-193
  general characteristics, 112-114
  of gin, 136-137
  marketing restrictions, 160-163
  by months, 119, 124-125, 135, 139, 141, 143, 146
  order of, by brands, 133
  overall relationships, 117-120
  personnel for, 184
  promotion, 186-196
  reports on, 179-180
  of rum, 142-144
  by sizes, 120-121
  of vodka, 145-146
  volume of, 93-96
  of whiskey, 125-135
Saloons, 10
Samples, 161
Saturday Evening Post, 176
Schenley Distillers, 15
Schenley Industries, Inc., 115
Schenley Reserve, 16, 47
Schiedam gin, 53
Schieffelin & Co., 116
Scotch Mist, 154
Scotch and soda, 154
Scotch type whiskey, 48
Scotch whisky, 15, 48, 49-50
  sales statistics, 131-132, 134-135
Scotland, 41
Screwdriver, 159
Seagram, *see* Distillers Corp.–Seagram, Ltd.
Seagram's Ancient Bottle Gin, 180
Seagram's 7 Crown, 16, 47, 180
Seagram's whiskies, 16
Sealing material, plastic, 68

Season, consumer buying and the, 150
Selling costs, 96; *see also* Prices
Sex, in drinking, 87
Sidecar, 157
Silver Label rum, 144
Slave trade, in liquor history, 4-5
Slivovitz, 59, 142
Sloe gin, 55
Smirnoff Vodka, 146
Sociological factors, 148
Sodas, 152
Sour-mash whiskey, 41
Southern Comfort, 56
Southern Comfort Corp., 116
Spain, 57, 60
Specially Designated Distributors (SDD'S), 83
Spirit blends, 40, 47-49
  sales statistics, 127-129, 134-135
Spirits:
  defined, 35-36
  sales statistics, 117, 123-124
  see also Brandy, Cordials, Gin, Rum, Vodka, and Whiskey
Spirits, 190
Stamps, revenue, 20
Standard Brands, Inc., 116
Standards of Identity for Distilled Spirits, FAA Act text, 215-223
Star, 157
States:
  advertising in, 172-176, 188-192
  bootleg problems in, 92
  commissions, in monopoly states, 82-83
  marketing laws in, 162-163
  sales statistics, 117, 118, 122, 134-136, 138, 141, 143, 145
  wet and dry, 90-91
Still, 34-35, 72
Stillage, 33
Stinger, 157
Stitzel-Weller Distillery, Inc., 116
Straight whiskies, 9, 18, 41, 45, 151
  sales statistics, 127-128, 129, 134-135
Strega, 56
Strip stamps, 68
Sugar Act, 4-5
Supreme Court, U.S., 27
Sweden, 13
Swedish Punch, 56
Sweeteners, 152

T

Taft, W. H., 9
Taste preferences, 18
Taxes, 5-6, 20, 24, 25, 26
Tax gallon, 36-37
Teen-age drinking, 23-25
Temperance movements, 9-10
Tennessee, 41
Tequila, 63, 120*n*
Testimonials, 194
Theatre program advertising, 189
"Tied house," 21, 161, 162
Tobago, 63
Tom Collins, 152, 155
Tom gin, 52
Tom and Jerry, 159
Tourist areas, consumer buying and, 150

Trade papers:
- advertising and publicity in, 185, 192, 195-196
- reports on spirits, 179-180

Transportation advertising, 186, 189, 192, 194, 196

Treasury Department, 14, 20-21

Trinidad, 63

Triple sec, 55

Truck-panel advertising, 184, 192

Turkey, 13

Twenty-first Amendment, 13, 201

U

U.S. Supreme Court, 27

V

Vacation areas, consumer buying and, 150

Van der Hum, 56

Vermouth, 152

Vieille Cure, 56

Virgin Islands rum, 60, 142-144

Virginia, 41, 57

VO, 132

Vodka, 38
- drinks made with, 159
- prices of, 107-108
- production of, 62-63
- sales of, 120-125, 145-146

Vodka Martini, 159

Volstead Act, 11

"VSOP" (very special old pale) cognac, 60

W

Walker, *see* Walker, Hiram–Gooderham & Worts, Ltd.

Walker, Hiram–Gooderham & Worts Ltd., 15, 115

Ward 8, 154

Warehousing, 27, 37, 40-41

War Production Board, 16

Washington, George, 5

Washington (State), 57

Webb-Kenyon Act, 10

West Germany, 57

West Indies, 4

Wet areas, 90-91

Wheat, 41

Wheat whiskey, 44

Whiskey, 3, 38
- aging of, 39
- defined, 44
- domestic, 112, 114
- drinks made from, 153-154
- imported, 48-51, 112, 127
- labeling, *see* Labeling
- leading brands, 114-117
- in liquor history, 5-9
- prices of, 99-103, 107-108
- production of, 6-7, 41-51
- sales statistics, 112-135
- *see also* Standards of Identity *and separate whiskies*

Whiskey Collins, 154

Whiskey Rebellion, 6

"Whiskey Ring," St. Louis, 8

Whiskey sour, 154

Whiskey Trust, 9

White Label rum, 61, 158

White whiskey, 44

Wholesalers:
- associations of, 30
- merchandising by, 196
- in open states, 80

Wickersham Report, 12
Wile Sons & Co., Inc., Julius, 116
Wine gallon, 36
Wine & Spirits Wholesalers of America (WSWA), 30
Wisconsin, 10
Withdrawals, statistical reports on, 178-179
Woman's Christian Temperance Union (WCTU), 10
Women's Association of Allied Beverage Industries (WAABI), 24, 32
World War II, 16-18
Wyoming, 83

Y

Yugoslavia, 57

Z

Zombie, 158